What Did
Miss Darrington See?

What Did Miss Darrington See?

An Anthology of Feminist Supernatural Fiction

Edited by Jessica Amanda Salmonson

Introduction by Rosemary Jackson

The Feminist Press
at The City University of New York
New York

Published 1989 by The Feminist Press at The City University of New York,
311 East 94 Street, New York, N.Y. 10128
Distributed by The Talman Company, 150 Fifth Avenue, New York, N.Y.
10011

Permission acknowledgments begin on page 262.

92 91 90 89 6 5 4 3 2 1

Library of Congress Cataloging-in-Publication Data

What did Miss Darrington see? : an anthology of feminist supernatural
fiction / edited by Jessica Amanda Salmonson; introduction by
Rosemary Jackson.
   p.   cm.
  Bibliography: p
  ISBN 1-55861-005-7 : $29.95.—ISBN 1-55861-006-5 (pbk.) : $10.95
   1. Fantastic literature—Women authors. 2. Horror tales—Women
authors. 3. Feminism in literature. 4. Feminist literature.
I. Salmonson, Jessica Amanda.
PN6120.92.W65W47 1989
808.83'8729—dc20   89-7506
                                                                CIP

This publication is made possible, in part, by public funds from the New
York State Council on the Arts.

Cover art: Le Passage (1956) by Kay Sage, American (1898–1963), oil on
canvas, 36 × 28½ in. (91.4 × 72.4 cm.); from the collection of Mrs. Wirt
Davis II, Dallas, Texas; photograph courtesy of Stephen R. Miller, Cohasset,
Massachusetts

Text design: Paula Martinac

Printed in the United States on acid free paper by McNaughton & Gunn, Inc.

Contents

Preface

ι||ι

The twenty-four stories in this book, written between 1850 and 1988, are the work of women from the United States, England, and Latin America. The authors, for the most part, were or are active in movements for women's rights and other social change; they also are (or were) writers with a vision of the short story as art, not lecture, though art that reflects their social concerns. This anthology restores to print a number of nineteenth- and early twentieth-century stories by authors who typically were popular in their own day but who have since been unjustly neglected. Also included are stories by authors who are familiar to readers today, but not generally as writers of supernatural fiction. Another source is contemporary Latin American magic realist fiction, a vital modern form of supernatural fiction that is known in this country by only a few of its practitioners. Together these tales represent a tradition of women's writing that has seen print only sporadically and in fragments, unrecognized by most scholars and, with one notable exception, by editors of anthologies.

I selected stories for this volume on the basis of both literary quality and feminist content. A good story that had only marginal feminist interest, or a feminist story that was not good fiction, was not suitable. Fortunately there is no shortage of fiction meeting both criteria. In fact, supernatural fiction written in English in the last two hundred years has been *predominantly* women's literature and much of it is clearly feminist. Among Latin American magic realists, as well, there is an abundance of feminist practitioners.

The links between feminist goals and values and the concerns of supernatural fiction are elucidated by Rosemary Jackson in her Introduction. She looks at the history of women's supernatural writing in the West since its inception with the work of Ann Radcliffe and other eighteenth-century Gothic writers, and discusses each of the stories in this volume in the context of this feminist literary tradition. I have supplied a brief biographical note preceding each story. As there was by no means room to include the majority of the finest stories available, I have included a further reading list, which itself only hints at the scope of this rich body of women's work.

While the reader is welcome to sample these stories in any order she or he pleases, I hope many will choose to read the volume as given. I decided to begin with a tale of the period in which the psychological ghost story especially flourished, "The Long Chamber." This story seems to me to illuminate the tone of all that follows: the sample of an early, almost folklorist theme rendered literary in "A Ghost Story"; next, a classic example of the regional methods of the late nineteenth-century United States, "Luella Miller"; followed by something almost purely gothic, the title story, "What Did Miss Darrington See?"; and so on, with variety the impression, the pace never flagging through repetition. The overall effect is to convey the constancy of feminist thought and struggle in the nineteenth and twentieth centuries— expressed, in this case, through the supernatural tale—subverting what was merely fashionable decade by decade in favor of what remains timeless in short story art and in feminist consciousness.

My interest in fantastic literature and especially the short story began in childhood and is unabating after more than thirty years. Although my interest does not focus exclusively on authors with feminist concerns, the ghostly writings of women have become, over the last ten years or so, of particular interest to me, whether in English or in translation from various languages. Several years ago I began collecting first editions of short story collections (for women's work, these are all too often the *only* editions and far too rare), and I soon discovered that the finest supernatural tales are absent from modern retrospectives. I also collect British and especially North American Victorian magazines (a dusty hobby, to be sure) and have found as much as seventy percent of the supernatural fiction therein was the work of women, the majority of it never reprinted in any form and only haphazardly preserved.

From the 1830s through the 1920s women were the dominant presence in British and U.S. magazines as poets, essayists, story writers, readers, and often enough as editors; hence, women dominated the fashions in literature. The closed community of the magazine trade meant that these women knew one another's writing, supported one another's careers, and were not individually "reinventing in the dark." A sizable percentage were consciously feminist and, depending on the degree of radicalism decade by decade, at certain historical moments feminists were the majority. Their supernatural stories amounted to a veritable school, yet almost no one in this century has commented on it. "The Yellow Wallpaper" (1892) by Charlotte Perkins Gilman has been treated as an exception, as nearly the only feminist shocker in a genre assumed by many to be inherently conservative. Few realized that Gilman's classic was only the best known in an enormous body of similar fiction.

When I first undertook the task of uncovering this body of fiction, no anthology of this nature had before been attempted. That is not to say women writers of the macabre have lacked for partisans; indeed, women's dominion over the ghost story of Victorian England has been widely acknowledged, and though few seem to have noticed it, this was true in the United States as well. What might without denigration be aptly termed "gentlewomen's" ghost story anthologies have appeared from time to time, nearly always edited by men who may have genuinely loved the genre but who lacked feminist concerns or viewpoint. "Gentlewomen" was the term of choice among the Victorian ghost story writers themselves, and has been adopted by modern anthologists as designating this veritable subgenre of ghost story. The most recent examples of the gentlewomen's ghost story anthology formula are Richard Dalby's commendable *The Virago Book of Ghost Stories* (1987) and *The Virago Book of Victorian Ghost Stories* (1988). Together, this pair of volumes presents an impressive overview chiefly of British authors, which tends to be the case with gentlewomen selections. Of broader scope are the young adult volumes from the sister team of Sean Manley and Gogo Lewis, who delight in such subtitles as "Spectral Stories by the Gentle Sex." I recommend their *Ladies of Horror* (1971), *Ladies of Fantasy* (1975), *Ladies of the Gothics* (1975), *Sisters of Sorcery* (1976), and *Ghostly Gentlewomen* (1977). The stories, both British and U.S., tend to be randomly chosen, which has the benefit of showing an extremely wide range of writings that just happen to be by women. Unfortunately, all of these books were only briefly marketed and none were easily obtained. Some lesser but still worthwhile examples of gentlewomen anthologies include Peter Haining's British *Gentlewomen of Evil* (1969) and *A Circle of Witches* (1971), Marcia Muller and Bill Pronzini's *Witch's Brew* (1984), Alan Ryan's *Haunting Women* (1988), both of which include both British and U.S. authors, and Alex

Hamilton's British *The Cold Embrace* (1967), this last issued only in England.

None of these volumes could be construed as feminist per se. But a feminist anthology did appear while *What Did Miss Darrington See?* was seeking a publisher. This is Alfred Bendixen's splendid *Haunted Women: The Best Supernatural Tales by American Women Writers* (1985), which is exemplary in its choices and theoretical discussions, even if it does lack guidance to further reading. Much more remains to be done before the true scope of women's feminist contribution to supernatural literature is adequately presented to modern readers.

More typical of the representation and availability of women's work is the so-called "definitive" anthology, Herbert A. Wise and Phyllis M. Fraser's *Great Tales of Terror and the Supernatural* (1944). This volume remains influential because it is perpetually in print; however, in more than one thousand pages room has been found for only four women. More recently Jack Sullivan's *Lost Souls* (1983)—a selection of British ghost stories by a U.S. editor—also nearly excludes women.

In the United States, it remains accepted practice for "leading" anthologists, nearly all male, to exclude women altogether. Some typical recent examples, randomly chosen, reflect the usual poor ratio of women to men: Alan Ryan's *Halloween Horrors* (1986), 0 to 13; J. N. Williamson's *Best of Masques* (1988), 3 to 18; Dennis Etchison's *Cutting Edge* (1986), 3 to 17; Karl Edward Wagner's *Year's Best Horror* (1986), 3 to 18; Charles L. Grant's *Terrors* (1982), 2 to 16; William Winter's *Prime Evil* (1988), 0 to 13; and David Schow's *The Silver Scream* (1988), 1 to 18.

Among British anthologists the exclusion is slightly less severe, perhaps because a larger number of the anthologists are women. The tradition of women editing ghost story anthologies, dating back to the 1920s, has provided a significant legacy of stories by women that would not otherwise have been commissioned or published. The anthologies of Lady Cynthia Asquith, Mary Danby, Christine Thompson, and Rosemary Timperley would by themselves fill an eight-foot shelf. Only from England's women anthologists have I occasionally encountered a general volume of supernatural stories (as opposed to a gentlewomen's ghost story selection) in which women "just happened" to outnumber men, as in Mary Danby's selections for children, though the heavily weighted ratios shown above are never reversed.

Women's literary endeavors have been overlooked by many means, as Joanna Russ has described in her brilliant *How to Suppress Women's Writing* (1983). The history of women's supernatural and horrific writings could provide textbook cases for all of Russ's points. A few years ago at one of the annual World Fantasy Convention gatherings, for example, I had the unpleasantly comic experience of viewing from the audience a panel exclusively of men addressing the problem of "Why Women Don't Write Horror." The possibility that these men might decline to publish women's stories if given the chance was not discussed. The likelihood that their limited world-views left them incapable of recognizing excellence in women's horrific imaginings was not discussed. The possibility that the misogynist nature of their own writing and editing tastes had turned many talented women to other arenas was not thought part of the trouble. The fact that women do manage to publish a good deal of excellent horror in spite of the obstacles was not mentioned. That none of these panelists' own works sold as well as those of Anne Rice or Shirley Jackson was outside the realm of the discussion. At the heart of their combined belief, though poorly expressed, was the idea that the exceptions proved the rule and women basically had nothing horrible to express.

Yet these stories by women abound, languishing in old magazines, forgotten in out-of-print single-author collections, or the rare good anthology. The problem has not been so much getting published, as staying in print. Women's writings, much more so than those of men, simply vanish. This is not to say that all these women were feminists, but conservative women have fared no better in having their work kept before the public eye.

No complete understanding of supernatural fiction is possible without an understanding of women's central importance to its development, as exemplified by the work of the short story artists presented here. Nor is a full understanding of women's fiction in general possible without an awareness of the supernatural stories that have been an important aspect of women's creative expression, beginning with the instructive fairy tales of oral tradition. I and The Feminist Press hope that *What Did Miss Darrington See?* will contribute to this broader awareness and understanding of, at least, the short story of women's fantastic imagination.

The chief authority in the preparation of this volume has been myself, admittedly an obsessive creature who has read far more in this vein than is altogether rational. Unattributed opinions expressed in the headnotes are for the most part my own, and anything foolish or incorrect is very likely my fault. Much of the material I refer to is part of my own personal library, but I am also indebted to the sizable periodical collections of the University of Washington's Suzallo Library and the Seattle Public Library.

I've received miscellaneous support and aid from a number of people who have made my task easier. I am grateful to Wendy Wees, Jules Faye, Joanna Russ, Susannah Driver, Susan Lee Cohen, R. Alain Everts, Alfred Bendixen, Rosemary Pardoe, Darroll Pardoe, Holly Tuttle, and others who, no doubt, I shall be chagrined to have forgotten at the moment.

Introduction

Every thing possible to be believed is an image of truth.

—William Blake,
The Marriage of Heaven and Hell

We must assume our existence as *broadly* as we in any way can; everything, even the unheard-of, must be possible in it. That is at bottom the only courage that is demanded of us: to have courage for the most strange, the most singular and the most inexplicable that we may encounter.

—Rainer Maria Rilke,
Letters to a Young Poet

An anthology of feminist supernatural fiction may appear, at first sight, a rather incongruous undertaking. Can there really be any direct link between feminism and literature dealing with supernatural themes? Isn't the very idea of relating feminism—concerned, primarily, with effecting social change and raising consciousness about gender and sexual politics in *this* world—to the supernatural—a realm supposedly outside nature and culture altogether—rather contradictory and something of a paradox? It is true that many of the women whose stories are reproduced here were actively engaged in struggles for female emancipation and equality. Olivia Dunbar, Inez Irwin, Elizabeth Phelps, and Olive Schreiner, for example, were influential figures in voicing women's rights and campaigning for women's suffrage, but is this enough to define their excursions into supernatural fiction as "feminist"? By comparing these stories, discussing some of the issues they raise, and placing them in relation to various literary traditions that they both comply with and defy, this introduction will explore whether it is possible to make a deeper link between feminism and supernatural fiction than merely biographical coincidence on the part of the authors. It will ask what it is that has driven women towards the wide range of writing covered by the term "supernatural fiction"—Gothic romance, ghost story, fantasy, allegory, parable, surrealism, psychological drama, inner-space fiction, dream vision; how this movement towards "non-realistic" narrative might be interpreted as parallel to feminist struggles on social and political fronts; and how it might extend an understanding of women's consciousness and experience.

The term "supernatural," as it is used here, is loose and all-embracing. It suggests that which is above or outside nature, more than the actual or ordinary, abnormal, extraordinary, marvellous, surreal. Fantasy or supernatural fiction reveals a preoccupation with themes, events, incidents, or characters normally described as impossible, implausible, incredible, uncanny, fanciful, imaginary, delusory, or mad, and with experiences that are excluded from so-called realistic literature. It is a fiction dealing with an extension of the idea of what is possible or "true": people returning from the dead as ghosts, vampires, substantial bodily presences; selves becoming doubled into mirror images and reflections, or split into multiple projections; sudden magical transformations and metamorphoses, distortions, swapping of roles and identities; mythical figures, such as angels and devils, manifesting in the midst of everyday life; spirits invading and inhabiting different bodies, able to break the boundaries of time and space, or to transcend the ordinary limits of matter; waking dreams of flying or of being haunted or having extraordinary powers. Far from being decried as nonsensical, or described as merely imaginary delusions, such experiences are represented in supernatural literature as both credible and valuable. Various narrative techniques—the common-sense narrator, for example, as in **Clay-Shuttered Doors** by Helen Hull (1926)—insist on the authenticity of events and prevent any dismissal of them as purely escapist fantasy, while a recurrent reflection on the meaning of the experiences reinforces a sense of their seriousness. The stories in this volume, for all their occasionally archaic or conventional form, are far from being frivolous or formulaic supernatural fictions—rather, they use the form to provide serious explorations and dramatizations of issues at the heart of human existence. They raise profound questions about the nature of identity, about the limitations surrounding earthly experience, the restrictions of body, mind, space and time, the distinction between life and death—profound philosophical, metaphysical, psychological and spiritual questioning.

The wide variety of stories in this volume reveals shifts in both literary form and in preoccupations and ideas; women's supernatural writings over the last two centuries have undergone significant transformations that mirror historical changes and changes in the history of ideas, as well as in the personal inclinations of their authors. Before examining these differences in detail, it is important to stress what these fictions share, their common exploration and expression of a world *other* than that represented in mainstream, "realistic" fiction. The dominant literary forms in Western culture from the eighteenth century onwards have been realistic and mimetic—it has been the novel of manners, then the classic Victorian novel, that have been seen as constituting the "great tradition."[1] According to this tradition, novels such as Jane Austen's *Mansfield Park,* George Eliot's *Middlemarch,* Tolstoy's *Anna Karenina,* D. H. Lawrence's *Sons and Lovers,* and Henry James's *Portrait of a Lady* are *realistic* works, reproducing a known, defined, visible social reality. There has been no room in such fiction, nor in such a world view, for anything not immediately knowable, for anything invisible, unseen, inexplicable. These areas have been prohibited from mainstream literature just as they have been tabooed by culture at large; a rationalistic, materialistic, scientific, and secular culture has restricted its definition of the "real" to what is familiar and under rational control. This culture is also a patriarchal one, and many of its values and definitions are male-determined. Indeed, some feminist critics have gone so far as to argue that the very history of reason, or rationality, and the materialistic, atheistic philosophy that accompanies it, are inseparable from masculinity and phallocentric power. Literature has supported and reinforced this dominant position. As Hélène Cixous explains, "Nearly the entire history of writing is confounded with the history of reason, of which it is at once the effect, the support, and one of the privileged alibis."[2] To challenge this history of writing by producing texts that are *outside* the frame of reason, that are anti-reason, unreasonable, unrealistic, is to simultaneously challenge the "reality" that frame contains and upholds—the "real" as it is defined by a materialistic, masculine, patriarchal culture.

It is hardly surprising, then, that women, in their protest against a social system that has defined reality and, particularly, women's reality and identity in such restrictive ways, should have been strongly drawn towards non-realistic narrative. It is as if their sense of things has been too large, too elusive, to be easily contained in the narrow perspectives of mainstream fiction, and they have had to evolve more fluid, transformative ways of writing in which to express questions, situations, and apprehensions that were impossible to include in the more respectable genre of the realistic novel or short story. In this general sense, the very existence of supernatural writing by women can be seen as a feminist enterprise, for it is a challenge to the dominant notions of reality and representation upheld by a patriarchal culture. It explores and thereby threatens to dissolve many of the structures upon which social definitions of reality depend, those rigid boundaries between life and death, waking and dream states, self and not-self, bodily and nonbodily existence, past and future, reason and madness, that have insisted on the substantiality of matter—which is all there is to a materialistic mind—and the insubstantiality of spirit.

Women writers of the supernatural have overturned many of these assumptions and definitions—not, as with some of their male counterparts, to investigate "horror" for its own sake, but in order to extend our sense of the human, the real, beyond the blinkered limits of male science, language, and rationalism. It is no accident that their work has been dismissed or derided by literary history—ghost stories have hardly had a respectable position in the literary canon—for their work constitutes as much of a threat, in its own implicit way, to masculine culture as any explicit militancy against patriarchy's silencing and disempowering of women that these authors may have enacted on a social level. They are intimating a world, a consciousness, a reality, *larger* than the one that man has controlled. This world of communion with spiritual beings is anathema to the atheistic, secular thinking of our capitalistic and patriarchal society. They are also attempting to find a language, a different literature, *other* than the one forged by men, to articulate senses and experiences which are frequently *beyond* words, beyond social definitions altogether. If, as Cixous claims, "writing is precisely the *very possibility of change,* the space that can serve as a springboard for subversive thought, the precursory movement of a transformation of social and cultural structures,"[3] then this form of women's writing is particularly powerful, and provides a clear connection between the politics and aesthetics of its authors. Seen at its most ambitious and far-reaching, supernatural fiction by women attempts to change the very way of thinking of Western minds, to dissolve the whole edifice of positivism, rationality, and secularism that has become synonymous with patriarchal culture, and to suggest that there is more in heaven and earth than is dreamt of in this culture's narrow philosophy and art—that its "realism" is in fact a misnomer and an anomaly.

The many different forms of supernatural story represented in this anthology indicate the wide range of non-realistic writing by women from the 1850s to the present. Closely related to, if not determined by, the historical and literary contexts in which they were written, they move in form and style from Gothic romance, through the archaic moralizing of Victorian ghost stories, to surrealistic visions, feminist allegories and fables, violent psychological fantasies, and modern therapeutic psychodramas.

Women have long been associated with the telling of supernatural tales; oral traditions seem to have depended on women, grandmothers, nurses, maids, to pass down legends, folk tales, superstitions, and fictions of haunting spirits by word of mouth, a kind of female collective memory. It is Nelly Dean, the old nurse, who "tells" rather than writes the ghost story of Heathcliff and Cathy in *Wuthering Heights,* for example. From the time when the supernatural entered Western literature in the form of Gothic tales of terror in the mid-eighteenth century, it became shaped and used by women and found a predominantly female readership. Ann Radcliffe's major novels, *The Mysteries of Udolpho* (1794) and *The Italian* (1797), experimented with supernatural terrors in a new way, relating them to the fears and anxieties of her female protagonists. This psychological use of Gothic by women was confirmed in Mary Shelley's influential fantasies *Frankenstein* (1818) and *The Last Man* (1826), which redeployed popular supernatural themes—terror, destruction, haunting, persecution, doubling—to dramatize her peculiarly *female* experience of alienation, isolation, and women's relation to the body, birth, and death.[4] This powerful line of supernatural fiction, running from Radcliffe and Mary Shelley, has been defined by Ellen Moers as a tradition of "female Gothic"—a tradition of women's writing that uses Gothic themes and conventions to articulate some of the difficulties, terrors, and pains of female experience, both physical and psychic.[5] Moers suggests that it is a tradition that runs from Radcliffe's eighteenth-century Gothic, through Mary Shelley to Victorian writers, and is evident in Emily Brontë's *Wuthering Heights* (1847), Charlotte Brontë's *Jane Eyre* (1847) and *Villette* (1853), Ann Brontë's *The Tenant of Wildfell Hall* (1848), Christina Rossetti's narrative poem *Goblin Market* (1849), and in their twentieth-century counterparts, including Djuna Barnes's *Nightwood* (1936), Isak Dinesen's Gothic tales, the work of Carson McCullers, Anne Sexton and Sylvia Plath, and some of the writings of Margaret Atwood and Angela Carter.

More important than critical quibbling over the terms "Gothic" or "non-Gothic," "supernatural" or "non-supernatural," are the issues these writings are trying to address, and the specific use of female Gothic in Victorian fiction provides a strong clue to its feminist potential. Less well known than the writings of the Brontës but similarly exploring the relation between women's social and psychic experiences are the works of Elizabeth Gaskell, whose novels and short macabre tales exemplify a certain type of women's subversive use of the supernatural. Gothic elements intrude into Gaskell's predominantly realistic novels of the 1840s, for example, to suggest that all is not well—that the perception and definition of the real world is threatened with disintegration.[6] Her novel *Mary Barton* (1848) lapses from its realism into unreal, surreal, hallucinatory scenes at crucial moments of crisis and when its female protagonist fears she is collapsing into insanity. It edges towards supernaturalism when the "normal" way of seeing is undermined, and when Mary, under intense psychological pressure, loses control and in some sense articulates her sexual longing, her female desire, which she apprehends as "madness."

What is happening unconsciously in *Mary Barton,* and more explicitly in Gaskell's short stories and the tales of other nineteenth-century women writers of the supernatural, is a use of terror, abnormality, even madness, to explore the edges, the limits of female sanity, and its relation to social control and propriety. Gaskell's *Lois the Witch* depicts a woman ostracized and haunted through her sexual difference—because she sees and lives differently, she is destroyed, "a witch, abhorred of all men"—while her Gothic story *The Grey Woman* (1861) anticipates many of the tales in this collection in its clear association of the issue of ghosts, ghostliness, and the supernatural with female exclusion. Here, an abandoned wife lives on the edge of society, deemed to have no social identity without her husband and doomed to a kind of living death. Metamorphosed from vital woman into deadly ghost, she becomes spectral, withdrawn, an allegorical version of many of the female figures in these tales, who slide between life and death, simultaneously inside yet outside the society or body or marriage to which they do not really belong. One way of reading the sexual politics of these stories is to see their interest in ghosts, haunting, hallucination, insecurity, and insanity as expressions of women's position as outsiders, of women's not belonging, of social and cultural alienation. Displaced from their society and history, dislocated from their bodies, minds and marriages, they move into another realm, *in between* things, to a kind of no-man's land. Feeling that they do not belong socially, they come to occupy the ultimate non-social, asocial position—that of the specter, madwoman, or ghost.

Unlike their social counterparts, these anti-social reflections are not confined within the limits of time, space, matter, or rationality. They can move freely through material form, as in Anna Maria Hall's *La Femme Noir* (c. 1850): "A form passed through the solid oak from her chamber, without the bolts being withdrawn . . . nothing opened, but it passed through—a shadowy form, dark and vapory, but perfectly distinct," and brilliantly depicted in the insubstantiality of the narrator in *Since I Died* by Elizabeth Stuart Phelps (1873): "It occurred to me, still leaning on the banisters, that his heavy arm must have swept against and *through* me," and through time, as in *An Unborn Visitant* by Vita Sackville-West (1932). Their ghostliness serves both as a parable of their social alienation—unrecognized, refused access to a full life, many women occupy a position similar to that of the living dead—and a protest against these restrictive forms of life and reality. As Gillian Beer has suggested, the very interest in ghosts can be seen as disruptive and subversive, for it seeks to replace the known and normal by something other, something less substantial. "Ghost stories," writes Beer, "are to do with the insurrection, not the resurrection of the dead . . . [with the ghost story] the fictional *takes place* in the everyday: it takes space, and it is this usurpation of space by the immaterial which is one of the deepest terrors released by the ghost story."[7] Dissolving clear dividing lines between life and death, substance and nothingness, ghosts challenge a culture that defines life as real, death as unreal, and that metaphorically places women on the side of death and insubstantiality. Ghosts, continues Beer, "elide the distance between the actual and the imagined," so that "frail and cherished distinctions collapse." In many of the stories here, conventional discriminations between actuality and imagination have ceased to operate altogether; ghosts are as real as living people—the old devices for keeping disturbing things in their place, whether these disturbances are ghosts, death, madness, women, or spirits, have ceased to work.

In their movement into other realms, however, the women in these stories are simultaneously opening up visions of new possibilities. Their alternate worlds, hinterlands, no-man's lands, no-wheres, and utopias are also images of difference, potential, wholeness, which are lacking in the limited "natural" sphere. Their fantasies of life beyond the individual body, mind, or history provide an intimation of wholeness, fluidity, even transcendence, which social reality has failed to provide. They make up for this lack, coldness, and isolation, often by imaging unity and communion with kindred spirits, and in this respect they run parallel to feminist utopias and visionary writing. Alice Brown's *There and Here* (1897), for example, offers a concise parable of a remaking and replacing of the real by something different, something that is difficult to articulate because of its unfamiliarity and its existence outside the realm of the social, outside language: "Once upon a time there was a little child, and he was always crying because he didn't know the difference between Here and There. He was always hating to be Here, and longing to be There." Ruth, the protagonist, shares the child's longing and experiences a brief but blissful transportation to that "There," learning that there really is no distinction between the two states: "Here is There and There is Here." The separation is man-made, distancing and excluding supernatural, visionary experience. However, her understanding cannot be easily translated into (man-made) language—she apprehends a unity, a mystery, a sense of the connectedness of life and death, "the one thing, you know, that explains everything," but it eludes language. "I almost had the words, but they won't stay." "She learned the secret which explains everything. But she never could remember that dream."

A similar frustration that supernatural experience lies beyond words appears in *Since I Died* ("Utterance has fled." "Speech and language struggle over me. Mute articulations fill the air.") and in other stories in this volume; they frequently point to the serious limitations and inadequacy of language to capture something ineffable, beyond the human and therefore beyond words. Instead, they have recourse to a language of allegory and symbolism—suggestive, parabolic, dreamlike, surreal, hinting at supernatural events, sketching them in, for when they are made too literal, as perhaps in *Tamar* by Lady Eleanor Smith (1932), they can become dangerously clumsy and incredible. Speaking of things that man has declared non-existent has always made women vulnerable to charges of exaggeration, neurosis, madness, and many of the characters here exist on the edge of society, time, or sanity precisely because their way of seeing is not restricted to the central, normal, rational one. In *There and Here* Ruth insists that "You mustn't think I'm crazy. I'm not," while *Clay-Shuttered Doors* shows a woman driven into a kind of insanity/death through social denial of her reality. Madness appears here as that which society has not permitted, has not admitted, and which then must assume extraordinary, eccentric, weird, impossible, or supernatural forms.

Looked at chronologically, the stories in this volume can be seen to demonstrate some of the interesting shifts and transformations of supernatural writing over the past two centuries. The earliest two, both from the 1850s—Hall's *La Femme Noir* and Ada Trevanion's *A Ghost Story*—represent the supernatural in a form characteristic of much early and Victorian Gothic, as moralistic or redemptive, intervening to aid the living. *La Femme Noir* uses a legendary female ghost, the black lady of the title, to instill terror in a wicked uncle and persuade him toward a fairy tale happy ending of the marriage of his niece to his enemy's son, while *A Ghost Story* has a recently dead schoolteacher returning to her favorite pupil to reveal the secret location of vital family papers. Both insist on the authenticity of their ghostly narratives and despite their rather formulaic frameworks and moralistic structures, indicate some of the themes and areas that were to become so central to women writers of the supernatural. Both focus on women returning from the dead to correct social wrongs. As the protagonist of *There and Here* declares, "I told you death denied the laws of life." This theme later develops into female revenge and support of women in difficulty, defying the boundaries of death itself in order to identify and communicate with women. For all their didactic tone and archaic style, these pieces of Victorian Gothic anticipate the feminist purposes and implications of women's subsequent use of supernatural fiction.

Emma Cobb's **What Did Miss Darrington See?** (1870) may also be viewed as a sentimental Romantic Gothic tale, with its Byronic hero loving Miss Darrington from beyond the grave, his love bridging "the wider, deeper gulf that divides us from the unseen world." Yet it is also useful to provide a feminist reading of this, not only in terms of its characterization of a powerful, self-determining female protagonist who refuses to fall for the charming Don Juan, but more specifically in the insistence on her power to *see*. Throughout the tale there is a repeated emphasis on the strength of her *look*. She is unsubdued by the magnetism and gaze of the Romantic hero—whose power traditionally lay in his eyes, as in the poetry of Byron, Shelley, and in Gothic novels—despite his clear belonging to that prototype: "The eye was large and looked like black velvet, with the flash of a diamond in its centre." Undaunted by this "fiery and intolerable splendour," Miss Darrington returns his Byronic gaze, looking "steadily into the eyes whose bold, strong glance had at first beaten down her own." Feminist criticism and theory have stressed the centrality of *the look,* of understanding who controls the look, as part of the strategy of women regaining control over their lives and bodies. The male gaze is one of the means by which men subdue women; looking *at* women, making women the object of the look rather than subjects who see in their own right, is part of the mechanism of sexual control and the subjugation of women.[8] The fact that in this piece of Victorian supernaturalism there is such an awareness of the power of the look aligns Cobb's work with more recent attempts of women at self-determination, for the way in which Miss Darrington returns, sends back, the hero's magnetic male gaze reverses a literary convention that had kept women in their place throughout Romantic poetry and prose.

It is wholly appropriate, therefore, that it is this tale, with its reversal of that investment of power in the male look, that provides the title for the volume, for it stands for much more than a woman seeing ghosts. It also asks how women are to *see* rather than simply be seen, how women are to determine the power of looking, how women too can define how and what we see, how we are seen and see ourselves. Miss

Darrington is the forerunner of a feminism that refuses to give away power by serving simply as the passive object of the male gaze, and instead claims women's power to look, to see, to define, to control, to *make* reality, however unacceptable, mad, or irrational that might appear from the male way of looking.

The illusory quality of the supposedly real world and a sense of life itself as a waking dream continues in Elizabeth Phelps's ***Since I Died*** (1873) and Alice Brown's ***There and Here*** (1897), both of which contain metaphysical questionings on the nature of life, death, identity, time, matter, within a sometimes whimsical image of another world that makes up for the loss and lack experienced in this one. The fluidity of female selves they represent, moving in and out of life and the body, is close to that expressed by a contemporary female poet, Linda Pastan, when she writes, "I slip/out of my skin/each night, hold it up by the sleeves/to see its shape/ . . . And in dreams/where what has been lost/ is sometimes so briefly/found, I slip/out of my skin again/half hoping/ not to find my way/back in."[9] The body is experienced as a trap, a limitation, confining the woman inside a reality which is partial, and which her other senses, her intuitions, have told her is incomplete. It is towards this other, larger reality that more visionary and allegorical writers of the supernatural have turned.

Olive Schreiner's powerful allegorical visions are the clearest example of this kind of feminist utopianism, of bringing supernatural elements into a focus that is simultaneously spiritual and, in the broadest sense, political. Her ***Three Dreams in a Desert*** (1890) uses visionary devices not to disrupt nor invade the real, but to extend the possibility of that world by imagining it otherwise. She creates a utopian image of a future towards which women must struggle—a utopia achieved not without pain and difficulty, but fought for on social, political, individual, outer and inner levels. The intimate connection between supernatural literature and feminism is revealed here, for it is this visionary writing that provides the backdrop and inspiration to cultural and personal struggle, the idealism, in every sense of that word, from which women may take support. Schreiner writes that such an approach is neither superficial wish-fulfillment, nor blindness to actualities, but a new, stark way of seeing. "I have tried to wear no blinkers. I have not held a veil before my eyes, that I might profess that cruelty, injustice, and mental and physical anguish were not. I have tried to look nakedly in the face those facts which make most against all hope."[10] The visionary element enables her to continue and sustain everyday social, political, and personal struggles by a sense of their larger purpose: "And yet, in the darkest hour, the consciousness which I carried back with me [from the vision] has never wholly deserted me; even as a man who clings with one hand to a rock, though the waves pass over his head, yet knows what his hand touches." Like Doris Lessing, with whom she shares a sense of spiritual priorities, and who has acknowledged a considerable debt and influence to her, Schreiner writes in a way that refuses to *oppose* the visionary and the social. Far from being in conflict, they are presented in her stories as inseparable, one informing, idealizing, and inspiring the other. Their mutual interaction, like the "marriage" between the zones in Lessing's visionary novel, *The Marriages between Zones Three, Four and Five* (1980), is an attempt to open up possibilities, awareness, consciousness, not only on a small, personal dimension but also on cultural, global, and universal levels. It is the figure of the female visionary, like Cassandra, a mad prophetess, like the heroine of Lessing's *Shikasta* (1979) or her "madwomen" whose madness permits them to speak what is unspoken and see what is invisible, who are the ones who must voice visions of the future, mixed as they are with doom, warning, and optimism.

There is no straightforward, linear progression of literary history, and some of the stories reproduced here from the early decades of the twentieth century are marked by many of the conventions of previous supernatural fiction. Mary E. Wilkins Freeman's **Luella Miller** (1902), a cautionary tale of a vampiric female who draws people to their death, and Eleanor Smith's *Tamar,* with its crudely literal depiction of a revengeful Satan collecting a deviant, sinful woman, are both hampered by a moralistic framework, yet sustain some ambivalence in their investment of energy, beauty, and defiance in the damned figures of the demonic Luella and Tamar. Vernon Lee's **The Doll** (1927), like many of its Victorian predecessors, has little overt horror, but its burning of the doll, the child bride of the past, can be read as a ritualized ending, the exorcism of a passive female role. Mary Austin's **The Readjustment** (1908) dissuades a vengeful female ghost out of her desire to haunt her husband. The ghost has carried over into death the distress and dissatisfaction that the woman experienced in life, but is defeated in her vengeful restlessness by a common-sense, womanly neighbor. Precisely because the ghost's presence is disturbing, a reminder of the *inadequacy* of social life and relationships for women—"Emma had always wanted things different, wanted them with a fury of intentness that implied offensiveness in things as they were"—it is apprehended as being too powerful, too strong for her ineffectual husband to manage. The neighbor restrains the ghost in the way that women impose self-restraint on themselves, for fear of their own power, their sense that their energy and anger is too much for men to respond to, or for society to contain.

The remainder of the stories, all from the twentieth century, use the supernatural in ways that show the influence of both psychoanalysis, with its understanding of unconscious processes, and feminism, with its refusal of fixed or passive concepts of femininity. They are fictions that more explicitly dramatize the workings of the female psyche and depict women's relation to each other.

Georgia Pangborn's *The Substitute* (1914) shows the close link between two women, in that one can replace the other as mother of her children after death. Olivia Dunbar's *The Long Chamber*, from the same year, and coinciding with the suffrage movement, to which its author gave active support, uses a ghost from a long-past love scene to make it impossible for a woman to fake happiness in an unfulfilling marriage. Here, the supernatural intrudes to introduce an insistent reminder of a wider focus than this "marriage [that] had been complete self-annihilation." It recalls possibilities, truths repressed, ideals that have been compromised at incredible cost to the individual woman. As the narrator articulates it, "ghostliness" serves to put the human into perspective, to give a sense of what lies beyond the social, beyond cultural convention, and which is so often betrayed by it. "Immune as I then believed myself to spectral invasions of my own serenity, I did not know at that time, or until long after, how the reverberations of spent lives may sometimes sound so loud as to muffle the merely human cry."

Significantly, the spectral presences in *The Long Chamber* come from within a mirror, a central metaphor in supernatural literature. Not only a convenient device for transporting protagonist or reader into a world closely related to, yet different from, this one, as in Lewis Carroll's *Alice Through the Looking Glass* (1872) and numerous nineteenth- and twentieth-century fantasies, where a reflecting glass provides entrance into an inverted, surrealistic realm or underworld, the mirror is also a symbol for psychic exploration. It offers images of possibility, of different selves, unrealized aspects of oneself that have not yet come into being: "The mirror provides versions of self transformed into another, become something or someone else. It employs distance and difference to suggest the instability of the 'real' on this side of the looking-glass and it offers unpredictable (apparently impossible) metamorphoses of self into other."[11]

Mirror images, reflections, doubles, metamorphoses, and splittings are recurrent themes in women's supernatural fiction of the twentieth century. They are means of exploring female identity, of expressing women's relation to unacknowledged, unconscious aspects of themselves and their interrelation with others. From *Frankenstein* and *Jane Eyre* to Anne Sexton's *The Ghost* (1978), Sylvia Plath's poetry, or autobiographical tales of haunting such as Flora B. Schreiber's *Sybil* (1974), women have written of themselves as divided, haunted, alienated from themselves, mad.[12] Charlotte Perkins Gilman's *The Yellow Wallpaper*

(1892), is a classic example of a woman persecuted to the point of insanity, forced to occupy the position of her mad double in order to escape the intolerable pressures of a patriarchal marriage.[13] Its brilliant parable of women's oppression puts into fantasy form Gilman's political commitment to feminism, as does the parallel story reproduced here, Helen Hull's *Clay-Shuttered Doors* (1926). Equally powerful as an uncompromising indictment of male control within family and society, and similarly stemming from radical political concern, Hull's story repeats the tension of *The Yellow Wallpaper* by hollowing out the predictable, known world of male order, rationality, language, and convention, and opening up onto the unknown and uncontainable. Its "mad" wife, the ghost Thalia, seems abnormal to the world. She is queer, blurred, half dead, transparent—both literally, because she is a supernatural visitant, and symbolically, as a woman only half alive in a stultifying marriage. Her coldness and deathliness—"A stiff loneliness hedged her as if she were rimmed in ice and snow"—is an allegory of female isolation, and the difficulty she experiences in belonging, in finding a place in her body, marriage, family, society—"It is hard to get back in"—tells of the difficulty women have in feeling inside, at home, within society. Her ghostliness ("Her lovely face had the empty shallowness, the husklikeness of death") is a literal enactment of the idea of women denied access to a full-blooded and fully embodied life. Thalia, like the women in the more recent feminist allegory in Ira Levin's novel *The Stepford Wives* (1972), is permitted only a death-in-life condition, a travesty of life; she is called back into marriage only as a function, a necessity for her husband's business, and not for herself. Whatever her attempts to overcome or mask her ghostliness ("She rouged her hollow cheeks. It was as if she drew another face for herself") cannot give to her the full identity she is denied, as she is condemned to remain forever outside, reminiscent of the ghost of Cathy in *Wuthering Heights,* clamoring for re-entry into a place and a body: "I can never get in again! Never! The black agony of fighting back." Thalia's final capitulation to death is but a confirmation of her exclusion. Like *The Long Chamber* and *The Yellow Wallpaper, Clay-Shuttered Doors* realizes the potential of feminist supernatural fiction to provide a damning indictment of male power and ambition. Its mad ghost-wife prefers death to a social identity and relationship that are merely denial and limitation.

Both Inez Irwin's *The Sixth Canvasser* (1916) and Vita Sackville-West's *An Unborn Visitant* (1932) use supernatural elements to dramatize family relations: in the first, a bond between mother and son, structured around the moment of death; in the second, between mother and daughter, structured around conception and birth. A deep fear of death in *The Sixth Canvasser,* expressed through Lawrentian-like rhythmic repetition that punctuates ordinary existence with an insistent reminder of mortality—"The moment of death! The moment of death!"—is allayed by the reappearance of the women's son. However, a rich ambiguity about his status, as to whether he is a ghost, projection, or actual person, leaves the ending disturbingly open to interpretation.

In *An Unborn Visitant,* time-travelling reveals the influence of Einstein's discoveries of the relativity of space and time. His theories "forced us to abandon the classical ideas of an absolute space as the stage of physical phenomena and absolute time as a dimension separate from space. According to Einstein's theory, both space and time are relative concepts. . . ."[14] Fictions exploring the dissolution of space and time could no longer be dismissed as merely fanciful; they were shown to be valid possibilities. One could say that these discoveries of science and physics were logical "proofs" of what women had long known and explored in their supernatural excursions—truths hitherto denied by the materialistic thinking of Western philosophy. Sackville-West's dialogue between mother and unborn daughter reintroduces the ideas that a person might be able to stand outside her body, to "select" her incarnation, to see chronological, linear time as a merely relative and arbitrary notion—ideas that are taken for granted in much Eastern mysticism as truths and that supernatural fiction represents in its different, secular Western form. Certainly the dissolution of time is a recurrent theme in these stories, as in *Since I Died:* "I miss the conception of that for which *how long* stands index"; "I see the watch now, in your pocket; I cannot tell if the hands move, or only pulsate like a heart-throb, to and fro; they stand and point, mute golden fingers, paralysed and pleading, forever at the hour of three," like Salvador Dali's famous surrealist painting of dissolving watches, *The Persistence of Memory.*

Largely due to the impact of relativity theories, psychoanalytic discoveries, and aesthetic movements like surrealism, the later stories in this volume are less hampered by the conventionial impulse to authenticate, defend, or explain their improbable events. Armonía Somers's **The Fall** (1967) melds together dream, imagination, and actuality in a surrealistic prose that fantasizes a black man's erotic union with the Virgin Mary. It identifies women with blacks as social outsiders and insists on woman's sensuality, refusing the hierarchical, institutionalized position that the Church has used to deny women's sexuality. Defying her image—"I was not what they have painted. I was different, certainly less beautiful."—and collapsing the myth of the Virgin Mother— "I cannot be the Immaculate. . . . I need to walk, hate, cry on this earth. I need to be of flesh, not cold and lifeless wax"—the fallen mother of God, like Michèle Roberts's feminist version of Mary Magdalene in *The*

Wild Girl,[15] speaks for women, opposing the false idolatry of femininity and the cult of virginity which has made women ashamed of their bodies. "I won't go on. I want no more pearls, prayers, tears, perfume, soaps." The visionary prose leads to a violent, volcanic ending, an apocalypse in which the masculine institution of the Church is exploded and the mask is dropped. An elemental female power has been re-released in a moment of simultaneous destruction and creation, death and resurrection.

Similarly dreamlike and exploding a restrictive, respectable mother/ virgin role for women, are the tales by Leonora Carrington, Barbara Burford, and Luisa Valenzuela. Carrington's Kafka-esque allegory, *The Debutante* (1939), has a raging hyena of hunger and anger, intolerant of pretence and maternal prohibition, lurking behind a decorous female image. Burford's *Dreaming the Sky Down* (1988) makes a compensatory dream of flight into an adolescent reality, while Valenzuela's *The Teacher* (1976) portrays the multiplicity of selves hidden within or behind the conventional one of female teacher. Blowing apart a fixed, feminine nurturing role are the realities of her other selves—mad, uncontained, unrestrained, unmotherly, laughing, desiring, needing, dirty, dishevelled, unpredictable, many-voiced—terrifying to the young man who has wanted to fetishize her in her teacherly role, and who now perceives her as "fiendish," "damned, possessed by the devil." Joanna Russ's *The Little Dirty Girl* (1983) shows how hard it is for women, too, to integrate these "unacceptable" aspects of themselves; they tend to be split off and projected into others, as "child" sides, mad parts women have had to leave behind as intolerable or taboo.

While the stories by Russ, Carrington, and Valenzuela are examples of what might be termed "intra-psychic" fantasies, employing supernatural elements to dramatize the female psyche as it encounters buried, repressed, and forbidden sides of itself, "explicable" in psychoanalytic terms as unconscious projection and splitting, the tales by Phyllis Eisenstein, Anne Sexton, and Lisa Tuttle could be called "inter-psychic," looking at the relation between separate psyches. Their implication that minds might be able to leak into one another, that the boundaries between selves, between "I" and "not I" are permeable, extends the supernatural into realms of telepathy and inner communication that are inexplicable and again challenge dominant notions of what is possible or real.

Eisenstein's *Attachment* (1974), perhaps one of the most innovative and original of these stories, draws on a modernist stream-of-consciousness narrative to explore the inner relation between two women who have never physically encountered one another. Ellie Greenfield, a young U.S. student, shares consciousness with an elderly

Catholic woman, the German Johanna—a mutual double-consciousness that began with Ellie's birth. Their thoughts, experiences, sensations, pleasures, and pains are felt simultaneously, sometimes in the foreground of their consciousnesses, at other times receding into background awareness. "To Ellie, Johanna's memories and experiences both waking and sleeping existed as a constant hum in the back of her mind, just below the threshold of consciousness . . . the dreamer's imaginary experiences were influenced by the waker's real ones." Their inner dialogue and communication is a powerful and convincing portrait of complete sharing of another's life and consciousness, beyond geographical distance, social difference, and physical separation—an interweaving of inner and outer worlds, memories, dreams, perceptions, and reflections that extends their experience beyond anything defined as normality. Aware that conventional psychiatry, with its limited notion of the "I," would categorize their claim to communicate in this way as mad, they learn to confine it to themselves, a rich source of extended inner experience, the joining into another human consciousness, with all the pain, delight, and expansion of knowledge and understanding that this implies.

The more sinister version of almost symbiotic possession in Sexton's *The Ghost* (1978) could be read as a sado-masochistic fable: a woman's anger and violence directed not outward but inward, eroding and destroying the self, a woman vampirically preying upon her namesake/ herself in a self-destructiveness whose ultimate expression would be suicide, as it was for Sexton. Tuttle's *A Friend in Need* (1981), on the other hand, presents a secret link between two women as a more positive, if puzzling, experience, as in *Attachment*. Again, there is a leakage of inner worlds, a complex mutual mirroring in which each woman is the imagined companion of the other and each constitutes the other's reality. The vertiginous effect of their meeting raises questions about their identity and subjectivity: Who imagines whom? Are we nothing more than the imaginary projection of another consciousness, nothing but the figment of someone else's dream?

Inner communication, telepathy, minds travelling toward and into one another, have become popular themes in modern supernatural fiction, but it might be that women have depicted them differently than men. John Wyndham's *The Midwich Cuckoos* (1957), a famous example of male supernaturalism, represents inter-psychic communication as a source of threat and terror. Evidence of deviancy, of alienation, demonic power, and possession that might attempt to take over society as we know it, it is treated with hostility, fear, and violent opposition, yoked into a narrative of good against bad in which supernaturalism is linked to all that is potentially evil—a contrast that repeats the difference between previous male and female writers of Gothic: Whereas M. G. Lewis's *The Monk* focuses on external violence and horror, for example, Mary Shelley's *Frankenstein* prioritizes psychological and existential issues, and inner, psychic experience. Women writers seem to have been driven less by this fear of difference, and to have welcomed the possibility of inner communication as a source of extended consciousness that might be put to beneficial service in the world.

This becomes clear if we compare male fantasy with the more visionary work of a writer like Doris Lessing, whose fiction can be seen as representing a position towards which many women using supernatural elements in their art have been moving. The recurrent themes and preoccupations of these stories—women transcending time, space and matter, collapsing individual identities, defying definitions of madness and sanity, moving beyond life and death—surface in Lessing's novels not as extraordinary, supernatural occurrences, but as the very stuff of reality. Her attempts to dissolve the limited world of the ego identity, first in *The Golden Notebook* (1962), with its merging of characters and its fusion of dream and waking perceptions, followed by the mystical dissolution of material form in *The Memoirs of a Survivor* (1974) and an extended exploration of different states of awareness, personal and collective, in her *Canopus in Argos* series, reveal Lessing's sense of *responsibility* to expand and extend our understanding of what is possible, natural, and real. Impossible to dismiss as allegorical, fanciful, or supernatural, her fictions open up an awareness of *this* world in a broader, deeper perspective.

The final novel in Lessing's five-volume *Children of Violence* series, *The Four-Gated City* (1969), suggests that it is *women* who are more able to perceive and receive this larger reality. Two of her female characters, Martha Quest and the mad woman Lynda Coldridge, possess an ability similar to that of Ellie and Johanna in *Attachment* to tune in to a consciousness beyond their own and to communicate inter-psychically. What they have access to is a dimension of experience that has always been there, but that has become invisible and inaudible because of man's reluctance to be open to anything beyond the control of his reason, sight, and language. Whereas their male friend, a science fiction writer called Jimmy Wood, presents supernatural events as artificially induced, mere fictional devices, Martha is interested in them as actualities. While he capitalizes on the supernatural for his art, she holds it to be important in fiction because it is *real*. "Odd in itself . . . a man has written half a dozen books about people with this or that sense out of the normal: but he is embarrassed when asked if people might in fact have this or that sense." He is unable to receive, to hear, to tune in to these other possibilities: "He could not listen: his experience did not connect with what she said. He was not able to hear."[16]

Lessing's description of Martha and Lynda experiencing this "abnormal" state of being, outside and beyond any easy translation into fixed language or conceptual thought, could serve as an epigraph to the supernatural stories in this volume. It suggests that women are drawn towards non-realistic literature not, as with many male writers, for purposes of horror, sadism, violence, or suspense, not to arouse fear for its own sake, but as means of intimating a wider sense of reality:

> . . . *in their own inner experience this was a time of possibility. It was as if doors kept opening in their brains just far enough to admit a new sensation, or a glimmer of something—and although they closed again, something was left behind. . . .* But to lay hands on it, to net it, that was different. It was as if the far-off sweetness experienced in a dream, that unearthly impossible sweetness, less the thing itself than the need or hunger for it, a question and answer sounding together on the same fine high note—as if that sweetness known all one's life, tantalisingly intangible, had come closer, a little closer, so that one continually sharply turned one's head after something just glimpsed out of the corner of an eye, or tried to refine one's senses to catch something just beyond them. . . . *They did not really know what they were doing, or how, really, they did it. Yet out of all this material gathered, they began to get glimpses of a new sort of understanding.*[17] (Italics mine.)

Materialistic, man-made culture has dismissed such understanding as madness, yet as Lessing continues, "Perhaps it was because if society is so organised . . . that *it will not admit what one knows to be true, will not admit it that is, except as it comes out perverted, through madness,* then it is through madness and its variants it must be sought after." (Italics mine.) Supernaturalism could be seen as another such "variant." If a rationalistic and secular culture will not admit what other cultures know to be true, it will come out "perverted" through various disguised forms. Spiritual truths and realities that are experienced as natural in less secular societies must assume unnatural, supernatural form in Western culture, and it may be that the themes of haunting, doubling, possession, internal communion, metamorphoses, time travelling, permeability of selves, and the interchangeability of life and death found in supernatural writing by women are precisely this—intimations of a suppressed world of spirituality, an area in many ways as taboo now as sexuality used to be.

Patriarchy's denial of this other world may be as damaging to women's attemps to find wholeness as its parallel frustration of their social and political yearnings. For, as Rainer Maria Rilke has written, the neglect of this world threatens both individual and society with a severely depleted awareness:

> That mankind has in this sense been cowardly has done life endless harm; *the experiences that are called "visions," the whole so-called "spirit-world," death, all those things that are so closely akin to us, have by daily parrying been so crowded out of life that the senses with which we could have grasped them are atrophied. To say nothing of God. But fear of the inexplicable has not alone impoverished the existence of the individual; the relationship between one human being and another has also been cramped by it,* as though it had been lifted out of the riverbed of endless possibilities and set down in a fallow spot on the bank, to which nothing happens.[18] (Italics mine.)

By re-introducing these "endless possibilities" of self and world, refusing to be intimidated by accusations of eccentricity or madness, extending the boundaries of fiction to the limits of language and beyond, women writers of the supernatural have continued to try to lift the veil imposed by a materialistic, rationalistic, and male-dominated culture, to enlarge consciousness and bring spiritual realities back into a predominantly secular age, and to *see* for themselves once again. As the lost goddess figure in Jules Faye's oneiric vision **Pandora Pandaemonia** (1988) declares,

> I am the spirit of every woman who has ever fought or loved fiercely. I am Death and the Spirit of Life in Death. My body is burdened with the things which have murdered women's lives. . . . And yet I live. I wait. I weep. I ache violently to be remembered.

Rosemary Jackson
Bristol, England

Notes

1. Coined by the British critic F. R. Leavis in 1948, the term "the great tradition" refers to an idea that has dominated studies of fiction writing, giving priority to realistic over non-realistic forms. Some of the philosophical, theoretical, and political implications behind realism in art are explored in Damian Grant's *Realism* (London: Methuen, 1970; New York: Routledge Chapman and Hall) and Terry Eagleton's *Criticism and Ideology* (London: New Left Books, 1976).

2. Hélène Cixous, "The Laugh of the Medusa," in *New French Feminisms,* ed. Elaine Marks and Isabelle de Courtivron (Brighton, England: Harvester, and New York: Schocken, 1981), 249.

3. Ibid.

4. Rosemary Jackson, "Frankenstein: A Myth for Women," *Women's Review* (London) 12 (October 1986): 16–17.

5. Ellen Moers, "Female Gothic," chap. 5 in *Literary Women* (London: W.H. Allen, and New York: Doubleday, 1977), 90–110.

6. This surfacing of supernatural elements is discussed further in my article on the Gothic in the nineteenth century: "The Silenced Text: Shades of Gothic in Victorian Fiction," *Minnesota Review* 13 (1979): 98–112.

7. Gillian Beer, "Ghosts," which reviews *Night Visitors* by Julia Briggs, *Essays in Criticism* 28 (1978): 259–64; 260.

8. One of the identifying features of the Byronic hero in Romantic literature was his mesmerizing male gaze, the power of the eye to fix and transfix women. For contemporary analyses of men's control of women through the eye, through determining who looks and how, see John Berger, *Ways of Seeing* (London and New York: Penguin, 1972) and E. Ann Kaplan, "Is the gaze male?" in *Women and Film: Both Sides of the Camera* (London: Methuen, and New York: Routledge Chapman and Hall, 1983).

9. Linda Pastan, "Night," in her *Selected Poems* (London: John Murray, 1979), 41.

10. Olive Schreiner, "The Dawn of Civilisation," in *Stories, Dreams and Allegories* (London: T. Fisher Unwin, and Darby, Pa.: Darby Books, reprint of 1923 ed.), 172.

11. Rosemary Jackson, *Fantasy: The Literature of Subversion* (London: Methuen, and New York: Routledge Chapman and Hall, 1981), 87–88. Also from that passage: "A mirror produces distance. It establishes a different space, where our notions of self undergo radical change." As Leo Bersani writes of the mirror: "The mirror [serves] as a metaphor for the inaccessibility of one's possible selves to one's present consciousness. It is a spatial representation of an intuition that our being can never be adequately enclosed within any present formulation—any formulation here and now—of our being. It is as if the experience of perceiving ourselves elsewhere suggested the possibility of our becoming something else. Mirrors represent as a phenomenon of distance our capacity for unpredictable metamorphoses." (Leo Bersani, *A Future for Astyanax: Character and Desire in Literature* [Boston and Toronto: Little, Brown, 1976], 208.)

12. Sandra M. Gilbert and Susan Gubar, *The Madwoman in the Attic: The Woman Writer and the Nineteenth Century Literary Imagination* (New Haven and London: Yale University Press, 1979); Elaine Showalter, *A Literature of Their Own: British Women Novelists from Brontë to Lessing* (Princeton: Princeton University Press, 1977); and *The Female Malady: Women, Madness and English Culture 1830–1980* (New York: Pantheon, 1985); Juliet Mitchell, *Women: The Longest Revolution* (London: Virago, and New York: Pantheon, 1984).

13. On *The Yellow Wallpaper,* see Elaine Hedges's afterword to *The Yellow Wallpaper,* Charlotte Perkins Gilman (New York: The Feminist Press at

C.U.N.Y., 1973), 37–63, and Gail Parker, ed., *The Oven Birds: American Women on Womanhood 1820–1920* (New York: Anchor Doubleday, 1972), 315–87.

14. Fritjof Capra, *The Turning Point: Science, Society and the Rising Culture* (New York: Simon and Schuster, 1982, and London: Fontana, 1984), 79.

15. Michèle Roberts, *The Wild Girl* (London: Methuen, 1984).

16. Doris Lessing, *The Four-Gated City* (London: Panther, and New York: Knopf, 1969), 387.

17. Ibid., 388.

18. Rainer Maria Rilke, *Letters to a Young Poet,* trans. M. D. Norton (New York and London: W. W. Norton, 1934), 67–68.

Proem

The Immortal

Since my soul and I are friends,
  I go laughing on my road;
Whether up or down it wends,
  I have never felt my load.

For the winds keep tryst with me,
  And the stars shine in my joy;
Meadow, hill or sky or sea,
  I create and I destroy.

Hope or fear or bliss or woe
  Flits a shadow on the sod;
Life and Death perpetual flow,
  Underneath them I am God.

Smaller than the smallest part,
  Larger than the moving Whole;
One in the divided heart
  And the Universal Soul.

Neither curse nor creed I know,
  Doubts that darken, faiths that shine;
Time and space are empty show,
  All that ever was is mine.

Silent, deathless, centered fast,
  Ancient, uncreated, free,
I came not to birth at last,
  Universes are of me.

Ellen Glasgow, 1908

What Did
Miss Darrington See?

The Long Chamber

ıllıₛ

Olivia Howard Dunbar

In a 1905 issue of The Dial, *Olivia Howard Dunbar lamented "the decay of ghost-fiction," which she perceived as becoming rare in the periodicals and, when it was published, too esoteric after the manner of Henry James. She advocated a new type of ghost story that was at once literal and psychological, ending her criticism on the positive note: "There is hope for a renaissance of the literary ghost [and] there may indeed develop a regenerated ghost-literature well worth acquaintance." This hope was fulfilled by the best ghost fiction of the following two decades, such as that composed by Ellen Glasgow, May Sinclair, Georgia Wood Pangborn, Katherine Fullerton Gerould, and Oliver Onions. Dunbar herself was to be part of that renaissance.*

Dunbar was a staunch activist in the women's suffrage movement. She wrote, in a 1917 issue of Everybody's Magazine, *of "the great matter of woman's freedom" and of women as "half-citizens to the world." As it was for many women writers of that decade, the right to vote, not yet won, was prominent in Dunbar's artistic as well as political consciousness.*

Born in West Bridgeport, Massachusetts, in 1873, Dunbar graduated from Smith College and worked for The New York World *until 1902. She quit her newspaper career in order to focus on feature articles and short fiction for the day's leading magazines and spent the rest of her life in New York as a noted fiction writer and biographer. She married poet Ridgeley Torrence in 1914, after establishing her independent career, and continued to use her own name. Torrence died in 1950 and Dunbar followed three years after.*

When "The Long Chamber" was published in the September 1914 issue of Harper's Magazine, Dunbar was deeply involved with the suffrage movement and at the same time pleasantly involved with a New York writers' group—and with Ridgeley Torrence. Understandably, the theme of romantic love runs through the story, though in a pensive and unconventional manner. The tale is first and foremost an entertainment, as any good ghost story must be. It is also decidedly feminist in its psychological investigation of a woman who has subjugated her own genius to the furtherance of her husband's career. The fact that the husband remains off-stage renders the story more than an indictment of overbearing masculinity; it is, rather, about the struggle within a reticent woman whose destiny is largely in her own control.

Dunbar seems to have had no champion since Dorothy Scarborough, who mentioned "The Long Chamber" in her classic overview The Supernatural in Modern Fiction *(1917) and reprinted another of Dunbar's feminist ghost stories, "The Shell of Sense" (1912), in* Famous Modern Ghost Stories *(1921). Dunbar's many other stories, some of them supernatural, remain uncollected.*

ılllı

There was perhaps no warrant for the vaguely swelling disquiet that possessed me from the moment that, late in the sultry August afternoon, there arrived the delayed telegram that announced the immediate coming of Beatrice Vesper.

. . . Beatrice Vesper abruptly on her way to me, and alone—it was the most strangely unlikely news. Yet I had no cause for real concern. She would find ready conveyance over the three steep miles from the railroad—our pleasantly decaying village being unlinked with the contemporary world. And, as the others reminded me, it wasn't as though the redundant spaciousness of Burleigh House didn't seem to invite, almost to select and compel, unaccustomed guests; or as though the Long Chamber, our supreme source of pride, hadn't that morning received the final touches that consecrated it to the utmost hospitality we could offer. As for Beatrice, she would delight in the survival of Burleigh House as unfailingly as she herself would prove its most harmonious ornament. And that matter of ornament wasn't one that David and I could be said to have taken at all lightly. How prodigally, how passionately, we had spent our love and labor on the precious house, in the months since it had so unexpectedly fallen into our hands—only to admit to each other, at the end of it all, in almost hysterical dismay, that the stately interiors seemed always empty, however vociferously we strove to be at home in them. There were void, waiting spaces that not the sum of all our alien, cheerful presences could fill. We had achieved a background, but a background for brilliant life; and it was as though we, living in terms of the palest prose, defiled past it almost invisibly. The truth was that we had established no spiritual tenancy, and that we didn't, ourselves, belong there. But though I was far from guessing with what mysterious tentacles the past would seize her, I knew that Beatrice Vesper would belong.

It was plain enough, however, from the first sight of my old friend, that she had come to me in no unhappy stress. Her secure and unvexed air was for an instant disconcerting; I had, in my panic, so prepared myself for haggard pathos. And indeed it was almost incredible that the hurrying, untender years should not have bruised so delicate a creature. With swiftly relaxing nerves I surrendered to the flattery of her explanation that when, only the day before, her husband had been summoned to Europe by cable—she herself being kept behind by the important final proof-reading of a technical work of Dr. Vesper's, to be published in the early autumn—she had from all her social resources chosen Burleigh House as her temporary refuge. . . . So that, after all, it seemed stupid to have taken fright. Beatrice and I had been the closest companions in earlier days. And doubtless I had exaggerated those conditions of her life which, for years past, had led her friends into the way of speaking of her ruefully, reminiscently, almost as if she were dead.

It was in this latter spirit that I had been speaking of her to David, only the day before, picturing her as the only woman I knew whose marriage had been complete self-immolation. Those of us who wore our fetters with a more modern jauntiness had resented, from our ill-informed distance, what seemed to be her slavish submission. She might as well have been chained in a cave—the rest of the world had not a glimpse of her. Dr. Vesper—a mild enough tyrant in appearance—did not care for society, so they had literally no visitors. There prevailed a legend that he was the most miserable of dyspeptics; and that Beatrice devoted most of her time to preparing the unheard-of substances that fed him. His financial concerns—for important mining interests had sprung from the geological work in which he had become famous—kept him in the city throughout the year, and Beatrice had never left him for a day, even in torrid midsummer.

But David, who is sturdily unmodern, refused to be astonished. "Why not, if she's in love with him?" he asked.

"But she's not," I insisted "or—she wasn't. It's her husband who's in love, and with the most unheard-of concentration. He has cared for her ever since she was a child, so the thing hung over her—though I suppose that's not a romantic way of putting it—for years before they were married. So isn't it rather extreme for her to relinquish everything else in the world for the sake of the man she merely—likes?"

David may have submitted a discreet version of this to our old friend

Anthony Lloyd, who had been with us all that summer, and I imagine that in consequence both men looked to find in Beatrice Vesper the dull, heavy-domestic type. So when, an hour after her arrival, they saw her vivid smile and smooth black hair and her young, slim figure in its mulberry-colored taffeta against the dark panels of our candle-lighted dining-room, they both bore very definite evidence of response to her loveliness. Anthony even betrayed his admiration a shade too markedly, for he had rather an assured way of paying court to women who attracted him. But his advance was deftly and unmistakably cut off. Beatrice Vesper's wifely attitude remained true, I saw, to its severely classic pattern.

However, pitfalls of this order were easily avoided, teased as we all were by the irresistible topic of our dazzling inheritance. And David was shortly embarked upon his familiar contention that we cared much more for the place than if he had been the direct heir and we had been able to anticipate the glory of ownership.

"Oh, we're very humble" David conceded, "but we do claim credit as resuscitators. That's what we've really felt ourselves to be doing for months—breathing life into a beautiful thing that had been left for dead. And it has begun to live again, don't you think, in a feeble way? But it's as showmen that we're so shockingly deficient. You see a house that Judge Timothy Burleigh built in 1723 and that was continuously lived in until they deserted it a generation ago, must—well, must have its secrets. But we have to admit we don't know them!"

"Oh, do you think you *can* live here without knowing?" Beatrice broke out with an intensity that surprised us all. "You'll divine them, if you learn them in no other way. Family traditions can never be smothered, you know—they cling too imperishably!"

"But the legend famine has already been relieved," Anthony announced, "or we assume that it has. At least, we've found a group of old trunks, filled with papers, and they've all been assigned to me, to dig secrets from. I'm going to begin in the morning."

"It's not that Molly and I haven't longed to dig for ourselves," David hastily defended us, "but we haven't had time. And as for divination— our imaginations lack the necessary point of departure because our cousins have kept all the portraits. That's the really serious gap, you'll notice, in our conscientious furnishing—that apparently we've sprung from the soil, that we haven't an ancestor. Though of course we have seen the old pictures, long ago, or I have."

"Oh, what were they—" Beatrice began.

"Mrs. Vesper, need you ask?" Anthony interrupted. "Wigged men with heavy, hawk-nosed faces—"

"And meek-eyed women," David assented, laughing. "Yes, they do look like that, mostly. The Burleighs were a formidable race and their wives must have been unnaturally submissive."

"But that's according to the Colonial portrait-painter's conventions," Anthony argued. "The very earliest of your portraits must have been painted less than two hundred years ago. Well, that's time enough for fashions in portraits to change; but do human beings alter essentially? The old Burleighs cannot have been so different, inside their Colonial purple and fine linen, from you and Molly. Your hawk-nosed grandfathers must have enjoyed a joke, now and then, and those meek-eyed Patiences and Charities—mustn't they have had their emotions?"

"There must be conditions so harsh that emotions remain latent," I suggested, carelessly.

But Anthony never missed an occasion to dogmatize, after his own fashion: "I admit there are temperaments that cannot love, for instance. But to those that can the opportunity doesn't fail."

"But surely," he roused me to protest, "there is a type of woman who never learns her own capacity, who remains ingenuous, undeveloped—"

"Only until her appointed time," Anthony extravagantly persisted.

"What you are trying to express," David flouted, "is the old-fashioned school-girlish belief in predestined lovers. And perhaps it has remained for you to explain what happens in case the predestined lover dies?"

"In that case he'll come back from the dead to teach her!" But this point was made amid a shout of laughter, and we all conceded that the subject had been carried as far as it could be.

Almost immediately after dinner, Beatrice confessing that she was very tired, I rather self-consciously took a pewter candlestick from its stand in the lower hall and guided her up-stairs. And I found myself weakly unable to bid her good night without a fond proprietary emphasis on the treasures of the Long Chamber, its ancient oaken chests and still more ancient powdering-table, its carved bed and woven counterpane, even the long mirror, faintly time-blurred, in which we had been told that Anne Burleigh, the first mistress of the house, used once to contemplate her charming face and towering head-dress.

"Then, of course, it contains her image still." Beatrice's smiling, confident glance seemed to penetrate with singular ease the delicate clouds with which two centuries had lightly flecked the glass. "I shall see it, of course, after she gets used to me. I wonder if this was her room?"

"That is one of the thousand things we don't know," I lamented. "But it may well have been. It is the finest, we think, of all the rooms. Judge Timothy's lovely young wife *should* have had it!"

"Don't you think it's almost heartless to have preserved her mere possessions," Beatrice admonished me, "and yet allow the memories of her life to be so scattered? We must gather them up and piece them together!"

"Reconstruction ought not to be too difficult in her case," I laughed. "I imagine she was a simple creature."

It was our household custom to breakfast in our rooms, and after that to pursue our independent occupations throughout the greater part of the day. But Beatrice's proof-sheets and documents, which were of the most inordinate bulk, and which further depressingly renewed themselves by express every few days, often consumed her evenings likewise. It had struck me that we might achieve an arid semblance of friendly intercourse if she would assign to me some clerkly and mechanical part of her labors. But I saw from her look that it was as though I had asked a priestess to delegate to me her hieratic function. Her fealty to her dingy religion of ink and paper and chemical symbols was inflexible. And unreasoning, I thought, since it had cost her the look of freshness and vigor she had worn on coming to us. The thing was consuming her—her altered face told the story. Two weeks, indeed, after she had come, I realized that we had not yet had a comfortable talk together. What, after all, did I know of this new Beatrice, except that her highly decorative presence justified our otherwise empty splendor, and that for her own part she was working herself into an illness. She had come to us, she said, for rest and country peace and a season of friendship, but it was patent to the point of irony that she was profiting by none of these. And I did confess to myself, I remember, a secret hurt that there were so many days when she was unable, or ostensibly so, to join us at the hour of frank idleness when we took our tea under the oak-tree on the lawn, and when we always, sooner or later, fell to talking of our somewhat shadowy guest.

"Is it I whom Mrs. Vesper is avoiding?" Anthony asked, rather wistfully, one afternoon. "I'll admit I didn't seize her tone directly she arrived, but I have it now—completely! She would find me irreproachable if she would only mingle with us a little. How comforting it would be if she had a human liking for tennis and riding!"

"My dear Anthony, I don't think she knows you are under the same roof, except when she sees you at dinner," I assured him. "But she's under the thrall of an inhuman husband who is overworking her from the other end of the world and practically denying us any share in her."

"Are you so sure it's overwork," David demanded, "and not the beginning of typhoid? She does look downright ill, you know. My own impulse would be to send for a doctor. Could there be anything unwholesome about the house—any eighteenth-century germ that has escaped our scourings?"

We all brooded for a moment on the possibility this opened.

"Do you think distraction would help her?" Anthony asked. "Because I have it here!"—he tapped his breast-pocket, triumphantly. "I've patched together in the last few days a good part of the history of Burleigh House. I had meant not to tell you yet, but secrecy is consuming me."

"Dole the stories out to us one at a time," David lazily suggested, his interest half-paralyzed by the sheer weight of the August atmosphere. "We'll inaugurate a series of Nights—if not a Thousand and One, then as many as you please. And you'll begin to-night, of course. Can you go as far back as Judge Timothy?"

"Yes—if you would rather begin there. Though I hadn't planned—"

"Then it's settled," I interrupted. And this was indeed so precisely what we had all been thirstily waiting for that I thought it a sufficient pretext for disturbing Beatrice on the spot. Moreover, David's hints had freshly stimulated my own smoldering anxiety in regard to my friend. I had been too passive—I should have forced her to spare herself. The unnamable fears that I had felt on the day of her arrival recurred and pierced me.

In the Long Chamber I found her rather wearily putting away her work for the day. She stood by her table, a slender, drooping figure with a sheaf of fluttering papers in her hand, and faced me—still without the look of affectionate welcome I had so missed of late; merely with a sweet patience and courtesy. I should perhaps have approached my end by gentle, gradual arts, but my concern for her abruptly overflowed in unconsidered words. I begged her to admit to me that she wasn't well, that I might insist on proper care for her. I blamed bitterly my own laxity in allowing her to wear herself out as she had done. The publication of her husband's book on a certain day could not, I urged, be a matter so imperative that she must sacrifice her youth, her life, to it. By every obligation of our old friendship I implored her to intrust herself to me—and I laid especial stress on my responsibility to her absent husband.

"You were all vigor and loveliness when you came to us," I reminded her. "And now—now—you are so changed!"

She looked at me in a half-startled fashion as I said this, and a dim, ambiguous smile trembled on her lips.

"Yes—he will find me changed." She spoke thoughtfully, but quite without emphasis. "But that is something I must face alone."

If she had said no more than this she would have left me with the impression that the distant Dr. Vesper was a subtler Bluebeard. And indeed a look of secrecy and dread that I now for the first time caught flowing darkly over her candid face was wretchedly that of the wife

The Long Chamber/7

who has opened the forbidden door and is haunted by the intolerable knowledge that must shortly betray her. Could it, after all, be a worse than physical suffering that was draining her eyes of their look of life? She had begun to move uneasily about, and I felt that she would have been glad to have me leave her. But unable longer to endure the intervening shield, I made a desperate effort to demolish it, to force her reluctant confidence; and with hot cheeks and trembling voice I stammered crude, disconnected sentences on the frequent failure of men to understand women and situations, . . . on the indulgence with which we were forced to regard many masculine traits. . . .

"Oh, you have thought that?" she interrupted me, almost shrilly—"that my husband caused me suffering? Why, Molly, I supposed you knew, that *everybody* knew, how utterly, stainlessly good he is. It is I, oh, always I, who fall short." She took my hand gently. "You must not go until I have told you how it is." And we sat down together.

Much of what she then told me I did indeed already know, but under a different complexion from that with which she now invested it—how at nineteen she had married Edward Vesper almost frivolously, with no sense of sacredness, lightly assuming—though this was, of course, true enough—that she was bestowing a blessing by becoming the wife of the man for whom she felt a merely childlike affection. How, afterward, she had discovered that the marriage had been urged, hurried, by her poor, desperate mother, who, with four younger children, was at the end of everything; and how Dr. Vesper's money had supported them all ever since. . . .

"Then I saw," Beatrice slowly went on, after a little, though I saw what the words were costing her, "how narrowly my own foolish ignorance had saved me from baseness. I had married for my own advantage a man who gave me perfect love. Facing this, I saw that from that moment I was bound to give more than I had ever dreamed of giving. And that, if I couldn't love my husband as he so wonderfully loved me, I must at least offer him the most sedulous counterfeit I could muster. That the least abatement of unremitting devotion would be treachery. . . . Well, that has been my life, and always, until now, I have known that no woman could do more—"

She would have gone on, the momentum of an impulsive confidence is so great, but at that point the maid came in search of me, announcing dinner. So, after a violent flurry of dressing, Beatrice and I contrived, ten minutes later, to be with the others in the dining-room. The disclosure she had made to me, with its intensely characteristic light on the apparent enigmas of her marriage, seemed for the time to have loosed a painful restraint. She talked with gentle gaiety, exchanging swift jests with the imperturbable Anthony, for whom I knew she had come to have a genuine liking, and seeming humanly at home with all of us, rather than driven, as one could fancy her latterly to have been, by some invisible harriers.

It even seemed natural and expected when, after dinner, Beatrice, who had so often spent her evenings alone, chose to seat herself at the old spinet and coax from it a few dim spectral chords.

"There's the prelude for your story, Anthony," David remarked when she had finished.

"It's a perfect one," Anthony declared. "Those are, of course, the very sounds with which Anne Burleigh beguiled her solemn days."

I had caught a note in his voice that awed me a little. "Anne Burleigh—you're to tell us of her! Then it won't, of course, be a cheerful story. Why is it that it has always been she, rather than any of the others, for whom our hearts have vaguely ached?"

"Cheerful? But of course not," Anthony rejoined with energy. "It can't be that you wanted me to discover simple tales of domestic lethargy. That isn't the sort of thing that leaves its impress on a family—and a house. That wouldn't be a story."

Then, as we urged him to begin, he altered his tone and turned to David a serious face. "You'll have to understand," he said, "that I'm taking a great liberty—with you and with your ancestors. This story that I've made out and that I'll repeat to you is, as a matter of fact, very largely—inferred. It's by no means an explicit tradition. But the inference seems to me so plain—and after living here in the house it is, oddly, so credible—and, well, you must forgive me, if, after all, you prefer to leave the inference unformulated."

None of us spoke; and I let my sewing drop in my lap.

"As you know," Anthony began, "Judge Timothy Burleigh married Anne Steele when she was seventeen. A year or two afterward, when they were living in this new and splendid Burleigh House, Sophia Steele, the young wife's sister, came to pay a visit. In this young girl's diary, which tells so much else, and which I've had the astonishing fortune to discover, she records her impression of her sister, who looked 'very maidenly, though the wife of so great a man and the mistress of so fine a house.' But I won't read you her crabbed little sentences—you can see them for yourselves later; I'll simply try to make a connected story. . . .

"Judge Timothy does not appear to have markedly played the lover to his charming little bride, but Sophia heard him praise her for her obedience, saying that it was the prime virtue in a wife. I had supposed that the housewives of that day had exacting responsibilities, but possibly because it was so fine a thing to be the Judge's wife, or else because her youth exempted her, little Mistress Burleigh seems to have had abundant leisure. She would play the spinet for hours at a time or she would sit with her baby boy—"

"The boy must have been Colonel Jonathan," David, who has always been rather too fond of facts, interposed. "Anne Burleigh had but one child."

"You see her, don't you, as I do," Anthony went on, "forlorn little Maeterlinckian heroine, treated as a child by her husband and practising rigidly the submission he exacted of her? It must have been a dull household, in spite of the splendid entertaining that took place at intervals, or sister Sophia wouldn't have had so much leisure to write in her diary. And it must have been an unnatural one, or—the climax wouldn't have flamed so suddenly. Something had to happen in such a house—and it did happen, as I make out, when a young relative of the Burleighs from Virginia came North to seek advancement in the law through his distinguished relative, the Judge. This young man, Brian Calvert, was asked to Burleigh House as a guest. It is very plain that he was keenly admired from the first by little sister Sophia, who meticulously describes his height and beauty and 'merry manners.' The Judge, I imagine, did not diffuse much merriment through the house. But the Virginian probably didn't see little Sophia; his attention was too completely and frankly absorbed. So she stayed apart, a sad, involuntary little spy, not critical or even fully comprehending, but vaguely and innocently envious, I gather, of an unknown mysterious thing with which the air about her had suddenly become surcharged. Anne Burleigh herself, poor child, was doubtless almost as far from understanding what had befallen her. At all events, there seems to have been no concealment. Anne and Calvert spent long days together, sitting under the trees in the garden. No one knows whether he said a word of love to her—I could almost believe that he did not. But the young, innocent creatures were none the less firmly in the grasp of the elemental force that was about to shatter them. It may have been love of the kind that absolutely cannot yield to reason, and that could never adapt itself to a slow cooling and decline—"

"Of course, they had to die," Beatrice Vesper broke in. "One cannot love like that—and live."

Her voice held somber secrets. It was as though she were speaking of something intimately real. I tried to see her face, but the shadow veiled it.

Anthony paused for a moment as though he, too, were amazed at her interruption. "Yes," he said, "there had to be a tragic issue. . . . The happenings of a certain day were told long after, but vaguely, in Sophia's journal. Perhaps the child herself only suspected. . . . One day Brian Calvert was ill and remained in his room. When evening came

Anne suggested taking some supper to him. The Judge reminded her, and rather ungently, that such an errand was for a servant to perform. . . . An hour later she burst into her sister's bedroom in a passion of fear. She had for the first time eluded and disobeyed her husband, taking to Calvert's room a porringer of gruel that she had made herself. The Judge, whom she doubtless supposed busy with his books, heard her step, followed her, and, entering the room a moment later, discovered her in Calvert's arms. I am sure they had never kissed before, but to her husband this was no extenuation. The Judge forced Anne from the room. Listening outside, she heard the sound of swords—and more—and worse. . . . Brian Calvert was never seen again. Anne Burleigh herself fell ill, and a few months later she died."

I felt that we had heard as much as we could bear, but David did not understand my signal, and advanced his literal and perfectly reasonable inquiry:

"Are you sure that Calvert was killed?"

"Entirely sure," Anthony said, a little dryly, "though there isn't a shadow of proof. Can you imagine such a husband hesitating or failing of his purpose?"

"You believe that they fought each other in this house?" David went on, in his solemn effort to realize the thing. "And there is no record of it? But where can it have been? You don't know that, of course?"

"Yes, I know," Anthony admitted, slowly. "It was in the guestroom. They called it the Long Chamber."

"The Long Chamber!" David repeated. And he turned toward Beatrice his honest, unperceiving eyes.

Beatrice had been sitting motionless. Now she rose hastily. "Why should you feel it tragic that he died?" she demanded, almost with brusqueness, but without looking at any one of us. "He would have chosen it. It was no unwilling death—that much I know." Her voice, usually so calm, was roughened with agitation. "I have stayed too long," she added. "I am very tired and should have gone earlier. But the story held us so."

She was gone before I had found words to detain her, and we all sat silent. Then Anthony said:

"I felt it before I had half finished the story. I know it now. *She has seen Calvert's ghost!*"

"That's preposterous!" David exclaimed.

"Because you haven't seen it yourself?" our friend inquired, quietly. "But, my dear David, have you ever slept in that room? And in any case what would the ghost of that young lover have to say to you?"

"Or to Beatrice Vesper, for that matter?" I added.

Anthony shrugged his shoulders. "Who knows?" he said. "I admit that if it were the usual family specter, I can't conceive her risking a second encounter. But Calvert's apparition—that might perhaps be less formidable. . . . Still, it's all much queerer than I like—and I'm not even sure I want her to tell."

David began to be troubled. "Molly, you know her. We don't. Is she so infernally secretive? Could she see a ghost in our house without telling us? And why shouldn't she tell?"

I sat brooding, conscious that I was trembling a response to every lightest breath of air. There were secrets about; the troubled atmosphere was heavy with them. Something had happened to Beatrice, as any one but my dear dull David could have seen. But since we three were so blindly in the dark, how and whence could it have come? Anthony was, of course, uncommonly astute, yet I had no curiosity as to the guesses I saw him shrewdly elaborating. He did not know Beatrice's sound, unassailable simplicity as I knew it.

We were all, indeed, unnaturally alert, tensely awaiting we knew not what, so that when the door-bell rang we all started as though the sound had some portentous significance—holding our breath, fairly, until the maid came in with an envelope which she said was for Mrs. Vesper.

"It's a cable," I said. "I'll take it up to her."

A half-hour must have passed since she had gone up-stairs, yet when I knocked she came to her door fully dressed. When she saw the envelope she asked me to stay until she had read the message—which was, she told me, a moment later, from her husband. He was sailing and would arrive in a week.

With a sense of relief that was almost disloyal I welcomed this definite, prosaic event. At least it would dissipate the vapors that had gathered.

"Can't we send for him to come directly here?" I suggested. "Must you meet him in New York when it is so hot and you're not really well?"

She laid her hand gently on my arm, instinctively trying to soften the harsh abruptness of what she was about to say.

"Why shouldn't I tell you? I shall never see him again."

The words sounded so unreasoning that I felt myself growing literally cold. "But, dear Beatrice—it was such a little time ago—in this very room—that you told me—"

"Of his goodness and his love. And of the obligations they imposed on me. But now—if I can't fully meet them—if I'm not the same—"

Her phrases were still without meaning to me. I tried vaguely to protest. "But your courage—"

"Oh, I had courage—for a lifetime. But I was mercifully blindfolded. Now, when I *know*—"

Anthony's confident statement recurred to me, precipitating dim suspicions, intimations, of my own.

"Beatrice, what is it that you have learned to know?" I demanded, firmly. "What is it that you have—seen?"

She cast a quick glance toward the old mirror, dull-rimmed, garlanded, in which she had gaily told me that she expected to see Anne Burleigh's child-like face. "Seen?" she repeated. "Oh, dear Molly, it's not alone what I have *seen*. . . . But there is something that lives on here, in this room, of which I merely knew the name. . . . I have felt it almost from the first moment. And there have been hours when I have so shared in it—when I have lived with an intensity I had never dreamed of—"

"Beatrice,"—I pressed her for something more definite—"you have seen Anne Burleigh?"

"Oh, it's not she who has left the deathless element," Beatrice said. "It's the man who loved her, who loved so well that he did not need to live. You see his love was so complete that it gained an earthly immortality of its own. It is here—now. I did not know such things could be. And, oh, Molly, I have tried *not* to know! You have seen how I have struggled to fill up my time and thought with work. I have not welcomed this other new thing, I have shrunk from it. But it has seized me and stripped my eyes and dazzled them—and I know what love can be."

"Brian Calvert has taught you!" I could not help the words. And, in spite of me, they sounded like an accusation.

"If it were only a lesson I could unlearn," she answered, quietly. "If I could only forget the sweet terror of it all."

"The terror of dreams and visions? But, dear Beatrice, that fades and vanishes."

"It is already vanished. But not before it has changed me past all helping. You can see how, after this, I can never—*pretend* to love."

I did not try to press her further, for I hoped that the next day, when Anthony's story would be less vivid to us all, I could prevail on the desperation of her attitude. I did insist, however, that she should not spend the night alone, and she consented, after a little, that I should sleep with her. Or so, at least, we termed it. But my patient vigil told me plainly enough that poor Beatrice slept no more than I. It is true that I assumed—though how could I be sure?—that I had dispelled her disturbing phantasms. I did not, though I lay there expectant at her side, feel the clutch at my own heart of Brian Calvert's strangely inextinguishable love; and though in the first few pale moments of dawn I saw Beatrice's strained eyes bent steadily on Anne Burleigh's garlanded mirror, to me its unrevealing surface presented merely a reticent blur.

It did not surprise me when, an hour later, Beatrice told me that she must leave Burleigh House that morning. And indeed it seemed that to let her go—out of the reach of the ghostliness that had so preyed upon her sensitive spirit—was, at that critical moment, the best that I could do for her. Yet, strangely, even after all that she had told me, I did not guess into what utter darkness she was going. Immune as I then believed myself to spectral invasions of my own serenity, I did not know at that time, nor until long after, how the reverberations of spent lives may sometimes sound so loud as to muffle the merely human cry. All that Beatrice Vesper saw and felt as she sat in the Long Chamber and battled ineffectually with the insistent presence, or presences, that may have abided within the distances of the dim, garlanded mirror, is still, I know, beyond my vain conjecture. And there are certain bare and almost intolerable facts that seem indeed to close the door on such imaginings. . . . For Edward Vesper never saw his wife again, and a month after Beatrice's going word came to me that she was dead. We have closed the Long Chamber for all time.

A Ghost Story

Ada Trevanion

Little is known about Ada Trevanion beyond the fact she was born into a prominent London family in the early nineteenth century. She contributed to numerous magazines on both sides of the Atlantic and was an early translator of fantasist Hans Christian Anderson. A collection of her poetry published in 1858 was reviewed by the London Atheneum; *excerpts from the collection were reprinted in the little magazine* Fantasy & Terror *in 1987. Her ballad "Cathleen's Ghost" is about a woman returning from the dead to accuse her faithless lover and frighten him to death. The much shorter poem "Spirits of the Dead" expresses a darkly romantic view of death.*

In the folk tradition of ghost lore, the return of a spirit with a mission to complete, a wrong to right, or who is compelled by guilt or sadness to reveal a hidden will or lost treasure is a typical concern. This ancient theme has been adapted to numerous short stories. Alice Morse Earle spoofed the motif in the final chapter of her nonfiction volume Stage Coach and Tavern Days *(1900), in which the ghost of an American Indian causes a gullible family to dig holes all over their property, seeking a non-existent treasure.*

Though many stories adopting this theme must be dismissed as cliché, "A Ghost Story," reprinted here from the January 1858 issue of New York's National Magazine, *uses the formula to explore an atypical subject: the relationship between student and teacher in a Victorian girls' school. The story is successful not only as a tale of haunting, but also as a portrait of the school and of the friendship, bordering on romance, between the heroine and her slightly older in-*

structor. With its almost entirely female cast, the tale was unquestionably tailored for the typical magazine reader of the nineteenth century, who was female. Since teaching was the primary professional role for women, the story offers a character that young Victorian readers would admire, with the spice of the supernatural making it sensational and dramatic.

ıllı

There are many incidents on record which resemble the following plain narrative, and in the books of wise men may be found attempts, more or less plausible, to account for similar facts without having recourse to anything supernatural. The reader will draw his own inferences. It is for me simply to relate the whole history, from the beginning to the end, only premising that it is true in every particular.

Some years ago my father sent me to Woodford House, a young ladies' school, of which a Mrs. Wheeler was the principal. The school had fallen off, before I went, from fifty pupils to thirty; yet the establishment was in many respects a superior one, and the teachers were very efficient.

Mrs. Wheeler and a parlor-boarder, with the two teachers, Madame Dubois and Miss Winter, and we thirty girls, composed the household. Miss Winter, the English teacher, slept in a small room adjoining ours, walked out with us, and never left us. She was about twenty-seven years of age, and had soft, thick, brown hair, and peculiar eyes, of which I find it difficult to give a description. They were of a greenish brown, and, with the least emotion, seemed to fill, as it were, with light, like the flashing brilliancy of moonshine upon water. At half past six in the morning it was her duty to call us, and about seven we came down stairs. We practiced our scales, and looked over the lessons we had prepared the evening before, till half past eight o'clock, when Mrs. Wheeler and Madame Dubois made their appearance; then prayers were read, and after that we had breakfast of coffee, and solid squares of bread and butter, which was very good the first part of the week. Breakfast over, Mrs. Wheeler took her seat at the head of the table, and the business commenced.

Mrs. Wheeler was a tall, stout person, with a loud voice, and a very authoritative manner. She paid assiduous attention to our deportment, and we were often assured that she was gradually falling a victim to the task of entreating us to hold up our heads.

Madame Dubois was a little old, shriveled woman, with a very irascible temper. She wore a turban on her head, and kept cotton in her ears, and mumbled her language all to mash. At one o'clock Mrs. Wheeler shut up her desk, and sailed out of the room, while we proceeded up-stairs to dress for our walk. The dinner was ready on our return at three. This was a plain meal, soon over; and after it Miss Winter took Mrs. Wheeler's place at the long table, and presided over our studies until tea at seven. I thought this interval the pleasantest part of the day, for Miss Winter was clever, and took great pains where she saw intelligence or a desire to learn. I was less with her, however, than many of the girls, because, as one of the elder pupils, I was expected by Mrs. Wheeler to practice on the piano for at least three hours daily. The study was a large, uncarpeted room, with a view of a spacious flower-garden. Some part of most fine spring and summer days was spent in this garden. I liked being there better than going for a walk, because we were not compelled to keep together. I used to take a book, and when the weather was not too cold I sat much near a fountain, under the shade of a laburnum-tree which hung over it. I wonder if the fountain and laburnum-tree are there still.

Woodford House was rather famous for mysterious inmates. There was Mrs. Sparkes, the parlor-boarder, who always took her breakfast in her room, and was rumored to have come by sea from a distant part of the earth, where she and the late Captain Sparkes (her husband) had rolled in gold. It was understood that, if she had her rights, she would be worth fifty thousand a-year. I am afraid she had them not, for I suspect her annual income amounted to little more than five hundred. She was very good-natured, and we all liked her; but our vague association of her with the sea, and storms, and coral reefs, occasioned the wildest legends to be circulated as her history. Then there was a fair pale girl, with bright curling hair, who, we found out, or thought we found out, was the daughter of a father who did not like her. She was a very suggestive topic; so was a young Italian, who had in her possession a real dagger, which many of us believed she always carried about her. But I think all these were outshone, on the whole, by Miss Winter, who never talked about her relations, called at the post-office for her letters, in order that they might not be brought to the school; and, further, had a small oak wardrobe in her room, the key of which she wore around her neck. What a life she had with some of the girls! and how lonely she was, too! for she belonged neither to Mrs. Wheeler nor to us; and it was impossible to be on very friendly terms with Madame Dubois.

Poor Miss Winter! I never troubled her with impertinent questions; and perhaps she felt grateful to me for my forbearance; for my companions, one and all, declared that she "favored Ruth Irvine." I was not popular among them, because I studied on half-holidays, and in the hour before bed-time, when we were left to our own devices. They tried to laugh me out of this; but they couldn't; so they hated me as school-girls only can hate, and revenged themselves by saying that "my father was poor, and I was, for this reason, anxious to make the most of my time while at Woodford House." This taunt was intended to inflict severe mortification, as a profound respect for wealth pervaded the school, which was, of course, derived from its head.

I suspect I over-studied at this period, for I became a martyr to excruciating headache, which prevented me from sleeping at night; and I had, besides, all kinds of awkward habits and nervous affections. O! Mrs. Wheeler's earnest endeavors to make me graceful; her despair of my elbows; her hopelessness in my shoulders, and her glare of indignation at my manner of entering a room!

I spent the summer vacation this year at Woodford House, for my father was abroad, and I had no relation kind enough to take pity on my homeless state. I was very dispirited: and my depression so much increased the low, nervous fever which was hanging about me, that I was compelled for some days to keep my bed. Miss Winter nursed me of her own accord, and was like a sister to me. Now that the other girls were gone she was quite communicative. I learned that she was an orphan, and had a brother and three sisters, all younger than herself, who were used to consult her on every occasion of importance. I liked to hear about them much; I believed them to be wonders of talent and kindness. The brother was a clerk in some mercantile house in the city; the sisters were being educated at a private school. The affection which united her to this brother and these sisters seemed to me to be stronger than either death or life.

The teachers' holidays never began until long after ours; but in the long vacation they were allowed to take pedestrian excursions; and Miss Winter would return from these to my sick chamber, laden with mosses and wild flowers. I used to feel it a great consolation, amid the neglect and contempt of others, that she was attached to me. When the day for her departure came she gave me Coleridge's "Rhyme of the Ancient Mariner;" and I was to keep it always, and never to forget her if I never saw her again. I do not think she spoke thus because she felt any foreboding of ill, for she was very happy in her quiet way; but she never allowed herself to look forward with much hope to the future. I got a letter from her to say that she had arrived safely at her brother's in the city, and begging me not to fret for her sake. I tried to be cheerful, but time passed wearily without her. Every morning, at breakfast, I heard for the twentieth time of Miss Nash, who so appreciated the advantage of spending the vacation with such a person as Mrs. Wheeler that she could scarcely be induced to leave Woodford House. *She* never complained that the piano in the back parlor had several dumb notes, or that Rollin's "Ancient History" was not the most cheerful specimen of polite literature. It was uncharitable; but I couldn't help it; I hated Miss Nash. The latter part of the day was more agreeable; I was usually invited to tea and supper by Mrs. Sparkes, and was regaled in the front parlor with seed-cake and rolls, likewise with currant wine. I should have enjoyed these entertainments exceedingly, but I had written a poem in four cantos, in which the late Captain Sparkes figured as a pirate, and was shot for a voluminous catalogue of atrocities; and this secret lay like a load of lead on my mind, and prevented me from feeling at my ease with Mrs. Sparkes. It was after an evening spent with this lady, and in the absence of Mrs. Wheeler, who had gone to the city to arrange about receiving a new pupil, that—*that it first happened.*

It was a still, sultry night; the moon very bright. I was lying in my narrow, white bed, with my hair disordered all over the pillow; not just falling asleep, by any means, but most persistently and obstinately broad awake, and with every sense so sharpened that I could distinctly hear the flow of the fountain without, and the ticking of the clock in the hall far down below. I had left the door of my chamber open, on account of the heat. Suddenly, at midnight, when the house was profoundly silent, a draught of cold air seemed to blow right into the room; and almost immediately after I heard the sound of a footfall upon the stairs. Sleep seemed many thousand miles farther off than ever, or I should have thought I was dreaming; for I could have declared the step was Miss Winter's; and yet I knew that she was not expected back for at least a fortnight. What could it mean? While I listened and wondered the footsteps drew nearer and nearer, and then suddenly halted. I looked around, and beheld at the foot of the bed the form of my friend! She was attired in the plain dark dress she usually wore; and I could see on the third finger of her left hand the sparkle of a ring, which was also familiar to me. Her face was very pale, and had, I thought, a strange, wistful expression. I noticed, too, that the bands of hair which shaded her forehead looked dark and dank, as if they had been immersed in water. I started up in my bed, extending my arms, and exclaiming, "You here! When did you come? What has brought you back so soon?" But there was no answer, and she was gone the next moment. I was startled, almost terrified, by what I have described. I felt an indefinite fear that something was wrong with my friend. I arose, and passing through her chamber, which was unoccupied, went above and below, looking for her, and softly calling her by name; but every room I entered was empty and silent; and I presently returned to bed, bewildered and disappointed.

Toward morning I grew drowsy, and a little before my usual hour for rising I fell asleep. When I awoke the bright sunlight was shining in through the window. I heard the servants at their work below, and I was sure that it was very late. I was dressing hurriedly, when the door was softly opened. It was Mrs. Sparkes.

"I would not have you disturbed," she said; "for I heard you walking about last night. I thought, as it was holiday-time, that you should sleep when you could."

"O, thank you," I replied, scarcely able to restrain my impatience. "Where is Miss Winter, Mrs. Sparkes?" She looked surprised at the question, but answered, without hesitation,

"With her friends, no doubt. We need not expect her for this fort-night yet, you know."

"You are jesting," I said, half offended. "I know that she is returned. I saw her last night."

"You saw Miss Winter last night!"

"Yes," I answered; "she came into my bed-room."

"Impossible!" and Mrs. Sparkes burst out laughing, "unless she have the power of being in two places at once. You have been dreaming."

"I could not dream," I said; "for I was broad awake. I am sure I saw Miss Winter. She stood at the foot of my bed, and looked at me; but she would not tell me when she came, or what had brought her back so soon."

Mrs. Sparkes still laughed. I said no more on the subject, for I thought there was some mystery, and she was trying to deceive me.

That day passed. I was little inclined to sleep, though I was very tired when night came. I kept thinking about Miss Winter, and wondered if she would come again. After I had been in bed a few hours I became terribly nervous; the slightest sound made my heart leap. Then the thought came into my head that I would get up and go down stairs. I slipped on a few things, and softly left my room. The house was so silent, and everything looked so dusky that I felt frightened, and went on trembling more than before. There was a long passage in a line with the school-room, and there was a glass door at one end of it, which opened upon the garden. I stood at this door for several minutes, dreamily watching the silvery light which the moon threw upon the dark trees and the sleeping flowers without. While thus engaged I grew contented and serene. I had turned, to creep back to bed, when I heard, as I thought, some person trying the handle of the door behind me. The sound soon ceased; yet I almost believed the door was opened, for a rift of wind blew through the passage which made me shudder. I stopped, and looked hurriedly back. The door was closely shut, and the bolt still fast; but standing in the moonlight, where I had lately stood, was the slight figure of Miss Winter! She was as white, and still, and speechless as she had been on the preceding night; it almost seemed as if some dreadful misfortune had struck her dumb. I wished to speak to her, but there was something in her face which daunted me; and besides the fever of anxiety I was in began to dry up my lips, as if they would never be able to shape any words again. But I moved quickly toward her, and bent forward to kiss her. To my surprise and terror her form vanished. A cry escaped me, which must have alarmed Mrs. Sparkes, for she came running down stairs in her nightdress, looking pale and frightened. I told her what had happened, and very much in the same way that I have just been telling it now. There was an expression of uneasiness on her face as she listened. She said kindly, "Ruth, you are not well to-night; you are very feverish and excited. Go back to bed, and before tomorrow morning you will forget all about it."

I returned to bed; but I did not next morning forget what I had seen on the previous night; on the contrary, I was more positive than before. Mrs. Sparkes was disposed to think that I had seen Miss Winter in a dream on the first night, and that on the second, when broad awake, I had been unable to divest myself of the idea previously entertained. However, at my earnest and often repeated request, she promised she would pass the coming night with me in the girl's sleeping-room. All that day she was most kind and attentive. She could not have been more so if I had been seriously unwell. She put all exciting books out of my way, and asked me from time to time if my head ached. In the evening, after supper, she showed me some engravings which had belonged to her husband. I was very fond of pictures. We remained looking at them till a late hour, and then we went to bed. Tired as I was, I could not sleep. Mrs. Sparkes said she should stay awake also; but she soon became silent, and I knew by her breathing that she was sound asleep. She did not rest long. At midnight the room, which had been oppressively warm, grew suddenly cold and draughty; and again I heard Miss Winter's known step on the stairs. I laid hold of Mrs. Sparkes's arm, and shook her gently. She was sleeping heavily, and awoke slowly, as it seemed to me; but she sat up in bed, and listened to the approaching steps. I shall never forget her face at that moment. She seemed to be beside herself with terror, which she tried to hide, and uncertain what it would be the best for her to do; she caught my hand at last, and held it so tightly that she quite hurt me. The steps drew nigh, and halted, as they had done before. Mrs. Sparkes's gaze followed mine to the foot of the bed. The form of my friend was there. I can scarcely expect to be credited. I can only state on my honor what followed.

A night-lamp was burning in the room, for Mrs. Sparkes never slept in the dark. Its light showed me the pale still face of Miss Winter more clearly than I had seen it on the previous nights. The features were like those of a corpse. The eyes fixed direct on me, the long-familiar, grave, shining eyes. I see them now; I shall see them till I die! O how sad and earnest they looked! A full minute, or it seemed so, did she gaze in silence; then she said, in a low, urgent tone, still looking through me with her eyes, "Ruth, the oak wardrobe in the room which was mine, contains papers of importance, papers which will be wanted. Will you remember this?"

"I promise that I will," I replied. My voice was steady, though the cold drops stood on my brow. The restless, wistful look in her eyes changed, as I spoke, to a peaceful and happy expression. So, with a smile upon her face, she passed away. No sooner had Miss Winter's form disappeared than Mrs. Sparkes, who had been silent only because she was paralyzed with terror, began to scream aloud. She did more: she sprang out of bed, and rushed round the foot of it, out on the landing. When she could make the servants attend her she told them that somebody was in the house; and all the women, a cook and two housemaids, went armed with pokers and shovels, and examined every room from cellar to attic. They found nothing, neither in the chimneys nor under the beds, nor in any closet or cupboard. And as the servants went back to bed I heard them agree what a tiresome and wearying thing it was when ladies took fancies. Mrs. Sparkes wanted to leave the house the next day; but the thought of the ridicule to which she should expose herself, if the matter oozed out, induced her to summon up her courage, and remain where she was.

The morning after Mrs. Wheeler returned. She and Mrs. Sparkes were talking together in the study for a long while. I could not help wondering what they were talking about, and so anxious did I feel that I could not settle to anything. At last the door opened, and Mrs. Sparkes came out. I heard her say distinctly: "It is the most shocking thing I have ever heard. She was a painstaking young person, and you will miss her sadly." At the sound of the opening door, with a sudden determination, I had rushed down-stairs, and was within a few steps of the study as Mrs. Sparkes came out.

Mrs. Wheeler was sitting at the table, with an open newspaper before her. She looked grave and shocked. After making some inquiries about my health, she said, "You will be sorry to hear Miss Winter will not return—an able teacher, and I believe you were much attached to her." She was going on; but I interrupted her with a wild cry—"Miss Winter is dead!" said I, and I swooned away.

It was noon when I awoke, and saw Mrs. Sparkes bending over me, as I lay on my bed, and trying to restore me. I begged her to tell me everything, and she did so. My dear friend was indeed no more. The story of her death was, like all the sad stories I have ever heard told in real life, very—very short. She had left the house where her sisters were lodging, late one evening; that was the last time they saw her alive. She had been found dead, lying along the rocks under the cliff. This was all that there really was to tell. There was nobody near her when she was found, and no evidence to show how she came there.

I cannot remember what happened for some days afterward, for I was seriously ill, and kept my bed; and often in the long nights I would lie awake, thinking about my friend, and fancying she would appear again. But she came no more.

Time passed on, and brought the last day of the vacation. I was sitting by myself in the study, Mrs. Wheeler and Mrs. Sparkes having both gone out, when a servant ushered in a strange gentleman, who, when I told him that Mrs. Wheeler was from home, immediately asked for Miss Irvine. On hearing that I was the person inquired for, he requested five minutes' conversation with me. I showed him into the back parlor, and waited, rather surprised and nervous, to hear what he had to say. He was a young man, not more than twenty-one or twenty-two years of age, and had a very grave manner; and though I was certain that he was a stranger, yet there was something in his face which seemed not altogether unfamiliar to me. He began by saying: "You were very fond of a teacher who was here, of the name of Winter. In her name and for her sake, I thank you for the love and kindness you showed her."

"You knew Miss Winter, sir?" I asked, as calmly as I could.

"I am her brother," he replied.

There was silence between us, for the tears had sprung to my eyes at the mention of my dear lost friend's name; and, I believe, at heart he was crying too. At last he mastered his feelings, and by an effort resumed his former calm manner. "I have been for this last week seeking for some papers which my poor sister must have left behind her, and always seeking them in vain," he said. "If you could give me any clew to where they may be, you would do a great kindness to my remaining sisters and myself."

He still spoke calmly; but there was a look in his eyes which showed me that he was suffering terrible anxiety. I hastened to relieve it by saying: "I have reason to think that you will find the papers you are in want of in a small oak wardrobe which belonged to dear Miss Winter. If you please, I will show you where it stands."

How his face lighted as he rose to follow me! his lips moving evidently with voiceless but thankful words on them.

We went up-stairs to the room that had been his sister's, where I pointed out the piece of furniture to which she had referred me on that dreadful night. And after using some considerable force, the lock yielded to his determined hand; and there, concealed under a false bottom, in

A Ghost Story/23

one of the drawers, were the papers he sought for. When he had taken them from the secret ledge, he turned to me, and said, "How much do you think these papers are worth to me?"

"Indeed, I can't tell," I replied; "but thank God you came hither to seek them, for I am so glad they are found."

"I thank you," he said; "I thank you, with all my heart."

We went down-stairs again into the parlor; and then he told me how a kinsman of theirs, who was very rich, but nevertheless a great miser, had borrowed a large sum of money from their dead father, which he now refused to repay, and was even wicked enough to deny he had ever received; how they had gone to law about the matter; and how, if the papers he had just found could not have been produced, he and his sisters would have been penniless; but as it was, they would recover the sum to which they were justly entitled, with interest for five years.

After this he begged my acceptance of a locket containing some of my dear Miss Winter's hair, and with her Christian name and the date of her death inscribed upon it; and bade me remember, if I should ever be friendless or in distress (which he prayed God I might never be) that he felt toward me as a brother. I was quite overcome, and hid my face on the table. When I looked up again he was gone.

A fresh surprise awaited me. The next day I met Mrs. Wheeler as she was coming to bid me go into the parlor; and her manner was so gracious that I obeyed her without fear. My dear father was there. He was so shocked at my ill looks that he resolved to remove me home without loss of time. I sought out my poor friend's grave, and made it as beautiful as I could with grass and flowers. There was no tombstone there then, but there is one now.

Luella Miller

⑃⑃⑃

Mary E. Wilkins Freeman

Mary E. Wilkins Freeman (1852–1930), whose byline exists in a half-dozen variants but is given here as she finally preferred it, was a prolific author of novels, poetry, children's books and, at her best, short fiction. The best known collections of her work, A Humble Romance *(1887) and* A New England Nun *(1891), are recognized milestones of New England regionalism and U.S. realism. Chronicling the decline of Yankee village life, she wrote of outcast, eccentric women, much as did Sarah Orne Jewett and Annie Trumbull Slosson, but with a far darker tone that better suited horrific imaginings. "The Furies existed for her," observed Van Wyck Brooks in* Literature in New England *(1944), while her few detractors have called her sordid and excessively morbid. She lived for many years in Boston with Mary Wales, a childhood friend from Vermont. She left Boston at the age of fifty, when she married a New Jersey physician. She continued to write, but not as well or as often; spinsterhood apparently served her creative urges better than her late marriage.*

Regionalists invariably included supernatural stories as part of their creative output. Harriet Beecher Stowe, Jewett, Slosson, Alice Brown, Rose Terry Cooke, Elizabeth Stuart Phelps, and Harriet Prescott Spoffard all wrote tales of the unknown, and mysticism runs through even their non-supernatural works. This cross-fertilization of regional and supernatural literature is pervasive, yet literary historians so compartmentalize their interest that the connection is obscured. The great horror writer H. P. Lovecraft was a Decadent, latter-day New England regionalist; his decaying villages of Dunwich and Arkham are indistinguishable from those of Jewett and Freeman. Yet horror researchers have excluded the majority of the regionalists' ghost stories even from the broadest studies. Similarly, scholars who focus on the flourishing of New England genre fiction have system-atically ignored or maligned the obvious supernatural elements in their favorite authors' works; Dr. Edward Foster in his 1956 biography of Freeman typically dismisses her ghost stories in a single sentence as "simply mediocre." The common prejudice against weird fiction blinded him to the fact that "The Lost Ghost" and "Luella Miller" are among the strongest of her works.

Yet Freeman's ghost stories have been less neglected than those of Jewett, Brown, Slosson and others; she shares, along with Edith Wharton and Henry James, a considerable audience for these stories. Several editions of her ghost story collection The Wind in the Rose-bush and Other Stories of the Supernatural *(1903) have been published in the last two decades, plus a partial* Collected Ghost Stories *(1973). Her story "The Shadow on the Wall" was adapted for television in the original* Twilight Zone *series and has been anthologized several times. Hence, Freeman's importance to supernatural fiction in the United States is al-most as well established as her pre-eminence as a regionalist.*

"Luella Miller" is reprinted here from The Wind in the Rose-bush; *the stories in that volume were collected from* Everybody's *Magazine of 1902. Like Freeman's non-fantasies, it gives us a portrait of nineteenth-century village life and of common people, especially eccentric women. The spunky old woman who narrates this tale is typical of Freeman's characters, though she is not as grimly miserable as many others. Luella herself is a vampire, for whom the narrator has genuine empathy and concern, despite the fact that she is dangerous. In Freeman's hands, vampirism is not the sexual symbol found in most vampire fiction, but represents self-destructive passivity.*

⁂

Close to the village street stood the one-story house in which Luella Miller, who had an evil name in the village, had dwelt. She had been dead for years, yet there were those in the village who, in spite of the clearer light which comes on a vantage-point from a long-past danger, half believed in the tale which they had heard from their childhood. In their hearts, although they scarcely would have owned it, was a survival of the wild horror and frenzied fear of their ancestors who had dwelt in the same age with Luella Miller. Young people even would stare with a shudder at the old house as they passed, and children never played around it as was their wont around an untenanted building. Not a window in the old Miller house was broken: the panes reflected the morning sunlight in patches of emerald and blue, and the latch of the sagging front door was never lifted, although no bolt secured it. Since Luella Miller had been carried out of it, the house had had no tenant except one friendless old soul who had no choice between that and the far-off shelter of the open sky. This old woman, who had survived her kindred and friends, lived in the house one week, then one morning no smoke came out of the chimney, and a body of neighbours, a score strong, entered and found her dead in her bed. There were dark whispers as to the cause of her death, and there were those who testified to an expression of fear so exalted that it showed forth the state of the departing soul upon the dead face. The old woman had been hale and hearty when she entered the house, and in seven days she was dead; it seemed that she had fallen a victim to some uncanny power. The minister talked in the pulpit with covert severity against the sin of superstition; still the belief prevailed. Not a soul in the village but would have chosen the almshouse rather than that dwelling. No vagrant, if he heard the tale, would seek shelter beneath that old roof, unhallowed by nearly half a century of superstitious fear.

There was only one person in the village who had actually known Luella Miller. That person was a woman well over eighty, but a marvel of vitality and unextinct youth. Straight as an arrow, with the spring of one recently let loose from the bow of life, she moved about the streets, and she always went to church, rain or shine. She had never married, and had lived alone for years in a house across the road from Luella Miller's.

This woman had none of the garrulousness of age, but never in all her life had she ever held her tongue for any will save her own, and she never spared the truth when she essayed to present it. She it was who bore testimony to the life, evil, though possibly wittingly or designedly so, of Luella Miller, and to her personal appearance. When this old woman spoke—and she had the gift of description, although her thoughts were clothed in the rude vernacular of her native village—one could seem to see Luella Miller as she had really looked. According to this woman, Lydia Anderson by name, Luella Miller had been a beauty of a type rather unusual in New England. She had been a slight, pliant sort of creature, as ready with a strong yielding to fate and as unbreakable as a willow. She had glimmering lengths of straight, fair hair, which she wore softly hooped round a long, lovely face. She had blue eyes full of soft pleading, little slender, clinging hands, and a wonderful grace of motion and attitude.

"Luella Miller used to sit in a way nobody else could if they sat up and studied a week of Sundays," said Lydia Anderson, "and it was a sight to see her walk. If one of them willows over there on the edge of the brook could start up and get its roots free of the ground, and move off, it would go just the way Luella Miller used to. She had a green shot silk she used to wear, too, and a hat with green ribbon streamers, and a lace veil blowing across her face and out sideways, and a green ribbon flyin' from her waist. That was what she came out bride in when she married Erastus Miller. Her name before she was married was Hill. There was always a sight of "l's" in her name, married or single. Erastus Miller was good lookin', too, better lookin' than Luella. Sometimes I used to think that Luella wa'n't so handsome after all. Erastus just about worshipped her. I used to know him pretty well. He lived next door to me, and we went to school together. Folks used to say he was waitin' on me, but he wa'n't. I never thought he was except once or twice when he said things that some girls might have suspected meant somethin'. That was before Luella came here to teach the district school. It was funny how she came to get it, for folks said she hadn't any education, and that one of the big girls, Lottie Henderson, used to do all the teachin' for her, while she sat back and did embroidery work on a cambric pocket-handkerchief. Lottie Henderson was a real smart girl, a splendid scholar, and she just set her eyes by Luella, as all the girls did. Lottie would have made a real smart woman, but she died when Luella had been here about a year—just faded away and died: nobody knew what ailed her. She dragged herself to that schoolhouse and helped Luella teach till the very last minute. The committee all knew how Luella didn't do much of the work herself, but they winked at it. It wa'n't long after Lottie died that Erastus married her. I always thought he hurried it up because she wa'n't fit to teach. One of the big boys used to help her after Lottie died, but he hadn't much government, and the school didn't do very well, and Luella might have had to give it up, for the committee couldn't have shut their eyes to things much longer. The boy that helped her was a real honest, innocent sort of fellow, and he was a good scholar, too. Folks said he overstudied, and that was the reason he was took crazy the year after Luella married, but I don't know. And I don't know what made Erastus Miller go into consumption of the blood the year after he was married: consumption wa'n't in his family. He just grew weaker and weaker, and went almost bent double when he tried to wait on Luella, and he spoke feeble, like an old man. He worked terrible hard till the last trying to save up a little to leave Luella. I've seen him out in the worst storms on a wood-sled—he used to cut and sell wood—and he was hunched up on top lookin' more dead than alive. Once I couldn't stand it: I went over and helped him pitch some wood on the cart—I was always strong in my arms. I wouldn't stop for all he told me to, and I guess he was glad enough for the help. That was only a week before he died. He fell on the kitchen floor while he was gettin' breakfast. He always got the breakfast and let Luella lay abed. He did all the sweepin' and the washin' and the ironin' and most of the cookin'. He couldn't bear to have Luella lift her finger, and she let him do for her. She lived like a queen for all the work she did. She didn't even do her sewin'. She said it made her shoulder ache to sew, and poor Erastus's sister Lily used to do all her sewin'. She wa'n't able to, either; she was never strong in her back, but she did it beautifully. She had to, to suit Luella, she was so dreadful particular. I never saw anythin' like the fagottin' and hemstitchin' that Lily Miller did for Luella. She made all Luella's weddin' outfit, and that green silk dress, after Maria Babbit cut it. Maria she cut it for nothin', and she did a lot more cuttin' and fittin' for nothin' for Luella, too. Lily Miller went to live with Luella after Erastus died. She gave up her home, though she was real attached to it and wa'n't a mite afraid to stay alone. She rented it and she went to live with Luella right away after the funeral."

Then this old woman, Lydia Anderson, who remembered Luella Miller, would go on to relate the story of Lily Miller. It seemed that on the removal of Lily Miller to the house of her dead brother, to live with his widow, the village people first began to talk. This Lily Miller had been hardly past her first youth, and a most robust and blooming woman, rosy-cheeked, with curls of strong, black hair overshadowing round, candid temples and bright dark eyes. It was not six months after she had taken up her residence with her sister-in-law that her rosy colour faded and her pretty curves became wan hollows. White shadows began to show in the black rings of her hair, and the light died out of her eyes, her features sharpened, and there were pathetic lines at her mouth, which yet wore always an expression of utter sweetness and even happiness. She was devoted to her sister; there was no doubt that she loved her with her whole heart, and was perfectly content in her service. It was her sole anxiety lest she should die and leave her alone.

"The way Lily Miller used to talk about Luella was enough to make you mad and enough to make you cry," said Lydia Anderson. "I've been in there sometimes toward the last when she was too feeble to cook and carried her some blanc-mange or custard—somethin' I thought she might relish, and she'd thank me, and when I asked her how she was, say she felt better than she did yesterday, and asked me if I didn't think she looked better, dreadful pitiful, and say poor Luella had an awful time takin' care of her and doin' the work—she wa'n't strong enough to do anythin'—when all the time Luella wa'n't liftin' her finger and poor Lily didn't get any care except what the neighbours gave her, and Luella eat up everythin' that was carried in for Lily. I had it real straight that she did. Luella used to just sit and cry and do nothin'. She did act real fond of Lily, and she pined away considerable, too. There was those that thought she'd go into a decline herself. But after Lily died, her Aunt Abby Mixter came, and then Luella picked up and grew as fat and rosy as ever. But poor Aunt Abby begun to droop just the way Lily had, and I guess somebody wrote to her married daughter, Mrs. Sam Abbot, who lived in Barre, for she wrote her mother that she must leave right away and come and make her a visit, but Aunt Abby wouldn't go. I can see her now. She was a real good-lookin' woman, tall and large, with a big, square face and a high forehead that looked of itself kind of benevolent and good. She just tended out on Luella as if she had been a baby, and when her married daughter sent for her she wouldn't stir one inch. She'd always thought a lot of her daughter, too, but she said Luella needed her and her married daughter didn't. Her daughter kept writin' and writin', but it didn't do any good. Finally she came, and when she saw how bad her mother looked, she broke down and cried and all but went on her knees to have her come away. She spoke her mind out to Luella, too. She told her that she'd killed her husband and everybody that had anythin' to do with her, and she'd thank her to leave her mother alone. Luella went into hysterics, and Aunt Abby was so frightened that she called me after her daughter went. Mrs. Sam Abbot she went away fairly cryin' out loud in the buggy, the neighbours heard her, and well she might, for she never saw her mother again alive. I went in that night when Aunt Abby called for me, standin' in the door with her little green-checked shawl over her head. I can see her now. 'Do come over here, Miss Anderson,' she sung out, kind of gasping for breath. I didn't stop for anythin'. I put over as fast as I could, and when I got there, there was Luella laughin' and cryin' all together, and Aunt Abby trying to hush her, and all the time she herself was white as a sheet and shakin' so she could hardly stand. 'For the land sakes, Mrs. Mixter,' says I, 'you look worse than she does. You ain't fit to be up out of your bed.'

" 'Oh, there ain't anythin' the matter with me,' says she. Then she went on talkin' to Luella. 'There, there, don't, don't, poor little lamb,' says she. 'Aunt Abby is here. She ain't goin' away and leave you. Don't, poor little lamb.'

" 'Do leave her with me, Mrs. Mixter, and you get back to bed,' says I, for Aunt Abby had been layin' down considerable lately, though somehow she contrived to do the work.

" 'I'm well enough,' says she. 'Don't you think she had better have the doctor, Miss Anderson?'

" 'The doctor,' says I, 'I think *you* had better have the doctor. I think you need him much worse than some folks I could mention.' And I looked right straight at Luella Miller laughin' and cryin' and goin' on as if she was the centre of all creation. All the time she was actin' so— seemed as if she was too sick to sense anythin'—she was keepin' a sharp lookout as to how we took it out of the corner of one eye. I see her.

You could never cheat me about Luella Miller. Finally I got real mad and I run home and I got a bottle of valerian I had, and I poured some boilin' hot water on a handful of catnip, and I mixed up that catnip tea with most half a wineglass of valerian, and I went with it over to Luella's. I marched right up to Luella, a-holdin' out of that cup, all smokin'. 'Now,' says I, 'Luella Miller, *you swaller this!*'

" 'What is—what is it, oh, what is it?' she sort of screeches out. Then she goes off a-laughin' enough to kill.

" 'Poor lamb, poor little lamb,' says Aunt Abby, standin' over her, all kind of tottery, and tryin' to bathe her head with camphor.

" '*You swaller this right down,*' says I. And I didn't waste any ceremony. I just took hold of Luella Miller's chin and I tipped her head back, and I caught her mouth open with laughin', and I clapped that cup to her lips, and I fairly hollered at her: 'Swaller, swaller, swaller!' and she gulped it right down. She had to, and I guess it did her good. Anyhow, she stopped cryin' and laughin' and let me put her to bed, and she went to sleep like a baby inside of half an hour. That was more than poor Aunt Abby did. She lay awake all that night and I stayed with her, though she tried not to have me; said she wa'n't sick enough for watchers. But I stayed, and I made some good cornmeal gruel and I fed her a teaspoon every little while all night long. It seemed to me as if she was jest dyin' from bein' all wore out. In the mornin' as soon as it was light I run over to the Bisbees and sent Johnny Bisbee for the doctor. I told him to tell the doctor to hurry, and he come pretty quick. Poor Aunt Abby didn't seem to know much of anythin' when he got there. You couldn't hardly tell she breathed, she was so used up. When the doctor had gone, Luella came into the room lookin' like a baby in her ruffled nightgown. I can see her now. Her eyes were as blue and her face all pink and white like a blossom, and she looked at Aunt Abby in the bed sort of innocent and surprised. 'Why,' says she, 'Aunt Abby ain't got up yet?'

" 'No, she ain't,' says I, pretty short.

" 'I thought I didn't smell the coffee,' says Luella.

" 'Coffee,' says I. 'I guess if you have coffee this mornin' you'll make it yourself.'

" 'I never made the coffee in all my life,' says she, dreadful astonished. 'Erastus always made the coffee as long as he lived, and then Lily she made it, and then Aunt Abby made it. I don't believe I *can* make the coffee, Miss Anderson.'

" 'You can make it or go without, jest as you please,' says I.

" 'Ain't Aunt Abby goin' to get up?' says she.

" 'I guess she won't get up,' says I, 'sick as she is.' I was gettin' madder and madder. There was somethin' about that little pink-and-white thing standin' there and talkin' about coffee, when she had killed so many better folks than she was, and had jest killed another, that made me feel 'most as if I wished somebody would up and kill her before she had a chance to do any more harm.

" 'Is Aunt Abby sick?' says Luella, as if she was sort of aggrieved and injured.

" 'Yes,' says I, 'she's sick, and she's goin' to die, and then you'll be left alone, and you'll have to do for yourself and wait on yourself, or do without things.' I don't know but I was sort of hard, but it was the truth, and if I was any harder than Luella Miller had been I'll give up. I ain't never been sorry that I said it. Well, Luella, she up and had hysterics again at that, and I jest let her have 'em. All I did was to bundle her into the room on the other side of the entry where Aunt Abby couldn't hear her, if she wa'n't past it—I don't know but she was—and set her down hard in a chair and told her not to come back into the other room, and she minded. She had her hysterics in there till she got tired. When she found out that nobody was comin' to coddle her and do for her she stopped. At least I suppose she did. I had all I could do with poor Aunt Abby tryin' to keep the breath of life in her. The doctor had told me that she was dreadful low, and give me some very strong medicine to give to her in drops real often, and told me real particular about the nourishment. Well, I did as he told me real faithful till she wa'n't able to swaller any longer. Then I had her daughter sent for. I had begun to realize that she wouldn't last any time at all. I hadn't realized it before, though I spoke to Luella the way I did. The doctor he came, and Mrs. Sam Abbot, but when she got there it was too late; her mother was dead. Aunt Abby's daughter just give one look at her mother layin' there, then she turned sort of sharp and sudden and looked at me.

" 'Where is she?' says she, and I knew she meant Luella.

" 'She's out in the kitchen,' says I. 'She's too nervous to see folks die. She's afraid it will make her sick.'

"The Doctor he speaks up then. He was a young man. Old Doctor Park had died the year before, and this was a young fellow just out of college. 'Mrs. Miller is not strong,' says he, kind of severe, 'and she is quite right in not agitating herself.'

" 'You are another, young man; she's got her pretty claw on you,' thinks I, but I didn't say anythin' to him. I just said over to Mrs. Sam Abbot that Luella was in the kitchen, and Mrs. Sam Abbot she went out there, and I went, too, and I never heard anythin' like the way she talked to Luella Miller. I felt pretty hard to Luella myself, but this was more than I ever would have dared to say. Luella she was too scared to go into hysterics. She jest flopped. She seemed to jest shrink away to nothin' in that kitchen chair, with Mrs. Sam Abbot standin' over her and talkin' and tellin' her the truth. I guess the truth was most too much for her and no mistake, because Luella presently actually did faint away, and there wa'n't any sham about it, the way I always suspected there was about them hysterics. She fainted dead away and we had to lay her flat on the floor, and the Doctor he came runnin' out and he said somethin' about a weak heart dreadful fierce to Mrs. Sam Abbot, but she wa'n't a mite scared. She faced him jest as white as even Luella was layin' there lookin' like death and the Doctor feelin' of her pulse.

" 'Weak heart,' says she, 'weak heart; weak fiddlesticks! There ain't nothin' weak about that woman. She's got strength enough to hang onto other folks till she kills 'em. Weak? It was my poor mother that was weak: this woman killed her as sure as if she had taken a knife to her.'

"But the Doctor he didn't pay much attention. He was bendin' over Luella layin' there with her yellow hair all streamin' and her pretty pink-and-white face all pale, and her blue eyes like stars gone out, and he was holdin' onto her hand and smoothin' her forehead, and tellin' me to get the brandy in Aunt Abby's room, and I was sure as I wanted to be that Luella had got somebody else to hang onto, now Aunt Abby was gone, and I thought of poor Erastus Miller, and I sort of pitied the poor young Doctor, led away by a pretty face, and I made up my mind I'd see what I could do.

"I waited till Aunt Abby had been dead and buried about a month, and the Doctor was goin' to see Luella steady and folks were beginnin' to talk; then one evenin', when I knew the Doctor had been called out of town and wouldn't be round, I went over to Luella's. I found her all dressed up in a blue muslin with white polka dots on it, and her hair curled jest as pretty, and there wa'n't a young girl in the place could compare with her. There was somethin' about Luella Miller seemed to draw the heart right out of you, but she didn't draw it out of *me*. She was settin' rocking in the chair by her sittin'-room window, and Maria Brown had gone home. Maria Brown had been in to help her, or rather to do the work, for Luella wa'n't helped when she didn't do anythin'. Maria Brown was real capable and she didn't have any ties; she wa'n't married, and lived alone, so she'd offered. I couldn't see why she should do the work any more than Luella; she wa'n't any too strong; but she seemed to think she could and Luella seemed to think so, too, so she went over and did all the work—washed, and ironed, and baked, while Luella sat and rocked. Maria didn't live long afterward. She began to fade away just the same fashion the others had. Well, she was warned, but she acted real mad when folks said anythin': said Luella was a poor, abused woman, too delicate to help herself, and they'd ought to be ashamed, and if she died helpin' them that couldn't help themselves she would—and she did.

" 'I s'pose Maria has gone home,' says I to Luella, when I had gone in and sat down opposite her.

" 'Yes, Maria went half an hour ago, after she had got supper and washed the dishes,' says Luella, in her pretty way.

" 'I suppose she has got a lot of work to do in her own house to-night,' says I, kind of bitter, but that was all thrown away on Luella Miller. It seemed to her right that other folks that wa'n't any better able than she was herself should wait on her, and she couldn't get it through her head that anybody should think it *wa'n't* right.

" 'Yes,' says Luella, real sweet and pretty, 'yes, she said she had to do her washin' to-night. She has let it go for a fortnight along of comin' over here.'

" 'Why don't she stay home and do her washin' instead of comin' over here and doin' *your* work, when you are just as well able, and enough sight more so, than she is to do it?' says I.

"Then Luella she looked at me like a baby who has a rattle shook at it. She sort of laughed as innocent as you please. 'Oh, I can't do the work myself, Miss Anderson,' says she. 'I never did. Maria *has* to do it.'

"Then I spoke out: 'Has to do it!' says I. 'Has to do it! She don't have to do it, either. Maria Brown has her own home and enough to live on. She ain't beholden to you to come over here and slave for you and kill herself.'

"Luella she jest set and stared at me for all the world like a doll-baby that was so abused that it was comin' to life.

" 'Yes,' says I, 'she's killin' herself. She's goin' to die just the way Erastus did, and Lily, and your Aunt Abby. You're killin' her jest as you did them. I don't know what there is about you, but you seem to bring a curse,' says I. 'You kill everybody that is fool enough to care anythin' about you and do for you.'

"She stared at me and she was pretty pale.

" 'And Maria ain't the only one you're goin' to kill,' says I. 'You're goin' to kill Doctor Malcom before you're done with him.'

"Then a red colour came flamin' all over her face. 'I ain't goin' to kill him, either,' says she, and she begun to cry.

" 'Yes, you *be!*' says I. Then I spoke as I had never spoke before. You see, I felt it on account of Erastus. I told her that she hadn't any business to think of another man after she'd been married to one that had died for her: that she was a dreadful woman; and she was, that's true enough, but sometimes I have wondered lately if she knew it—if she wa'n't like a baby with scissors in its hand cuttin' everybody without knowin' what it was doin'.

"Luella she kept gettin' paler and paler, and she never took her eyes off my face. There was somethin' awful about the way she looked at me and never spoke one word. After awhile I quit talkin' and I went home. I watched that night, but her lamp went out before nine o'clock, and when Doctor Malcom came drivin' past and sort of slowed up he see there wa'n't any light and he drove along. I saw her sort of shy out of meetin' the next Sunday, too, so he shouldn't go home with her, and I begun to think mebbe she did have some conscience after all. It was only a week after that that Maria Brown died—sort of sudden at the last, though everybody had seen it was comin'. Well, then there was a good deal of feelin' and pretty dark whispers. Folks said the days of witchcraft had come again, and they were pretty shy of Luella. She acted sort of offish to the Doctor and he didn't go there, and there wa'n't anybody to do anythin' for her. I don't know how she *did* get along. I wouldn't go in there and offer to help her—not because I was afraid of dyin' like the rest, but I thought she was just as well able to do her own work as I was to do it for her, and I thought it was about time that she did it and stopped killin' other folks. But it wa'n't very long before folks began to say that Luella herself was goin' into a decline jest the way her husband, and Lily, and Aunt Abby and the others had, and I saw myself that she looked pretty bad. I used to see her goin' past from the store with a bundle as if she could hardly crawl, but I remembered how Erastus used to wait and 'tend when he couldn't hardly put one foot before the other, and I didn't go out to help her.

"But at last one afternoon I saw the Doctor come drivin' up like mad with his medicine chest, and Mrs. Babbit came in after supper and said that Luella was real sick.

" 'I'd offer to go in and nurse her,' says she, 'but I've got my children to consider, and mebbe it ain't true what they say, but it's queer how many folks that have done for her have died.'

"I didn't say anythin', but I considered how she had been Erastus's wife and how he had set his eyes by her, and I made up my mind to go in the next mornin', unless she was better, and see what I could do; but the next mornin' I see her at the window, and pretty soon she came steppin' out as spry as you please, and a little while afterward Mrs. Babbit came in and told me that the Doctor had got a girl from out of town, a Sarah Jones, to come there, and she said she was pretty sure that the Doctor was goin' to marry Luella.

"I saw him kiss her in the door that night myself, and I knew it was true. The woman came that afternoon, and the way she flew around was a caution. I don't believe Luella had swept since Maria died. She swept and dusted, and washed and ironed; wet clothes and dusters and carpets were flyin' over there all day, and every time Luella set her foot out when the Doctor wa'n't there there was that Sarah Jones helpin' of her up and down the steps, as if she hadn't learned to walk.

"Well, everybody knew that Luella and the Doctor were goin' to be married, but it wa'n't long before they began to talk about his lookin' so poorly, jest as they had about the others; and they talked about Sarah Jones, too.

"Well, the Doctor did die, and he wanted to be married first, so as to leave what little he had to Luella, but he died before the minister could get there, and Sarah Jones died a week afterward.

"Well, that wound up everything for Luella Miller. Not another soul in the whole town would lift a finger for her. There got to be a sort of panic. Then she began to droop in good earnest. She used to have to go to the store herself, for Mrs. Babbit was afraid to let Tommy go for her, and I've seen her goin' past and stoppin' every two or three steps to rest. Well, I stood it as long as I could, but one day I see her comin' with her arms full and stoppin' to lean against the Babbit fence, and I run out and took her bundles and carried them to her house. Then I went home and never spoke one word to her though she called after me dreadful kind of pitiful. Well, that night I was taken sick with a chill, and I was sick as I wanted to be for two weeks. Mrs. Babbit had seen me run out to help Luella and she came in and told me I was goin' to die on account of it. I didn't know whether I was or not, but I considered I had done right by Erastus's wife.

"That last two weeks Luella she had a dreadful hard time, I guess. She was pretty sick, and as near as I could make out nobody dared go near her. I don't know as she was really needin' anythin' very much, for there was enough to eat in her house and it was warm weather, and she made out to cook a little flour gruel every day, I know, but I guess she had a hard time, she that had been so petted and done for all her life.

"When I got so I could go out, I went over there one morning. Mrs. Babbit had just come in to say she hadn't seen any smoke and she didn't know but it was somebody's duty to go in, but she couldn't help thinkin' of her children, and I got right up, though I hadn't been out of the house for two weeks, and I went in there, and Luella she was layin' on the bed, and she was dyin'.

"She lasted all that day and into the night. But I sat there after the new doctor had gone away. Nobody else dared to go there. It was about midnight that I left her for a minute to run home and get some medicine I had been takin', for I begun to feel rather bad.

"It was a full moon that night, and just as I started out of my door to cross the street back to Luella's, I stopped short, for I saw something."

Lydia Anderson at this juncture always said with a certain defiance that she did not expect to be believed, and then proceeded in a hushed voice:

"I saw what I saw, and I know I saw it, and I will swear on my death bed that I saw it. I saw Luella Miller and Erastus Miller, and Lily, and Aunt Abby, and Maria, and the Doctor, and Sarah, all goin' out of her door, and all but Luella shone white in the moonlight, and they were all helpin' her along till she seemed to fairly fly in the midst of them. Then it all disappeared. I stood a minute with my heart poundin', then I went over there. I thought of goin' for Mrs. Babbit, but I thought she'd be afraid. So I went alone, though I knew what had happened. Luella was layin' real peaceful, dead on her bed."

This was the story that the old woman, Lydia Anderson, told, but the sequel was told by the people who survived her, and this is the tale which has become folklore in the village.

Lydia Anderson died when she was eighty-seven. She had continued wonderfully hale and hearty for one of her years until about two weeks before her death.

One bright moonlight evening she was sitting beside a window in her parlour when she made a sudden exclamation, and was out of the house and across the street before the neighbour who was taking care of her could stop her. She followed as fast as possible and found Lydia Anderson stretched on the ground before the door of Luella Miller's deserted house, and she was quite dead.

The next night there was a red gleam of fire athwart the moonlight and the old house of Luella Miller was burned to the ground. Nothing is now left of it except a few old cellar stones and a lilac bush, and in summer a helpless trail of morning glories among the weeds, which might be considered emblematic of Luella herself.

What Did
Miss Darrington See?

ıllıı

Emma B. Cobb

Emma B. Cobb often contributed to the leading U.S. periodicals of the 1870s. I first encountered "What Did Miss Darrington See?" in a tattered, moldering 1870 issue of Harper's New Monthly Magazine *buried in the dusty loft of an enormous used-book shop in Seattle. This discovery sparked my wholehearted search for more ghost stories as consciously feminist as this one.*

In "What Did Miss Darrington See?" Cobb writes of a New England woman of independent spirit who is employed as a governess in the South. She wishes to be called a "gentlewoman," not a "lady," a term she finds demeaning, much as in recent years women have objected to being referred to as "girls." Miss Darrington wants to know others and be known intellectually, and she refuses to participate in an unrealistic, romantic prescription for the way women and men must relate to one another. The issues are so modern that, had the story been written as a period piece by an author of the present decade, there could easily be charges of anachronism. In fact, the period stories which are unrealistic are those which assume a lack of feminist ideology in the nineteenth century.

"What Did Miss Darrington See?", reprinted here from Harper's, *has many of the standard plot devices and characters of a typical gothic tale. It would be a fine example of the form even had it nothing "extra." But the characters are only conventional on the surface, which lends unusual vitality and realism to the gothic plot. The predictable sort of exaggerated, suffering love, the fainting spells, and*

the squeals of fright, are foreign to Miss Darrington's character; she is strong and self-determined. The standard Latin male lead, confronted with Miss Darrington's refusal to respond conventionally, is himself transformed into a character of finer depth.

⫿

It was not so very long ago, for it was only about a year before the outbreak of the great rebellion, that Colonel Sibthorpe, living at Catalpa Grove,——County, Kentucky, wrote to Mr. Allen, a merchant in Boston, with whom he had large dealings, to procure for him a governess. The correspondent was requested to look out for a young person capable of "finishing" the education of the colonel's two motherless daughters, aged respectively eighteen and sixteen, and of preparing his younger son for admission to a Southern college.

Mr. Allen was at first not a little embarrassed by a commission so entirely out of the ordinary course of business; but as he had a strong desire to oblige his Kentucky friend and customer, he at once set about making inquiries for a suitable person to "fill the order." Whether his search was attended with much or little difficulty I am unable to say; I only know that it resulted in the engagement, at a liberal salary, of Miss Elizabeth Darrington, from whom I have derived the chief incidents of the story I am about to relate, and who has reluctantly consented to my making them public.

Perhaps you have seen Miss Darrington? If so, I dare be sworn that you remember her more vividly than many a handsomer woman. At the time I speak of she was about twenty-four, a small figure, slight now, but promising fullness as time should go on; a face neither beautiful nor plain in feature, but showing intellect and *esprit,* and a manner unmistakably that of a gentlewoman. (It is a word little used now, but it expresses what I mean far more accurately than the flippant term "lady.") Sprung from one of the oldest and best families in Massachusetts—one which had produced governors and legislators in the early colonial time, and in nearly every generation since some man of shining mark—she had not only inherited a fair share of the family talent, but she had breathed an atmosphere of intellect and culture from her infancy. She had also been early forced by circumstances into a position of self-reliance, and had learned to think and act independently. The result was a character not so easily summed up as that of a woman of the model sort, made up after the ideal of newspaper homilists, and the reverend gentlemen who lecture on the "Woman Question." Such as these would have found something of a paganism in the very virtues of Miss Darrington, without, perhaps, perceiving that there was a touch of nobility even in her faults. Proud, certainly—every thing about her, from the curve of her well-cut lip to the high-arched instep of a rather small foot, attested to that fact. Cold? I am not so sure. Her best friends said so; and at least the glance of her eye was cool and steady. Yet she had a keen physical organization, and enjoyed life with a zest unknown to duller and narrower natures. In short, she was one of those women, peculiarly the product of our later civilization, in whom the brain is uppermost, feeling in abeyance, and gifted with a power of self-rule which, if they do suffer, enables them to hide it as skillfully as a Mohican. She liked men, but they seldom got farther with her than the point of good-comradeship. Very young men, by-the-way, were inclined to fight a little shy of her; but she liked shrewd elderly ones, and these were always her admirers. Her manner, too, was not the modest violet manner of the model woman; there was just a touch of conscious power in it—a fine, well-bred self-assertion, which stood her in good stead in her peculiar position at Catalpa Grove, and enabled her to keep the young ladies of the house very much in order. In those days Northern governesses of the meek sort used often to fare a little dismally among those high-spirited and not over-cultivated Southern girls. But one glance into the level gray eyes of Miss Darrington would have convinced a duller than the Sibthorpes that this was a woman on whom it would be dangerous to play off any airs of superiority. They had a wholesome fear of her at the end of the first hour, but they cordially liked her by the end of the first week, and their respect and liking never diminished while she remained with them. The truth is, real New England "blue blood" is the very bluest in America, and the pride it engenders is more than a match for the haughtiest "F. F. V."—a fact which our Southern friends did not know so well before the war as they do now, for the reason that in their isolated plantation life they were seldom brought in contact with the real thing. They had their estimate of the Northern spirit from second and third rate specimens. The Sibthorpes were fine girls, however, and when they found out the stuff the governess had in her they were ready enough to make Catalpa Grove a pleasant abode for her, and soon its gayeties were incomplete without her.

The grove was in a populous county, and within easy visiting distance of the city of L——. There was always open house, and a very delightful house at that. The colonel was a good specimen of the Kentucky gentleman, frank, hearty, hospitable, and well-bred, until you touched his prejudices. He greatly admired Miss Darrington, and, indeed, showed some disposition to give his feelings practical expression, but was skillfully checked by the lady before he had committed himself. It did not in the least suit her book to be made love to by her host. She had undertaken a profitable year's task, and she wanted the salary. She did not choose either to resign the chance of earning it or to be made uncomfortable by the presence in the house of a rejected suitor.

You think I am describing a hard and selfish woman. What do you think she was down there governessing for, that finely trained, thorough-bred creature, among those free-and-easy, not over-intellectual Kentuckians? She was the eldest of four children. Her father was dead, and her mother a delicate, fine lady, as lovely and as helpless as a baby or a flower. Elizabeth was the support of the family. She kept the children at school, and wrote every week to her mother a long letter, full of fun and nonsense and merry rattle, to make that dear woman believe she had not a care in the world. But, trust me, she had plenty.

Miss Darrington had been about six months at the grove when, one morning in March, the household was thrown into a little cheerful commotion by a letter from Tom Sibthorpe, the colonel's eldest son, announcing his return home. He wrote to say that he should bring with him a friend, a young Cuban, with whom he had been traveling, and whom—for I am compelled to give him a fictitious name—I shall call Raphael Aldama. The expected advent of this stranger caused not a little excitement to the young ladies of the grove. He was of Spanish birth, but his family had lived for years in Havana, and he had formerly been at school with Tom Sibthorpe in New Orleans. The girls had never seen him; but they told Miss Darrington the most remarkable stories about him, of his wonderful personal beauty, his astonishing strength, his terrible temper and reckless daring, his duels and scrapes. He was very rich, very haughty, very magnificent. They were wild to see him, but rather inclined to be afraid of him. He was said to be as irresistible with women as he was dangerous with men. Miss Darrington did not find their picture of the expected guest particularly attractive. She laughed to herself, mentally decided that the romantic Cuban was probably a very ordinary young savage, and thought no more about him.

The travelers reached Catalpa Grove on the day expected. It was in the afternoon that they arrived; and his imperial highness, Signor Raphael, was pleased to retire immediately to bed, where he spent the night and the whole of the next day. All day long the two Sibthorpe girls were in a little fever of excitement, and were not above showing it. Alice could not practice her music lesson, and Rosalie had more trouble than usual with French verbs. They laid out their prettiest toilets for the evening, and teased Tom Sibthorpe with all sorts of questions about his friend. Miss Darrington listened, a little *ennuyée,* checked a satirical smile, and yawned behind her fan. When they had fluttered away she arrayed herself in the plain white dress which was her ordinary evening wear, with no ornament, except some scarlet blossoms of the Japan quince in her dark braids, and went down to play galops and waltzes for the others to dance.

The evening was well-nigh spent, her fingers were getting tired, and she was playing half mechanically, her thoughts carried far away, when Alice Sibthorpe came toward her, leaning on the arm of a gentleman, and begged to present the Signor Aldama, who desired the pleasure of her acquaintance. She looked up, indifferently, and met the glance of an eye before whose fiery and intolerable splendor her own for an instant fell—for an instant only. She was quite too practiced a woman of the world to lose her self-possession, though for a moment compelled to acknowledge the force of a magnetism more powerful than her own. A voice peculiarly soft and melodious addressed her, and the sweet, measured tones in which she replied betrayed no disturbance. Alice took her place at the piano, and she moved to a sofa, the stranger placing himself at her side; and she found herself studying curiously the face before her.

It was a very handsome face. She acknowledged that instantly. A white forehead, smooth as a boy's, over which the black hair clustered in heavy rings; an arched nose, the wide delicate nostril of which had a quiver of pride in it, like what one sees in fiery young horses; lips full yet firm, a strange sweetness in their smile, yet a fierceness in their passionate curve which suggested possibilities of cruelty. The eye was large and looked like black velvet, with the flash of a diamond in its centre. With all this a figure strong yet slender, a springing, cat-like tread, and a manner full of lazy grace, yet marred by something of haughty indifference.

Miss Darrington looked now steadily into the eyes whose bold, strong glance had at first beaten down her own, and recognized the nature of the soul that looked out from them. "It is a case for Van Amburgh," she said to herself, "or Girard, the lion-tamer. What jungle can have reared a wild animal like this?" But the low musical voice in which he addressed her did not accord with his harsh impression, and his manner at the moment was almost reverent in its gentle respect.

From that evening an intimacy singularly close and confidential existed between these two. I say existed, for it was a thing which had no growth; it seemed to spring up, "full-statured, in an hour." But whether it were of the nature of love or friendship the lookers-on were puzzled to decide. But, at least, he seemed never willingly absent from her company, and she had an evident pleasure in having him near her. Yet she certainly made no effort to attract him. So much was admitted, even by the two Sibthorpe girls, who, having, perhaps, anticipated an admirer in their brother's friend, may have felt a twinge of resentment at seeing him immediately carried off by the governess. But they were not ill-natured, and they had no lack of admirers; so they soon accepted the situation, wondering a little, too, for it was not vanity in them to think that, in point of beauty as well as youth, they had the advantage. But Raphael had known plenty of beautiful women—had enjoyed to the full the incense of their admiration—while a woman with brains was a new revelation to him. The spell of intellect and culture he found irresistible. This was the more strange as he was the last man whom a superficial judgment would have supposed likely to be attracted by such qualities. He had very little culture himself, little education, indeed, in the ordinary sense of the word. But he had seen a great deal of *life* in his five-and-twenty years—a life of vivid impressions and keen emotions. He had always been his own master, knowing from boyhood no law but his own will. The result was a character fixed in its mould, yet giving the impression of immaturity. Though really older than Miss Darrington, he seemed to her like a grown-up child. His nature showed a tinge of barbarism, a certain antique simplicity, which seemed to belong to a past age. She could not fail to see that intellectually she was vastly his superior; and it is good evidence of the natural nobility of the man's nature that he, too, recognized that fact without resenting it. He had worshiped passionately at many a lovely shrine, but never quite free from the haughty feeling that his homage honored her on whom it lighted. Now, for the first time in his life, his boldness had become timidity, his audacity respect. The story of "Undine" may repeat itself in more forms than one. The soul in this half-savage breast sprang into conscious life with the first pure, unselfish love which had ever dwelt there. Unselfish, for he knew from the very first that it was hopeless. She was honest with him all through. She let him see that truly as she liked him, frankly as she admired him, she had only friendship to give him. Not that she told him so in words—a woman is a blunderer to whom such words are necessary—but he did not fail to perceive the truth.

Yet it must be confessed that she found in his companionship a wonderful charm, the secret of which she could never fully analyze. It might lie partly in his remarkable beauty—always a spell to any woman—or the intense personal magnetism by which he affected all who came near him. It might be the very contrast between her own complex but balanced nature and this romantic and ardent, though untutored soul. Then, too, he adored her, and what woman ever lived who did not love to be worshiped? His honest affection must have been inexpressibly soothing to her often-wearied spirit. I think she might even have loved him but for the recollection of—but that is *her* secret, and has nothing to do with my story.

So, though on the frankest terms of intimacy, they never talked of love. Without surrounding *herself* with any apparent defenses, she compelled *him* to a complete reserve in that direction. A coquette might have refused to listen to him; she assumed that he had nothing to say, and so persistently ignored the possibility of any thing else that he could not escape the position she assigned him.

Of course it was not to be expected that this sudden and close intimacy could escape comment in the little circle at the Grove. But after the first dash of surprise they treated the matter with indifference, good-naturedly, willing that the parties should please themselves. Only Tom Sibthorpe, gifted with a somewhat more acute observation than the rest, watched the pair with a puzzled interest.

"By Jove!" he said to his sister Alice, "I did not think the woman had lived who could so tame the tiger in Raphael Aldama. Can you tell me the secret of her power? It is not coquetry; she never throws out a lure; yet the very soul of the man is on its knees before her. It can not be beauty; she is not so pretty as you, or Rose; though in the real *air de grande dame* she beats you both out of the field—that little thing, not over five feet high! I don't know but it is in her pride, after all. For the first time in his life Raphael has found some one prouder than he is. Do you believe she will marry him?"

"I should think so, certainly," replied Alice, rather surprised at the doubt.

"Possibly you are right. Women should know women. But I am not sure that she is one to say, 'all for love, and a world well lost.'"

"How can you be so censorious, Tom?" cried Alice, indignantly. "Miss Darrington is no more cold-hearted than you are. Besides, if it is a question of worldly advantage, she has every thing to gain from such a marriage."

"You think so, my dear, but she knows better. To her the losses might outweigh the gains."

"What would she lose?"

"The whole world in which she has hitherto lived and moved and had her being. Don't you see how opposite they are in character, in education, in ideas of life? She has been reared in the stimulating mental atmosphere of the North, and is, to say truth, a very fine specimen of its culture; has grown up in sympathy with the living forces of thought which move the modern world. He is like the child of some past civilization, who does not even known himself out of harmony with this thinking nineteenth century. There can be no spiritual kinship between the two. If she were to marry him she would lose the freedom she prizes beyond every thing, and gain, not a *mate,* but merely an *adorer.* And such an adorer! A woman might as well trust herself to a typhoon."

"Don't you think his love for her would last?"

"How can I tell? He has loved a hundred times before; though, to speak the truth, I never saw him in such earnest as now. But if he did not weary, she would. His passion is too *exigeante;* it would bore her in a little while."

"You seem to think she does not care for him."

"Nay; that is where I am wholly at sea. She is not one to wear her heart on her sleeve for such daws as we to peck at. But, after all, what does it matter? These things are always unequal. *Il y a toujours l'un qui baise, et l'autre qui tend le joue.*"

"You are a horrid old cynic, Tom."

"Yes, dear; and a stupid one at that; so let us talk of something else."

So the warm spring days flew swiftly by, and the old house rang with the gayety of that careless Southern life; and these two floated on with the stream, enjoying the present, but knowing well that their pleasure could not last. At least she knew this. She understood that there could be no permanent tie between them. They had drifted together from opposite poles; they would soon drift apart again, and that would be the end. But it was not easy to keep him to this view.

"Why talk of the future at all?" he said, impatiently. "Let me at least dream that I have you forever. These hours are so sweet—I sip them slowly, like drops of some precious wine. I even fancy sometimes that the days go lingeringly, as if the very moments felt the joy they hold, and were loth to depart from us. We are but children playing in the sun; let us play that we are lovers—and love, you know, is eternal."

"Oh, but that is too idle."

"Yes; I will have it so," he said, evidently feeling that he was securing an advantage. "You insist that this companionship of ours is not any part of our real lives. It is a little dream we are dreaming together— a brief drama which we enact. In such a fictitious world it is no matter what *rôles* we take for our own. I choose the part of your lover. You can listen to my vows, for it is only play, you know."

She laughed, but made no reply. She was unwilling, by objecting, to seem to attach any importance to this new freak. He never relinquished the ground her silence conceded; yet he seemed always to feel that this advantage was a stolen one, and was careful not to press it too far. Though after that he would often hold toward her the language of a lover, he was strangely gentle for one so naturally fierce and wild, and he played with this whim in a half sad, half tender way, which sometimes moved her more than she chose to show.

Raphael was passionately fond of music, and sang well in a wild, lawless way of his own, though in that, as in every thing else, quite guiltless of scientific method. He often chose to be present when Miss

Darrington was giving her morning lesson to the young ladies; and, as what he chose to do it was rather difficult to prevent, both teacher and pupils soon learned to go on without paying any attention to him.

One memorable morning in May the two girls had finished their lesson and left the room. Raphael, who had been lying on a sofa by the window, with a newspaper over his face, as if asleep, flung it away as they closed the door.

"Now that those chatterers are gone, sing to me, Isabel," he said. It was one of his caprices to substitute for her stately English name of Elizabeth, whose consonants plagued his southern tongue, the softer Spanish form which is its equivalent.

"What will you have?" she asked, reseating herself. "Are you in a sober mood, or will something gay and sparkling suit you better?"

"Any thing you like will please me."

"That is a very flattering frame of mind in which to find one's audience. As a reward you shall hear this choice little bit from Tennyson's 'Maud,' which has just been set to music."

"Very well; I have not an idea who Tennyson is, and never heard of his 'Maud;' but if you like it I shall. I only want to hear your voice."

"What pretty things you say this morning! But I assure you that my grum tones do no justice to it. You should hear Alice."

"Alice screams like a macaw."

"That is not quite complimentary to my best pupil. But now, barbarian, be silent, and listen."

The song was the one, so familiar now, beginning, "There has fallen a splendid tear." She sang it in a way of her own, rolling out the words at the top, or rather bottom, of her voice, trying to imitate the deep, passionate tones of Maud's lover, as he stands, half stifled with impatience, listening in the hush of the summer night for the footfall that he loves:

"There has fallen a splendid tear
  From the passion-flower at the gate.
She is coming, my dove, my dear;
  She is coming, my life, my fate.
The red rose cries, 'She is near, she is near;'
  And the white rose weeps, 'She is late;'
The larkspur listens, 'I hear, I hear;'
  And the lily whispers, 'I wait.'

"She is coming, my own, my sweet;
  Were it ever so airy a tread,
My heart would hear her and beat,

Were it earth in an earthy bed;
My dust would hear her and beat,
  Had I lain for a century dead;
Would start and tremble under her feet,
  And blossom in purple and red."

During the singing of the first stanza Raphael kept his position on
the sofa, but the second had not proceeded far when, with a smothered
exclamation, he started upright, and sat leaning eagerly forward, listening with a flushed and working face. At the close he sprang to his feet,
and came toward her, his eyes burning like coals of fire.

"*Jesu Maria!* Why do you sing like that to me?"

The passion in his tones made her tremble, but she answered as calmly
as possible: "I had no special reason. I thought the song a pretty piece
of hyperbole, which would please you."

"It is not hyperbole; it is truth," he said, softly, a sudden paleness
replacing the flush on his face. He stood close behind her, and leaned
over to look at the sheet from which she had been singing. His fingers
rested for a moment with a light touch upon her hair—a touch inexpressibly soft and caressing—as he repeated:

" 'My dust would hear her and beat,
  Had I lain for a century dead;
Would start and tremble under her feet,
  And blossom in purple and red.'

Why, yes," he went on, dreamily, "surely the earth does not furnish a
grave so deep that the sound of her little foot above it would not send
a thrill through his heart."

"Raphael, I think you rave."

"Indeed no," he said, smiling softly. "Can not you see that if I were
really your lover, as we only play I am, neither death nor the grave
could divide me from you? In life, distance might divide us. Your own
coldness, the cruel *convenances* of the world in which you live, might
build themselves like a wall between us; but were this soul unchained
by death I should be free to seek you, and the universe of God is not
wide enough to divide me from her I love. Not highest heaven nor
deepest hell could keep me from my darling."

"You would not appear to her in the fashion of the spectre bridegroom, in the ballad of 'Leonora' we read the other day? Few ladies
would like that."

She spoke lightly, for the scene was becoming too painful, and she felt that she must end it at any cost. But her effort failed. He only smiled—a grave, patient smile, strangely unlike himself, she thought—as he answered:

"No, surely. Do you think I would frighten her, or harm one hair of her little head? Not to terrify, but to bless, would I seek her. And she would know my soul at last, and read all its love for her—a love she was too blind to believe in here."

Tears sprang to her steadfast eyes. "Dear Raphael," she said, "I will not wrong you by jesting any more. I do know your generous regard for me, and I am grateful for it. But if I were to listen to you it would be the bane of both. We are not suited to each other. We belong to two different worlds. The air of yours would scorch and blast me, as mine would chill and destroy you."

"You do not care for me, then?"

"Indeed I do care. I was cold and lonely here, away from all I love; you came, and I was warmed with the sun of the tropics. It is you who give the charm to these sweet spring days which are passing so swiftly. But when they are gone that will be the end. You will leave us, and though you will think of me kindly for a while, the world of excitement and adventure will quickly renew its charm for you, and you will thank me then that I have left you unfettered."

"And you?" he asked, in a tone of some bitterness. "You will forget me, doubtless?"

"I shall never forget you," she answered, sadly. "I shall remember you always as the kindest, the most generous of friends. My life is one of labor and care; and this brief holiday we have spent together has the charm which only rare pleasures have. To you it is like the rest of your life, and so its memory will fade the sooner."

"So you doubt alike my truth and constancy?"

"Doubt your truth? Ah, no! But for constancy—what is it? We are none of us constant—God be thanked, who gives us the power to change. How could we live if we had not that—if every sorrow held its keenness forever?"

"Do I cause you sorrow, Isabel?"

"Only when I see you unhappy. Did you not say that we were children playing in the sun? Then what have we to do with care? Let us play the play out merrily, for the end of it is near."

She staid for no reply, but smiling on him kindly, though with swimming eyes, she rose and left the room.

A week later Raphael went. Imperative business compelled Tom Sibthorpe's departure, and his friend had no pretext for lingering longer. In the interval he bore himself toward Miss Darrington with a fair degree of the coolness she had been teaching him, but whether from pride or acquired indifference she could not tell. The day before his departure he ordered his horse immediately after breakfast, and rode to L——. She noticed, as he passed the window, that he had exchanged the white linen suit which, in common with other gentlemen at that season, he wore constantly, for a complete black dress.

He was gone nearly all day, only making his appearance after dinner was over, and the whole family assembled in the drawing-room. He had resumed his usual garb, and seemed in very gay spirits. Several guests were present, and he made himself brilliantly agreeable to them, flirted with Rose Sibthorpe, and paid any number of compliments to Alice on her singing. Miss Darrington played superbly, but he did not approach her. When she had finished, however, and walked away from the others into the shelter of a window, he soon followed.

"Have you heard," he said, "that I go tomorrow?"

"So Tom has been telling me."

"You speak very quietly. Do you understand that we part finally— that we shall never meet again?"

"Yes, I know."

The words were almost inaudible, for pain choked her voice. He went on:

"Well, then, since it is so—since we shall never be any thing to each other any more, will you not give me something which shall at times remind me of you? Otherwise I might forget you, you know."

"What shall it be?" she asked, faintly. The smile on his lips was almost more than she could bear.

"Any thing which you have worn, so it will seem a part of you."

"Wear this, then," drawing from her finger a little plain gold ring.

There was a flash like triumph in his eyes as he received it, and touched it to his lips before placing it upon his own finger.

"Now," he said, still speaking in the same slow tone, as if he were controlling it by an effort—"now, will you look at what I have here?"

He took a small parcel from the breast of his coat and placed it in her hand. She removed the wrapper, and there appeared a common jewel-case of purple morocco, which, on being opened, revealed, reposing on its velvet bed, a trinket of singular and beautiful workmanship. It was a large drop, or globe, of exquisitely cut crystal, inclosed in a fine net-work of gold.

"Do you like it?" he asked, as she did not speak.

"Who would not? It looks like a soap-bubble tangled in a golden nest, or a great dewdrop bound round with threads of Titania's hair. Surely you did not find such a rare and curious thing at L——?"

"No; I carried it there to-day. For what purpose I am not sure that I dare to tell you. It is an heir-loom in our family, and has come down to me through many generations. There is a tradition among us that it is a talisman, and brings good fortune to her who wears it. Will *you* wear it in memory of the last Aldama?"

Miss Darrington hesitated. "Ought you to part with a thing of such peculiar value?"

He answered with a strange smile: "I do not part with it. I only make of it a link between myself and you. While you wear it you can not wholly forget me. If you wish to do so, reject it."

She answered by fastening it to her watch-chain. Again that triumphant flash broke from his eyes. Some one approached the window. Their *tête-à-tête* must come to an end. He leaned toward her and whispered hastily: "Some day, when you look at it, you will learn how high my presumption has soared. But the link between us is riveted now. You can never undo it." The next moment he had moved away, and was laughing gayly with a group of ladies.

That night, in her own room, as Miss Darrington was laying aside her watch, she once more examined curiously the crystal drop. As she turned it over and over her fingers must have touched a small spring concealed in the gold net-work, for the globe parted in the middle, and the sides falling open, revealed a small but perfect photograph likeness of Raphael himself. This, then, was the errand which had taken him to L—— that day; this was the piece of presumption which he had hesitated to confess to her. He had probably believed that she would not discover it till after he was gone. Should she tell him that she had done so, and reject a gift to which he evidently attached a half-superstitious importance? On consideration she decided against this course. It would bring about an exciting and perhaps stormy scene, and could do no good. They were not likely ever to meet again, so no embarrassment could ensue from her acceptance of his gift, and she need never wear it unless she chose.

The two travelers were to leave early next morning, as they had a ride of some miles to reach the nearest railway station. The heat was excessive, and Miss Darrington, who had not been well for some days, found herself languid and suffering; but she went down as usual. Alice Sibthorpe was in the room with her when Raphael came to say good-by. He spoke his farewells lightly and gayly to both ladies, and left the room. Alice followed to say another parting word to her brother, and to watch with the rest the bustle of departure. Miss Darrington remained alone, and yielding to the languor of indisposition and the oppressive heat she sank down upon a lounge. A sadness deeper than she was prepared to feel, and which she chose to attribute mainly to physical depression, sent the slow tears stealing through her closed eyelashes.

So sunk was she in the listlessness of her sorrowful mood that she did not heed the opening of the door, or perceive that she was not alone until, looking up, she saw Raphael again beside her. His face was pale, his lips trembled, his eyes flashed darkly through the tears that filled them. He bent over her; she extended her hand. He caught and pressed it in his own so fiercely as almost to draw from her a cry of pain. He seemed making an effort to speak, but his voice died away in his throat.

There was a sound of footsteps approaching the door. He heard it and started. Then suddenly dropping on his knees beside her couch, and bending down to her feet, he kissed them passionately, again and again, and rising, darted from the room. She heard him spring down the staircase, and the next moment the clatter of his horse's hoofs dashing away, and the voice of Tom Sibthorpe swearing at him to stop.

Miss Darrington was both shocked and pained by an incident which revealed a feeling on the part of her friend so much deeper than she had thought possible. But she consoled herself with the reflection that with him all emotions, though keen, were transient. Some other woman, she believed, would soon ensnare his fickle fancy, and efface from his mind all memories of pain. "I shall regret him longer than he will me," she said, and turned to work as the best cure for sorrowful thoughts.

The autumn of the year 1868 found Miss Darrington living in Boston. A busy woman now, for life with her had been steadily gathering new interests and occupations. Some youthful dreams, indeed, had faded out of sight, some triumphs anticipated once had been wholly missed; yet in the career she had marked out for herself a fair measure of success had rewarded her efforts, and won her the recognition so dear to us all. Without being a famous woman, she had secured a position which enabled her to make her social world what she would. She was happy and cheerful, for with her no sense was dulled, no power of enjoyment diminished; only the uneasy restlessness of youth had passed, and given place to the secure repose of one who has found her place and learned to fill it.

With a life thus pleasantly full, it was not surprising that the episode of her Kentucky sojourn gradually faded from her thoughts. As for her Cuban friend, it was seldom now that the idea of him returned to her. Beautiful as he had been to her, the passing *tendresse* she had felt for him had taken no hold upon her life. She had never woven his image with a single dream of the future; and the feeling with which she remembered him, though grateful and even tender, had no longing in it. The little globe of crystal still hung at her watch-chain, recalling, when it met her eye, a pleasant memory of those spring days they had spent together; but for that reminder she might perhaps not have thought of him at all. She had never seen him, and all that she knew of him could be briefly told. On the outbreak of the war he had entered the Confederate army, held the rank of colonel, and fought with reckless bravery. But becoming offended at some real or fancied slight put upon him by his commanding officer, he resigned his commission; and the next thing known of him he was enlisted on the Union side. Probably he was actuated each time more by a love of adventure than by any special sympathy with the cause either of Union or rebellion. Severely wounded in the third year of the war, he again withdrew from the service, and returned to Cuba. At Havana he had a quarrel—it was only about a dog—with an Englishman in the street; and the result was a duel, in which the Englishman was killed. To avoid the consequences of this affair he went to Mexico; and in that ever-seething caldron of revolution and tumult he was finally lost to view.

One evening late in September—it was the twenty-ninth, as she had reason afterward to note—Miss Darrington sat alone in the little room which served her as a study. It was a narrow but lofty apartment, its single high-arched window looked westward over the green trees of a square, with a glimpse of the Charles Riving shining beyond. A library table, a single tall book-case, a lounge, a bust or two, some flowers in the window—these were nearly all the objects noticeable in the room.

Miss Darrington, who had been unusually busy all day, laid down her pen, and, leaning wearily back in her arm-chair, turned her eyes on the glowing evening sky. It had been a day of unusual beauty, very warm for the season; and the sun was setting in a sky soft, brilliant, and clear. A flood of yellow light streamed on the quiet river and brightened the distant view. The spires and leafy domes of Cambridge swam in a golden haze. The softened radiance filled the little room, and, falling about the lady herself, seemed to wrap her in an atmosphere of reverie. She was dreamily conscious of the beauty of the parting day; but she was not thinking of that, or, indeed, of any thing definite. She was, in fact, physically and mentally tired; and it was perhaps owing to this that a kind of depression stole over her—not really a sense of pain or sorrow, only a heavy languor of spirit, a feeling more tinged with the hue of sadness than was habitual with her. A long time elapsed. The sunlight slowly withdrew; the splendor of the sky passed into the paleness of evening, and a few of the larger stars began to show themselves; but still she remained motionless, and half unconscious of place or time.

"Isabel!"

The name was uttered almost at her elbow in a low, clear voice, whose accents were unmistakable, even if she had not on the instant remembered who alone in all the world had ever called her by that name. She turned eagerly to welcome the unexpected guest. "Raphael!" she exclaimed, in accents of undisguised pleasure.

He was standing just within the room. The door, a heavy one, was closed; and she wondered in a flash of thought how it could have opened to admit him unheard by her. She half rose to meet him; but a strange thrill shot through her, and an irresistible force bound her to her seat. She looked at him fixedly. There was still enough of brightness in the fading twilight for her to recognize unmistakably his form and features. But his face was very pale, and there was a look upon it unlike any thing she had ever seen there. So sad, yet so still—so full of some strange calm—it filled her with awe. She noticed that he wore a dress half military in its character, with some tarnished gold embroidery upon the breast, and a large cloak, thrown back and falling from his shoulders as he stood, his hat in his hand, in an attitude of careless grace she well remembered. He was so near she could almost have touched him with her hand. But yet he never spoke; only his lips parted with a tender smile, and his eyes dwelt on her with a glance so intense, so full of fathomless love and sorrow, it was more than her heart could bear.

She tried to speak; but though her lips shaped his name, her voice died away in a husky whisper. Suddenly over the pale sad face broke a look of rapturous joy—a smile like the sunshine of heaven; and in that instant the figure vanished—was gone utterly in a breath; and the lady *felt* that she was alone.

Miss Darrington is not a nervous woman, but it was some minutes before she could summon sufficient calmness to act, or even to think. Then she rang her bell, and a servant came to the door. "Come in," she said, in answer to his respectful tap. But when he attempted to obey her the door was found locked on the inside. She remembered that she had herself turned the key some hours before to secure herself from interruption. Moreover, the man, on being questioned, declared with evident truth that no visitor had passed in or out of the house since noon. It was by a strong effort of will that she now drove back the superstitious feelings that assaulted her, and forced a smile at her own absurdity. Of course the thing was an illusion, a trick of the imagination played on by nerves overworn with work. It was odd, though, that imagination should have raised up so vividly the image of one who certainly had not recently been in her thoughts. Then, too, her memory could hardly have supplied some details of this vision; they were unfamiliar. Where could she have got the picture of her friend in that garb? The wide gray cloak, the gold-laced military dress—these were very unlike the negligent white linen suit in which she remembered him. Only on one occasion had she seen him dressed otherwise, and that was the day when he rode to L——, to sit for the photograph which

What Did Mrs. Darrington See?/53

still hung at her side. On that day he had put on a black evening dress. Then the voice which had uttered her name—a name which only he had ever applied to her. How could imagination have raised that sound in her ear with such suddenness as to give her a shock of surprise?

It was odd, certainly; but she did not choose to indulge herself in morbid fancies upon the subject. Convinced that a low physical condition was really responsible for the illusion of which she had been the victim, she resolutely put the whole thing out of her mind, and set herself to get back the healthy tone to which nature entitled her. She left off writing, rode and walked frequently, and went much into society. But she was not able to dissipate the impression made upon her mind by what she had seen. Whenever she thought of it it was with a renewal of the same strange thrill which she had contended with at the time. She could not help recalling certain words which Raphael had once spoken to her, how he had vowed to seek her through the universe when death should have left him free to do so. Could such things be? And had death really freed that fiery and generous spirit? If so, where and when had he passed away? In a country so full of political and social turmoil as Mexico it was easy to imagine all possible contingencies, especially with a man of his temper. She found herself frequently turning to the columns of "Mexican correspondence" in the newspapers, for the chance of lighting upon his name; yet she knew well how easy it would be, in the chaos of that country, for a single stranger to vanish out of life and leave no trace. And then she told herself again that this was all nonsense and nerves; that her old friend was probably alive and well somewhere, and that he had forgotten her as completely as if she had never crossed his path. So, by degrees, the intensity of her first impression wore off, and her mind was regaining its accustomed poise, when a new incident occurred.

Tom Sibthorpe, at the close of the war, had settled himself to the practice of law in New York. He and Miss Darrington often met, and a warm friendship had grown up between them, kept alive by a frequent correspondence, not sentimental, but much like that which two clever men are apt to enjoy. One day early in December the lady received a letter from her friend, in which, after discussing in a lively manner one or two items of personal gossip, a new book, and the last *bon-mot,* the writer said:

"Have you heard that it is all over with our poor friend Aldama? He was one of the few victims of the almost bloodless revolution with which sleepy old Spain has just been astonishing the world. I was not unprepared to hear of him as involved in that affair, for I knew that the dream of a free and regenerated Spain had taken strong hold upon him. You remember that, notwithstanding his long residence in Cuba, he was always intensely a Spaniard in feeling. Seven or eight months ago he went to London, and fell in with Prim and his conclave of schemers. Of course they made much of him, for he was just the man for their purposes. His reckless courage, his familiarity with every species of dangerous adventure, his indifference to the ordinary objects of ambition, which took him out of the list of rivals, and the immense wealth at his command, would make him invaluable to them. He entered heart and soul into their schemes; but he seems to have been haunted by a presentiment that his life would be the cost. Some time in the summer he wrote me a long letter, in which, though it had occasional flashes of his old self, it was plain to see that he was oppressed by some strong foreboding. His life, he said, had never been of any use to himself or any one. He had wasted it all in the pursuit of a pleasure he had never found, chasing a phantom of happiness which had forever fled before him. It might partly redeem the worthlessness of such a life if he could strike one blow for Spain and liberty. If his country was to be free, some of her sons must bleed for her, and he could at least die as well as a better man. Then suddenly changing both his tone and topic, he referred to our school-days together, recalling certain wild frolics we two had shared, in a gay and witty way that made me laugh then, but which now I can only think upon with tears. That was the last I heard from him until a few days ago, when a letter from my sister Alice, who, as you know, is married to Mr. Manners, an Englishman living in Madrid, gave me the whole sad story.

"It was in the month of August that Raphael, choosing, as usual, the post of greatest danger, went from Paris to Madrid, to communicate with the heads of the conspiracy there. The southern provinces were already alive with insurrection, but none of his friends in the city thought of connecting him with the movement. Only George Manners, a young relative of my brother-in-law, became, to some extent, his confidant, and was deeply infected with his enthusiasm. The thing must have been well managed, for the extent and power of the uprising would seem to have been quite unrecognized. But events, as you know, moved very fast. The absence of the Queen from her capital furnished the insurgents with just the opportunity they required, and immediately the revolt became a revolution. Raphael, who must have held in his hands some important threads of the affair, remained in the city until the resignations of the Queen's ministry; but on the 20th of September he left Madrid to put himself in communication with Serrano, who was marching to give battle to the royalist forces. George Manners went with him, telling Alice that there was going to be a row, and he wanted to see it. A fortnight later George came back alone. The account he gives is not very clear as to details, but the main facts are plain enough.

"They succeeded in joining Serrano's forces a day or two before the engagement, which occurred on the 28th of September, not very far from Cordova; my recollection of the place, as named in the newspaper reports, is a little at fault. Raphael had a command, and in the action became separated from his friend. When the fight was over, the Queen's troops defeated and scattered, Manners tried in vain to find him. The young man had himself been taken prisoner, and only released when his captors found him a hinderance to flight, so his knowledge of the incidents of the fight was a good deal confused. After a two days' search, however, he learned that a wounded officer had been carried by some of his men into the hut of a peasant, the locality of which was pointed out to him, and had since died there. He hastened to the place, and in the still, cold form that lay there alone on a rude bench, covered with a rough cavalry cloak, he recognized his friend and ours."

Miss Darrington paused in her reading, and her breath came short and quick. The 28th of September! And he had lived for some hours after—how long she would never know. But she recalled with a shock that made every nerve quiver that it was on the evening of the 29th of September that she had seemed to see him in her own room!

It was some time before she could command herself sufficiently to go on with the letter.

"Poor Raphael," the writer continued; "there were splendid possibilities in him, if a bad education had not spoiled their promise. I hardly knew until he was gone how dear he had been to me. We were almost like brothers; and yet I know that he never fully revealed himself to me, and never would. After that visit to Catalpa Grove he was more than ever reserved. He was greatly changed, too; his boyish high spirits had vanished, and he seemed colder, graver, older by many years. I could not fail to see that his nature had been stirred to its profoundest deeps by some experience—whether of joy or pain I never knew. The key to his secret was not in my hands. Dear friend, I believe that if any one possessed such a key it was yourself. You knew him but a little while, but you read him far better than I. No need to tell *you* how rich in high impulses, in noble aspirations, was that generous, ungoverned soul. But the world was out of joint for him always. Only once did any hope to set it right seem offered him, and he missed that. If he had not— But forgive me. I am speculating upon contingencies which, perhaps, were never possible."

Miss Darrington read no farther. The letter dropped from her hands, and her face was buried in them, while hot tears forced themselves through her fingers—tears of remorseful tenderness, as she thought how little she had prized, how little deserved, that strong, true, generous love which had held her to the last in such tender remembrance; which had made its way across the ocean, across the wider, deeper gulf that divides us from the unseen world, to give to *her* the greeting of lips that were sealed, the last loving look of eyes that were forever closed to all on earth beside!

She believed that. If you doubt it—if you think it can not be—will you tell me *what it was* that Miss Darrington saw?

La Femme Noir

⫘

Anna Maria Hall

Anna Maria Hall was born in Ireland on January 6, 1800. She died in London at the age of 81. Her distinguished career included numerous short story collections, novels, and plays, productions of which starred such notable actors as the elder Tyrone Power. Among her voluminous output are numerous fantasies, of both the light and brooding varieties. Among her works are Tales of a Woman's Trials *(1834),* Tales of Irish Peasantry *(1840), and* A Woman's Story *(1857) and many volumes of "tales and sketches." She was a contributor to major magazines on both sides of the Atlantic and editor of* Sharpe's London Magazine *and* The St. James's Magazine, *like ghost story writers Mrs. Henry Wood (née Ellen Price) and Mary Elizabeth Braddon, who edited prestigious Victorian monthlies. Although Hall's books are rare today, a few have been restored to print in facsimile editions, so that she continues to reach an audience across more than 150 years.*

Hall was active in many philanthropic pursuits, including the establishment of the Hospital for Consumptives in Brompton, the Governesses' Institute, and the Home for Decayed Gentlewomen. She was friend to numerous street musicians, generous to all in need, and a strong advocate of women's rights and temperance. She also believed in spiritualism; some of her fiction is an intriguing mixture of occult and feminist ideology.

"La Femme Noir," written in the mid-nineteenth century, was one of Hall's best known stories and was reprinted as late as 1891, in the magazine Littell's Living Age, *from which it is reprinted here. The story harks back to the earliest*

roots of women's supernatural storytelling. The manner in which the story is narrated—by a matriarch addressing the young women of her family—echoes the fact that most of the fairy tales that have been recorded and credited to "gentlemen collectors" were gathered by interviews with elderly women. Whether family legends or peasant lore, those old stories told for generations by forgotten women have greatly influenced today's supernatural literature.

The narrator of "La Femme Noir" is a strong-willed woman with definite ideas about men. The specter of the tale, sharing the narrator's philosophy, sides with the living of her sex against a patriarchal tyrant. This gives the story a curiously modern tone when compared to the traditional stories many of us are weaned on nowadays; it is likely that Hall, rather than the "gentleman collectors," more truly captured the spirit of oral tradition as it was passed from grandmothers to granddaughters of long ago.

〜

People find it easy enough to laugh at "spirit-stories" in broad daylight, when the sunbeams dance upon the grass, and the deepest forest glades are spotted and checkered only by the tender shadows of leafy trees; when the rugged castle, that looked so mysterious and so stern in the looming night, seems suited for a lady's bower; when the rushing waterfall sparkles in diamond showers, and the hum of bee and song of bird tune the thoughts to hopes of life and happiness; people may laugh at ghosts then, if they like, but as for me, I never could merely smile at the records of those shadowy visitors. I have large faith in things supernatural, and cannot disbelieve solely on the ground that I lack such evidences as are supplied by the senses; for they, in truth, sustain by palpable proofs so few of the many marvels by which we are surrounded, that I would rather reject them altogether as witnesses, than abide the issue entirely as they suggest.

My great grandmother was a native of the canton of Berne; and at the advanced age of ninety, her memory of "the long ago" was as active as it could have been at fifteen; she looked as if she had just stepped out of a piece of tapestry belonging to a past age, but with warm sympathies for the present. Her English, when she became excited, was very curious—a mingling of French, certainly not Parisian, with here and there scraps of German done into English, literally—so that her observations were at times remarkable for their strength. "The mountains," she would say, "in her country, went high, high up, until they could look into the heavens, and *hear* God in the storm." She never thoroughly comprehended the real beauty of England; but spoke with contempt of the flatness of our island—calling our mountains "inequalities," nothing more—holding our agriculture "cheap," saying that the land tilled itself, leaving man nothing to do. She would sing the most amusing *patois* songs, and tell stories from morning till night, more especially spirit-stories; but the old lady would not tell a tale of that character a second time to an unbeliever; such things, she would say, "are not for make-laugh." One in particular, I remember, always excited great interest in her young listeners, from its mingling of the real and the romantic; but it can never be told as she told it; there was so much of the picturesque about the old lady—so much to admire in the curious carving of her ebony cane, in the beauty of her point lace, the size and weight of her long ugly earrings, the fashion of her solid silk gown, the singularity of her buckled shoes—her dark-brown wrinkled face, every wrinkle an expression—her broad thoughtful brow, beneath which glittered her bright blue eyes—bright, even when her eyelashes were white with *years*. All these peculiarities gave impressive effect to her words.

"In my young time," she told us, "I spent many happy hours with Amelie de Rohean, in her uncle's castle. He was a fine man—much size, stern, and dark, and full of noise—a strong man, no fear—he had a great heart, and a big head.

"The castle was situated in the midst of the most stupendous Alpine scenery, and yet it was not solitary. There were other dwellings in sight; some very near, but separated by a ravine, through which, at all seasons, a rapid river kept its foaming course. You do not know what torrents are in this country; your torrents are as babies—ours are giants. The one I speak of divided the valley; here and there a rock, round which it sported, or stormed, according to the season. In two of the defiles these rocks were of great value; acting as piers for the support of bridges, the only means of communication with our opposite neighbors.

"Monsieur, as we always called the count, was, as I have told you, a dark, stern, violent man. All men are wilful, my dear young ladies," she would say; "but Monsieur was the most wilful: all men are selfish, but he was the most selfish: all men are tyrants—" Here the old lady was invariably interrupted by her relatives, with "Oh, good Granny!" and, "Oh fie, dear Granny!" and she would bridle up a little and fan herself; then continue—"Yes, my dears, each creature according to its nature—all men are tyrants; and I confess that I do think a Swiss, whose mountain inheritance is nearly coeval with the creation of the mountains, has a *right* to be tyrannical; I did not intend to blame him for that: I did not, because I had grown used to it. Amelie and I always stood up and when he entered the room, and never sat down until we were desired. He never bestowed a loving word or a kind look upon either of us. We never spoke except when we were spoken to."

"But when you and Amelie were alone, dear Granny?"

"Oh, why, then we did chatter, I suppose; though then it was in moderation; for monsieur's influence chilled us even when he was not present; and often she would say, 'It is hard trying to love him, for he will not let me!' There is no such beauty in the world now as Amelie's. I can see her as she used to stand before the richly carved glass in the grave oak-panelled dressing-room; her luxuriant hair combed up from her full round brow; the discreet maidenly cap, covering the back of her head; her brocaded silk, (which she had inherited from her grand-mother,) shaded round the bosom by the modest ruffle; her black velvet gorget and bracelets, showing off to perfection the pearly transparency of her skin. She was the loveliest of all creatures, and as good as she was lovely; it seems but as yesterday that we were together—but as yesterday! And yet I lived to see her an old woman; so they called her, but she never seemed old to me! My own dear Amelie!" Ninety years had not dried up the sources of poor Granny's tears, nor chilled her heart; and she never spoke of Amelie without emotion. "Monsieur was very proud of his niece, because she was part of himself; she added to his consequence, she contributed to his enjoyments; she had grown necessary; she was the one sunbeam of his house."

"Not the *one* sunbeam, surely, Granny!" one of us would exclaim; "you were a sunbeam then."

"I was nothing where Amelie was—nothing but her shadow! The bravest and best in the country would have rejoiced to be to her what I was—her chosen friend; and some would have perilled their lives for one of the sweet smiles which played around her uncle, but never touched his heart. Monsieur never would suffer people to be happy except in his way. He had never married; and he declared Amelie never should. She had, he said, as much enjoyment as he had: she had a castle with a draw-bridge; she had a forest for hunting; dogs and horses; servants and serfs; jewels, gold, and gorgeous dresses; a guitar and a harpsichord; a parrot—and a friend! And such an uncle! he believed there was not such another uncle in broad Europe! For many a long day Amelie laughed at this catalogue of advantages—that is, she laughed when her uncle left the room; she never laughed before him. In time, the laugh came not; but in its place, sighs and tears. Monsieur had a great deal to answer for. Amelie was not prevented from seeing the gentry when they came to visit in a formal way, and she met many hawking and hunting; but she never was permitted to invite any one to the castle, nor to accept an invitation. Monsieur fancied that by shut-ting her lips, he closed her heart; and boasted such was the advantage of his good training, that Amelie's mind was fortified against all weak-nesses, for she had not the least dread of wandering about the ruined chapel of the castle, where he himself dared not go after dusk. This place was dedicated to the family ghost—the spirit, which for many years had it entirely at its own disposal. It was much attached to its quarters, seldom leaving them, except for the purpose of interfering when anything decidedly wrong was going forward in the castle. 'La Femme Noir' had been seen gliding along the unprotected parapet of the bridge, and standing on a pinnacle, before the late master's death; and many tales were told of her, which in this age of unbelief would not be credited."

"Granny, did you know why your friend ventured so fearlessly into the ghost's territories?" inquired my cousin.

"I am not come to that," was the reply; "and you are one saucy little maid to ask what I do not choose to tell. Amelie certainly entertained no fear of the spirit; 'La Femme Noir' could have had no angry feelings towards her, for my friend would wander in the ruins, taking no note of daylight, or moonlight, or even darkness. The peasants declared their young lady must have walked over crossed bones, or drank water out of a raven's skull, or passed nine times round the spectre's glass on Midsummer eve. She must have done all this, if not more; there could be little doubt that the 'Femme Noir' had initiated her into certain mysteries; for they heard at times voices in low, whispering converse, and saw the shadows of two persons cross the old roofless chapel, when 'Mamselle' had passed the foot-bridge alone. Monsieur gloried in this fearlessness on the part of his gentle niece; and more than once, when he had revellers in the castle, he sent her forth at midnight to bring him a bough from a tree that only grew beside the altar of the old chapel; and she did his bidding always as willingly, though not as rapidly, as he could desire.

"But certainly Amelie's courage brought no calmness. She became pale; her pillow was often moistened by her tears; her music was neglected; she took no pleasure in the chase; and her chamois not receiving its usual attention, went off into the mountains. She avoided me—her friend! who would have died for her; she made no reply to my prayers, and did not heed my entreaties. One morning, when her eyes were fixed upon a book she did not read, and I sat at my embroidery a little apart, watching the tears stray over her cheek until I was blinded by my own, I heard monsieur's heavy tramp approaching through the long gallery; some boots creak—but the boots of monsieur!—they growled!

" 'Save me, oh save me!' she exclaimed wildly. Before I could reply, her uncle crashed open the door, and stood before us like an embodied thunderbolt. He held an open letter in his hand—his eyes glared—his nostrils were distended—he trembled so with rage, that the cabinets and old china shook again.

" 'Do you,' he said, 'know Charles le Maitre?'

"Amelie replied, 'She did.'

" 'How did you make acquaintance with the son of my deadliest foe?'

"There was no answer. The question was repeated. Amelie said she had met him, and at last confessed it was in the ruined portion of the castle! She threw herself at her uncle's feet—she clung to his knees; love taught her eloquence. She told him how deeply Charles regretted the long-standing feud; how earnest, and true, and good, he was. Bending low, until her tresses were heaped upon the floor, she confessed, modestly, but firmly, that she loved this young man; that she would rather sacrifice the wealth of the whole world, than forget him.

"Monsieur seemed suffocating; he tore off his lace cravat, and scattered its fragments on the floor—still she clung to him. At last he flung her from him; he reproached her with the bread she had eaten, and heaped odium upon her mother's memory! But though Amelie's nature was tender and affectionate, the old spirit of the old race roused within her; the slight girl arose, and stood erect before the man of storms.

" 'Did you think,' she said, 'because I bent to you that I am feeble? because I bore with you, have I no thoughts? You gave food to this frame, but you fed not my heart; you gave me not love, nor tenderness, nor sympathy; you showed me to your friends, as you would your horse. If you had by kindness sown the seeds of love within my bosom; if you had been a father to me in tenderness, I would have been to you—a child. I never knew the time when I did not tremble at your footstep; but I will do so no more. I would gladly have loved you, trusted you, cherished you; but I feared to let you know I had a heart, lest you should tear and insult it. Oh, sir, those who expect love where they give none, and confidence where there is no trust, blast the fair time of youth, and lay up for themselves an unhonored old age.' The scene terminated by monsieur's falling down in a fit, and Amelie's being conveyed fainting to her chamber.

"That night the castle was enveloped by storms; they came from all points of the compass—thunder, lightning, hail, and rain! The master lay in his stately bed and was troubled; he could hardly believe that Amelie spoke the words he had heard: cold-hearted and selfish as he was, he was also a clear-seeing man, and it was their truth that struck him. But still his heart was hardened; he had commanded Amelie to be locked into her chamber, and her lover seized and imprisoned when he came to his usual tryste. Monsieur, I have said, lay in his stately bed, the lightning, at intervals, illumining his dark chamber. I had cast myself on the floor outside her door, but could not hear her weep, though I knew that she was overcome of sorrow. As I sat, my head resting against the lintel of the door, a form passed through the solid oak from her chamber, without the bolts being withdrawn. I saw it as plainly as I see your faces now, under the influence of various emotions; nothing opened, but it passed through—a shadowy form, dark and vapory, but perfectly distinct. I knew it was 'La Femme Noir,' and I trembled, for she never came from caprice, but always for a purpose. I did not fear for Amelie, for 'La Femme Noir' never warred with the high-minded or virtuous. She passed slowly, more slowly than I am speaking, along the corridor, growing taller and taller as she went on, until she entered monsieur's chamber by the door exactly opposite where I stood. She paused at the foot of the plumed bed, and the lightning, no longer fitful, by its broad flashes kept up a continual illumination. She stood for some time perfectly motionless, though in a loud tone the master demanded whence she came, and what she wanted. At last, during a pause in the storm, she told him that all the power he possessed should not prevent the union of Amelie and Charles. I heard her voice myself; it sounded like the night-wind among fir-trees—cold and shrill, chilling both ear and heart. I turned my eyes away while she spoke, and when I looked again, she was gone! The storm continued to increase in violence, and the master's rage kept pace with the war of elements. The servants were trembling with undefined terror; they feared they knew not what; the dogs added to their apprehension by howling fearfully, and then barking in the highest possible key; the master paced about his chamber, calling in vain on his domestics, stamping and swearing like a maniac. At last, amid flashes of lightning, he made his way to the head of the great staircase, and presently the clang of the alarm-bell mingled with the thunder and the roar of the mountain torrents: this hastened the servants to his presence, though they seemed hardly capable of understanding his words—he insisted on Charles being brought before him. We all trembled, for he was mad and livid with rage. The warden, in whose care the young man was, dared not enter the hall that echoed his loud words and heavy footsteps, for when he went to seek his prisoner, he found every bolt and bar withdrawn, and the iron door wide open: he was gone. Monsieur seemed to find relief by his energies being called into action; he ordered instant pursuit, and mounted his favorite charger, despite the storm, despite the fury of the elements. Although the great gates rocked, and the castle shook like an aspen-leaf, he set forth, his path illumined by the lightning; bold and brave as was his horse, he found it almost impossible to get it forward; he dug his spurs deep into the flanks of the noble animal, until the red blood mingled with the rain. At last, it rushed madly down the path to the bridge the young man must cross; and when they reached it, the master discerned the floating cloak of the pursued, a few yards in advance. Again the horse rebelled against his will, the lightning flashed in his eyes, and the torrent seemed a mass of red fire; no sound could be heard but of its roaring waters; the attendants clung as they advanced to the hand rail of the bridge. The youth, unconscious of the *pursuit,* proceeded rapidly; and again roused, the horse plunged forward. On the instant, the form of 'La Femme Noir' passed with the blast that rushed down the ravine; the torrent followed in her track, and more than half the bridge was swept away forever. As the master reined back the horse he had so urged forward, he saw the youth kneeling with outstretched arms on the opposite bank—kneeling in gratitude for his deliverance from his double peril. All were struck with the piety of the youth, and earnestly rejoiced at his deliverance; though they did not presume to say so, or look as if they thought it. I never saw so changed a person as the master when he reentered the castle gate: his cheek was blanched—his eye quelled—his fierce plume hung broken over his shoulder—his step was unequal, and in the voice of a feeble girl he said—'Bring me a cup of wine.' I was his cupbearer, and for the first time in his life he thanked me graciously, and in the warmth of his gratitude tapped my shoulder; the caress nearly hurled me across the hall. What passed in his retiring-room, I know not. Some said the 'Femme Noir' visited him again; I cannot tell; I did not see her; I speak of what I saw, not of what I heard. The storm passed away with a clap of thunder, to which the former sounds were but as the rattling of pebbles beneath the swell of a summer wave. The next morning monsieur sent for the pasteur. The good man seemed terror-stricken as he entered the hall; but monsieur filled him a quart of gold coins out of a leathern bag, to repair his church, and that quickly; and grasping his hand as he departed, looked him steadily in the face. As he did so, large drops stood like beads upon his brow; his stern, coarse features were strangely moved while he gazed upon the calm, pale minister of peace and love. 'You,' he said, 'bid God bless the poorest peasant that passes you on the mountain; have you no blessing to give the master of Rohean?'

" 'My son,' answered the good man, 'I give you the blessing I may give:—May God bless you, and may your heart be opened to give and to receive.'

" 'I know I can give,' replied the proud man; 'but what can I receive?'

" 'Love,' he replied. 'All your wealth has not brought you happiness, because you are unloving and unloved!'

"The demon returned to his brow, but it did not remain there.

" 'You shall give me lessons in this thing,' he said; and so the good man went his way.

"Amelie continued a close prisoner; but a change came over monsieur. At first he shut himself up in his chamber, and no one was suffered to enter his presence; he took his food with his own hand from the only attendant who ventured to approach his door. He was heard walking up and down the room, day and night. When we were going to sleep, we heard his heavy tramp; at daybreak, there it was again; and those of the household, who awoke at intervals during the night, said it was unceasing.

"Monsieur could read. Ah, you may smile; but in those days, and in those mountains, such men as the master did not trouble themselves or others with knowledge; but the master of Rohean read both Latin and Greek, and commanded THE BOOK he had never opened since his childhood to be brought him. It was taken out of its velvet case, and carried in forthwith; and we saw his shadow from without, like the shadow of a giant, bending over THE BOOK; and he read in it for some days; and we greatly hoped it would soften and change his nature—and though I cannot say much for the softening, it certainly affected a great change; he no longer stalked moodily along the corridors, and banged the doors, and swore at the servants; he the rather seemed possessed of a merry devil, roaring out an old song—

Aux bastions de Genève, nos cannons
  Sont branquez;
S'il y a quelque attaque nous les feront ronfler,
  Viva! les cannoniers!

and then he would pause, and clang his hands together like a pair of cymbals, and laugh. And once, as I was passing along, he pounced out upon me, and whirled me round in a waltz, roaring at me when he let me down, to practise *that* and break my embroidery frame. He formed a band of horns and trumpets, and insisted on the goatherds and shepherds sounding reveillés in the mountains, and the village children beating drums; his only idea of joy and happiness was noise. He set all the canton to work to mend the bridge, paying the workmen double wages; and he, who never entered a church before, would go to see how the laborers were getting on nearly every day. He talked and laughed a great deal to himself; and in his gayety of heart would set the mastiffs fighting, and make excursions from home—we knowing not where he went. At last, Amelie was summoned to his presence, and he shook her and shouted, then kissed her; and hoping she would be a good girl, told her he had provided a husband for her. Amelie wept and prayed; and the master capered and sung. At last she fainted; and taking advantage of her unconsciousness, he conveyed her to the chapel; and there beside the altar stood the bridegroom—no other than Charles Le Maitre.

"They lived many happy years together; and when monsieur was in every respect a better, though still a strange man, 'the Femme Noir' appeared again to him—once. She did so with a placid air, on a summer night, with her arm extended towards the heavens.

"The next day the muffled bell told the valley that the stormy, proud old master of Rohean had ceased to live."

A Friend in Need

Lisa Tuttle

Lisa Tuttle was born in Texas in 1953. She began selling her short fiction before her twenty-first birthday and won the John W. Campbell Award for best new science fiction writer in 1974. Her work has appeared in most major science fiction magazines and anthology series in the United States and England. Often nominated for the Hugo and Nebula Awards, she won the latter for her story "The Bone Flute" (1984) in The Magazine of Fantasy and Science Fiction, *despite having tried to withdraw it from consideration because of what she viewed as questionable behind-the-scenes goings-on in the nomination process. She has also worked as a journalist on the Austin* American–Statesman. *For the last several years, she has lived in England.*

Tuttle was a proponent of feminism in science fiction very early in her career. A portion of her novel Windhaven *(1981), co-authored by George R. R. Martin, was first published in 1975. It was one of many non-sexist science fiction works produced at that time that startled the old-guard science fiction writers. Her most recent collection is* A Spaceship Built of Stone *(1987).*

Tuttle is not chiefly a science fiction author, however, but often writes on the edge between categories. Although it has been science fiction magazines that have embraced her work, her finest achievements have tended toward horror, and she seems most comfortable as a fantasist.

"A Friend in Need" was first published in Rod Serling's The Twilight Zone Magazine *in August 1981 and afterwards was selected for* The Year's Best Fantasy Stories: 8 *(1982). It also appears in Tuttle's first-rate collection*

A Nest of Nightmares (1986), which has appeared only in England and which may be the most significant book of its kind yet to take a consistently feminist approach to horror fiction. "A Friend in Need" is a hauntingly strange piece; building innovatively on the common childhood phenomenon of invisible playmates, it addresses many feminist concerns, from child abuse to the supportive communication women can achieve with women.

⫙

Photographs lie, like people, like memories. What would it prove if I found Jane's face and mine caught together in a picture snapped nearly twenty years ago? What does it mean that I can't find such a photograph?

I keep looking. My early life is so well documented by my father's industrious camera work that Jane's absence seems impossible. She was, after all, my best friend; and all my other friends—including one or two I can't, at this distance, identify—are there in black and white as they run, sit, stand, scowl, cry, laugh, grimace, and play around me. Page after page of birthday parties, dress-up games, bicycle riding, ice-cream eating, of me and my friends Shelly, Mary, Betty, Carl, Julie, Howard, Bubba, and Pam. But not Jane, who is there in all my memories.

Was she ever really there? Did I imagine her into existence? That's what I thought for twelve years, but I don't believe that anymore.

I saw her in the Houston airport today and I recognized her, although not consciously. What I saw was a small woman of about my own age with dark, curly hair. Something about her drew my attention.

We were both waiting for a Braniff flight from New York, already five minutes late. A tired-looking man in uniform went behind the counter, made a throat-clearing noise into the microphone, and announced that the flight would be an hour late.

I swore and heard another voice beside me, like an echo. I turned my head and met her eyes. We laughed together.

"Are you meeting someone?" she asked.

"My mother."

"What a coincidence," she said flatly. "We've both got mothers coming to visit."

"No, actually my mother lives here. She went to New York on business. Your mother lives there?"

"Long Island," she said. It came out as one word; I recognized the New Yorker's pronunciation.

"That's where you're from?"

"Never west of the Hudson until two years ago." Her sharp eyes caught my change of expression. "You're surprised?"

"No." I smiled and shrugged, because the feeling of familiarity was

A Friend in Need/69

becoming stronger. "I thought I knew you, that's all. Like from a long time ago. Grade school?"

"I'm Jane Renzo," she said, thrusting out her hand. "Graduate of Gertrude Folwell Elementary School and Elmont High, class of '73."

Jane, Jane Renzo, I thought. Had I known someone by that name? There were distant resonances, but I could not catch them. "Cecily Cloud," I said, taking her hand.

"What a great name!"

Our hands unclasped and fell apart. She was grinning; there was a hint of a joke in her eyes, but also something serious.

"But it doesn't ring any bells?" I asked.

"Oh, it does, it definitely does. Sets the bells a-ringing. It's the name I always wanted. A name like a poem. I hated always being plain Jane." She made a face.

"Better than Silly Cecily," I said. "The kids used to call me Silly until I got so used to it that it sounded like my real name. But I always hated it. I used to wish my parents had given me a strong, sensible name that couldn't be mispronounced or misspelled or made fun of— like Jane."

Jane. Memory stirred, but it was like something deep in a forest. I couldn't get a clear sight of it.

"We all have our own miseries, I guess," she said. She looked at her watch and then at me, a straightforward, friendly look. "We've got time to kill before this flight gets here. You want to go sit down somewhere and have some coffee?"

The rush of pleasure I felt at her suggestion was absurdly intense, inappropriate, as if she were a long-lost friend, returned to me when I had nearly given up hope of seeing her again. Trying to understand it, I said, "Are you sure we haven't met before?"

She laughed—a sharp, defensive sound.

Hastily, afraid of losing our easy rapport, I said, "It's only that I feel I know you. Or you remind me of someone. You never came to Houston when you were a kid?"

She shook her head.

"College?"

"Montclair State." We had begun to walk together in search of a coffee shop, down the long, windowless, carpeted, white-lit corridor. It was like being inside a spaceship, I thought, or in an underground city of the distant, sterile future. We were in Houston, but we might as easily have been in New York, Los Angeles, or Atlanta for all the cues our surroundings gave us. It was a place set apart from the real world, untouched by time or season, unfettered by the laws of nature.

"It's like the future," I said.

70/Lisa Tuttle

Jane looked at the curving walls and indirect lighting and gave me an appreciative smile. "It is kind of *Star Treky*," she said.

We came to rest in a small, dim, overpriced restaurant which was almost empty, in contrast to the bar on one side and the fast-food cafeteria on the other. I saw by my watch that it was too late for lunch and too early for dinner. We ordered coffee, causing the middle-aged waitress to sigh heavily and stump away.

"Actually, I'd rather have a shot of Tullamore Dew," said Jane. "Or a large snifter of brandy."

"Did you want—"

She shook her head. "No, no. Better not. It's just that the thought of seeing my mother again has me wanting reinforcement. But I'd be less capable of dealing with her drunk than I am sober."

I looked at her curiously, because she had struck me from the first as a capable, almost fearless person. "You don't get along with your mother?"

"Something like that. I moved out here to get away from her, and she still won't let me be. She calls me every night. Sometimes she cries. She won't believe that I'm grown up and that I have my own life to live, a life I've chosen. She's still waiting for me to give up this silliness and move back home. My sisters got away because they got married. But in her eyes I'm still a child."

The waitress returned, setting our coffees down before us with unnecessary emphasis. I watched the dark brown liquid slide over the rim of my cup, to be caught in the shallow white bowl of the saucer.

"You're lucky if you and your mother can relate to each other as people," Jane said.

I nodded, although I had never given the matter any thought; I'd simply taken it for granted. "We have disagreements, but we're pretty polite about them," I said.

This made Jane laugh. "Polite," she said. "Oh, my." She peeled the foil top off a plastic container of coffee whitener. "You're so lucky . . . to have had a happy childhood and a mother who knows how to let go."

It seemed at first acceptable, the way she so calmly passed judgment on my life, as if she knew it; then, suddenly, strange.

"I think I had a fairly normal childhood," I said. "Very ordinary. At least, it always seemed that way to me." It had been suburban, middle-class, and sheltered. I saw my experiences reflected in the lives of my friends, and I found it hard to believe that Jane had come from a background terribly dissimilar. "You were unhappy as a child?"

Jane hesitated, stirring her coffee from black to brown. Then she said, "I don't remember."

"What do you mean?"

"Just that. I don't remember my childhood. Most of it, anyway. It's as if I went to sleep when I was five and didn't wake up until I was twelve. The years in between are a blank."

I stared at her, trying to understand. I couldn't believe it. I didn't doubt that I had forgotten much of my own childhood, but there remained a satisfying large jumble of memories that I could rummage around in when the need arose. Some of the things that had happened to me remained as vivid in my imagination as if they had just happened: the day I had broken my bride doll, a rabbit-shaped cake my mother had baked one Easter, the taste of water warm from the garden hose at the height of summer, the Christmas when I had been sick, games of hide-and-seek, classroom embarrassments . . . I had only to let down the barriers to be flooded by memories, most of them far more intense than the recollections of anything that had happened to me as an adult. To be without such memories was to be without a childhood, to lack a certain identity.

"I can remember a few things from when I was very young," Jane said into my stunned silence. "None of them pleasant. And my sisters have told me things . . . it's just as well I don't remember. The things I've forgotten can't hurt me."

"But why? What happened to you? What was so terrible?"

"I'm sure other kids survived a lot worse. In fact, I know that for certain. There's no telling what will make one kid break and another survive, or what kind of defense mechanisms are needed. I work with emotionally disturbed children, and some of them have every right to be, given their backgrounds, while others come from loving families and just . . . crack over things that other kids take in stride. All I can say about the things that happened to me—well, I had my way of dealing with them, whether it was a good way or not. Forgetting, blotting it out, was part of it."

She sounded defensive and apologetic. I tried to look reassuring. "You don't have to—If it makes you uncomfortable, don't talk about it."

"No, that's it, I *do* want to talk about it. But I don't want to bore you. I don't want to burden you with my old stories."

"I don't mind at all," I said. "I'm happy to listen, if it helps you to talk."

"I think it might help. Well . . ." She cleared her throat and took a sip of coffee, looking at me self-consciously over the cup. "One of my earliest memories is when I was about four. My mother was forty-nine and menopausal. She was crazy that year, more than usual. Any little thing could set her off, and when she got angry, she got violent. I can't remember what it was I did, but it was probably something as minor as interrupting her while she was thinking—I got swatted for that more than once. At any rate, she started screaming. We were in the kitchen. She grabbed the carving knife and came for me, yelling that she'd cut off my hands so I couldn't make any more trouble."

"Jane!"

She shrugged, smiling wryly. "I'm sure I remember the knife as bigger than it really was. And maybe she wouldn't have hurt me at all. But what did I know? I was a little kid. And when somebody comes at you with a knife, the instinct is to get the hell away. She chased me all through the house. I finally hid in a cabinet and listened to her looking for me. One of my sisters got my father, and he managed to calm her down. But nobody knew where I was, and I was afraid to come out. I crouched there in the dark, beneath the bathroom sink, for hours, until I decided it was safe to come out. I hadn't heard her screaming for a long time, but I was afraid that she might be tricking me and that I'd open the door to find her on the other side, the knife in her hand and a horrible smile on her face."

"Was she insane?" I asked quietly.

"No." The denial came too quickly. Jane paused and shrugged. "I don't know. Define the term. Generally, she could cope. Was she really over the edge, or just trying to scare me into being good? It's hard to decide even now. She was very unhappy at that time in her life, and she's always been a very self-dramatizing person. We all have our own ways of dealing with life. What's insane?"

"I don't know," I said, although I thought I did. "Was she violent toward you most of the time? Did you go in fear of your life?"

"Sometimes. It was hard to know where you stood with her. That's the worst thing for a kid. I couldn't count on her, I didn't know how to get the right responses. Sometimes she would be very loving, sometimes what I did would make her laugh. At other times the same thing would have her screaming at me. But more often she turned her anger against herself. She must have tried to kill herself—or at least she pretended to—half a dozen times. I remember her lying on the floor in the living room with an empty bottle of pills and a half-full bottle of vodka. She told us she was going to die, and she forbade us to call for help. We were supposed to sit there and watch her die, so that she could die looking at the faces she loved most. We didn't dare move. Finally she seemed to have passed out, and Sue, my oldest sister, tried to call Dad. But the second her hand touched the telephone, my mother sat up and started screaming at her for being a disobedient bastard."

"Lord," I said, when Jane paused to sip coffee. I tried to imagine it, but could not quite achieve the child's point of view. "How did you survive?"

"Well, I blotted it out, mostly. I had my imaginary life." She smiled.

"How do you mean?"

"When you were a kid, weren't there some things which seemed just as real to you as real life, although you knew they were different? The things you didn't tell grown-ups about, although they were every bit as real and important—if not more so—as life at school and at home?"

"You mean like pretend games?" I asked. "I used to pretend—" And suddenly I remembered. "Of course. That's who you remind me of." I laughed, feeling silly. "Jane. I had an imaginary friend named Jane."

Jane's smile was somewhat wistful. "What was she like?"

"Oh, she was everything I wanted to be and wasn't. Practical and neat instead of dreamy and disorganized. Her hair was dark and curly instead of straight and mousy. She read a lot, like me, and knew all kinds of wonderful games. She had my favorite name, of course." I shrugged and then laughed. "She was like a real person. She didn't have any magical powers—except, of course, that she disappeared from time to time. She was actually rather like you, I guess. Isn't that funny, that my imaginary friend should remind me of you?"

Jane didn't look as if she found it particularly odd or amusing. She said, "I had imaginary friends, too. Except, at the time, they weren't in the least imaginary to me. The life I made up for myself was more important to me than my real life. It was my escape. It was how I survived the childhood I don't remember—the things that *really* happened to me." She paused to sip her coffee and then went on.

"I was six years old. I was wearing a brand-new brown velvet dress with a white lace collar. I'm not sure why, but I think I was going to a party later in the afternoon. I was feeling very special and happy, and I was sitting at the dining room table eating my lunch. My mother sat next to me and nagged me. She kept warning me to be careful. She kept telling me how expensive the dress was, and how difficult it would be to clean if I got it dirty. She told me not to be as clumsy as I usually was, and she warned me that I'd better not spill anything on myself. So of course, I did. I slopped a little bit of milk onto my dress. At that, she grabbed me and pulled me up out of my chair, screaming at me that I was messy, disobedient, and a complete disgrace. I didn't deserve to have nice clothes. I was an animal. I ate like a clumsy pig, and I didn't deserve the nice meals she fixed for me. I should never have been born. Nobody could stand to be around me. I should be kept in a cage where I could spill my food all over me to my heart's content. Screaming all the way, she dragged me up to the attic and left me there to meditate on my sins."

My stomach clenched with sympathy at Jane's level, matter-of-fact tone.

"But the odd thing," Jane went on, "the odd thing was that I *liked* the attic. I always had liked it. Being taken up there and left was no punishment at all. I was always begging to be allowed to play up there, but she would never let me. I could only go up there when my father went, to help him clean, or to get out the Christmas ornaments, or to store old clothes away. I suppose I liked the attic so much because it was outside her domain. She would send my father up for things instead of going herself. It was the only place in the house that didn't belong to her.

"And that was where she left me. Where I couldn't mess up any of her things. I was left all alone up there under the roof. It was cold and quiet and filled with cardboard boxes. I was very far away from the rest of the house. I couldn't hear my family downstairs—for all I knew, they might have gone out, or just disappeared. And I knew my mother couldn't hear me or see me, either. I could do anything I wanted and not be punished for it. I could think or say whatever I liked. For the first time in my life, it seemed, I was completely free.

"So I pretended that my family didn't exist—or at least that I didn't belong to it. I made up a family I liked a lot better. My new mother was pretty and young and understanding. She never lost her temper and she never shouted at me. I could talk to her. My new father was younger, too, and spent more time at home with us. My real sisters were so much older than me that they sometimes seemed to live in another world, so my new sisters, in my made-up family, were closer to my age. I had a younger sister who would look up to me and ask me for advice, and I had a sister exactly my age who would be my best friend. She was good at all the things I wasn't. And instead of being ugly, with kinky hair like mine, she was pretty with long, straight hair that she would let me braid and put up for her." She stopped short, as if on the verge of saying something else. Instead, she sipped her coffee. I waited, not saying a word.

"I know I invented them," she said. "I know it was all a game. But still it seemed—it still seems—that I didn't make them up but found them somewhere, and found a way of reaching them in that faraway, warm place where they lived. I lived with them for a long time—nearly seven years. When I remember my childhood, it's the time I spent with my make-believe family that I remember. Those people."

I wanted to ask her their names, but I said nothing, almost afraid to interrupt her. Jane was looking at me, but I don't think she saw me.

"I sat all alone in that cold, dusty attic, and I could feel the house changing below me. I was in the attic of another house. I could hear the voices of my new family drifting up to me. I could imagine every room, how each one was furnished. When I had it all clear in my mind,

I went downstairs to see for myself. It was the same size as my real house, but completely different. There was a small chord organ in the living room that my make-believe mother played in the evenings, all of us gathered around to sing old-fashioned songs. The family room had a cork floor with woven Indian rugs on it. There was a deer head over the television set; my make-believe father liked to hunt. The wallpaper in the kitchen was gold and brown, and the cookie jar was shaped like a rabbit dressed in overalls. There was a big oak tree in the backyard that was perfect for climbing, perfect for playing pretend games in. It could be a pirate ship, or—"

My skin was crawling. It was my house she was describing. My parents. My childhood. "What about the front yard?" I asked.

"Another oak tree. We had lots of acorns in the fall. There was a magnolia tree on one side, and a big brick planter box built out of the front of the house. It was great to play in. I'm amazed those blue flowers managed to grow with us stomping on them all the time. Your mother—"

"It was you," I said.

She shut up and looked down into her coffee.

"Why didn't you say?" I asked. "Why this game? Why pretend you didn't know me? Did you think I'd forgotten? Jane?"

She gave me a wary look. "Of course I thought you'd forgotten. I wasn't sure myself that any of it had happened. I never thought I'd see you again. I thought I'd made you up."

"Made me up!" I laughed uneasily. "Come on, Jane! What are you talking about? What's the point of this whole story?"

"It's not a story," she said. Her voice was high and stubborn, like a child's. "I knew you wouldn't believe it."

"What is it you want me to believe? We were friends when we were children. We both remember that, But if you tell me that you grew up in New York, and I know that I—"

"Why did you say you had an *imaginary* friend called Jane?"

"Because I thought—" And I stopped and stared, feeling the little hairs prickling all over me as I remembered. "Because you disappeared," I said softly. "Whenever you left to go home, you just vanished. I saw you come and go out of nowhere, and I knew that real people didn't do that." I was suddenly afraid that I was sitting at a table with a ghost.

As if she read my thoughts, Jane reached across the table and gripped my hand. There was a sullen, challenging look on her face. Her hand was warm and firm and slightly damp. I remembered that, as a child, too, she had been solid and real. Once her firm grasp, just in time, had kept me from falling out of a tree. We had tickled each other and played tag and helped each other into dress-up clothes. She had liked to braid my hair.

Jane took her hand away to look at her wristwatch. "We'd better go," she said.

I thought of the first time I had seen her, coming down the attic stairs. I was surprised to find a stranger in my house, but she had looked back at me, perfectly at ease, and asked me if I wanted to play. We were friends in that instant—although I couldn't remember, now, what we had said to each other or what we played. Only that first moment of surprise remains hard and clear and whole in my mind, like the last time I saw her disappear.

Usually when Jane left she simply walked away, and I did not see where she went. She was different from my other friends in that I never walked her home and we never played at her house. I didn't even know where her house was; I knew only, from things she had said, that it was in a different neighborhood.

But that last day, I remember, we had been playing Parcheesi on the floor of my bedroom. Jane said goodbye and walked out. A few seconds later I thought of something I had meant to ask or tell her, and I scrambled to my feet and went after her. She was just ahead of me in the hallway, and I saw her go into the living room. She was just ahead of me, in plain sight, in daylight—and then she wasn't. She was gone. I looked all through the living room, although I knew she hadn't hidden from me; there hadn't been time.

I couldn't believe what I had seen. Things like that didn't happen, except on *The Twilight Zone*. I was eleven and a half years old, too old to have imaginary friends. I never saw Jane again.

Until today.

And now she was standing, preparing to leave me.

Hastily I stood up, pushing my chair away from the table. "I don't get it," I said. "I don't understand what you're saying."

She looked at me and shrugged. "Why do you think I know? I thought I'd imagined you, and here you are. But I grew up in New York, you grew up in Texas. We *couldn't* have known each other as kids. But that's what we both remember."

"And now what?"

She smiled at me ironically. "And now the plane is coming in. Let's go."

We walked together through the featureless corridors in silence. It felt right and familiar for me to be at her side, as if we'd never been apart, as if we'd walked together many times before.

"I wish she wasn't coming," Jane said suddenly. "I wish I could have told her no. I wish I didn't have to deal with her. Will I be running away from my mother all my life?"

I touched her arm. She was real. She was real. She was there. I felt very close to her, and yet I knew, sadly, that she must be lying to me, or crazy. One of us must be. I said, "You'll be all right. You're strong. You're grown up now, and you've got your own life. Just tell yourself that. Your mother's just another woman. She can't make you do anything you don't want to do."

She looked at me. "You always thought I was braver than I really was. It's funny, but your thinking that made me try to live up to it. In order to be as brave and strong as you thought I was, I did things that terrified me. Like the time I climbed from a tree up onto the roof of the house—"

"I was terrified!" I said. Her words brought it back vividly, those moments when, from my own precarious treetop perch, I had seen her thin, small figure drop to the dark shingles of the roof, the breath catching in my throat as if I were the one in danger.

"So was I," she said. "But it was worth it for the way you looked at me. I'd always been a quiet little coward, but to you I was wild and daring."

Through the big window we saw a bright orange plane land and roll along the runway.

"Thank you," said Jane. "I needed a friend today."

"Not just today," I said. "Now that we've found each other, we'll get together again, often."

She smiled and looked away. I followed her gaze and saw the plane docking.

"That's ours," I said, turning my head to look at her. She was gone.

I whirled away from the window, scanning the crowds for her dark hair, her white blouse, her particular way of moving. She was nowhere to be seen.

There hadn't been time. I had turned my head only for a moment. She had been right beside me; I could feel her presence. From one second to the next, she had simply vanished.

Feeling dizzy, I moved indecisively a few steps this way, a few steps that. There was no point in searching for her. I already knew I wouldn't find her. I wondered what airport she might be waiting in; I realized she had never said where she lived. Was she able to find me because our lives briefly intersected in the bland, anonymous limbo of an airport, or could she have come to me wherever I was, because of her need?

I am waiting, wondering if I will ever see her again. Jane is real; she exists; I know I didn't imagine her. But did she imagine me?

78/Lisa Tuttle

Attachment

Phyllis Eisenstein

Phyllis Eisenstein, ex-butcher and now full-time writer, was born in Chicago in 1946 and graduated from the University of Illinois. She currently lives with her husband, Alex, who is a writer and an artist. Her interests include anthropology, archeology, mythology, the guitar, and old movies.

Her writing was influenced early on by Andrew Lang's fairy tales (written mainly by his wife and her friends). Among Eisenstein's five novels are Born to Exile *(1978), which won the Balrog Award,* Sorcerer's Son *(1979), and* The Crystal Palace *(1988). Her short fiction has appeared in such leading genre magazines and anthologies as* Analog, The Magazine of Fantasy and Science Fiction, *and* New Dimensions. *Only occasionally are women at center stage in her stories, but the supporting casts almost always include interesting, complex female characters.*

"Attachment" was first published in the December 1974 issue of Amazing, *the oldest surviving magazine of the pulp era and the first science fiction magazine ever published in the United States. The story became a finalist for the Nebula Award the following year, so it is all the more puzzling that it has never been reprinted before now. Like Lisa Tuttle's "A Friend in Need," it is essentially a story of communication between women. Ellie and Johanna are of different generations and hold some quite dissimilar views. Yet at the heart of their story of joy and sorrow is a simple love, a cherishing of each other's existence.*

It rose from nothingness—a creature of nightmare, black as a stormwave, mountainous, inexorable. Ellie struggled, gasping beneath its Leviathan weight, striking out at velvet folds now solid, now fluid, now impalpable vapor; she twisted turned, thrashed, seeking air where there was none.

She woke, eyes wide to the soft glow of the nightlight, but in her mind the monster roiled still, and clutched. Her fingers tightened on rosary beads five thousand miles away.

Johanna! Ellie's scream was silent, but loud as a clap of thunder to one too distant to hear a voice.

The great black evil drew back, dwindled to a small, eight-legged ball of fur, and vanished. In a small German town, Johanna Peters escaped from sleep.

I'm sorry, Ellie.

It's all right. Ellie Greenfield peered at the bedside clock. *It's your morning. The doctor should come by to see you soon.*

Go back to sleep, child. You need your rest.

I think I'll have a cup of tea.

Forgive me. It won't be much longer.

Ellie donned robe and slippers and moved out into the hall. Her parents' bedroom door was closed, and no light showed beneath; she tiptoed past and descended to the ground floor.

You don't think about it, Ellie, but we both know . . .

I don't know anything.

Here is Marta with the breakfast I can't eat.

Eat it anyway. She turned on the kitchen light, filled the kettle and put it on to boil. Her father had left the newspaper on the table—she opened it at random and began to read.

"Is something wrong, Ellie?" Her mother, Sally Greenfield, stood in the doorway in a frilly blue robe.

Ellie shook her head. "I just couldn't sleep, Mom. I'm making some tea."

Mrs. Greenfield sat down beside her daughter. "You haven't been sleeping well for weeks, and you've lost weight. Is something bothering you?"

Ellie shrugged. "Exams are coming up."

"You always say that. You can't possibly have that many exams."

Ellie smiled. "You never went to the University of Chicago."

Mrs. Greenfield touched her arm. "Is it too rough for you, honey? Your father and I were wondering . . . do you want to transfer to some other school?"

"No, Mom. I love U of C."

"But are you sure it isn't too rough?"

"I'm sure."

"Then what is it, sweetheart? What's bothering you?"

"Nothing, Mom. Don't worry about me."

"Is it . . . Bob? Are you and he having some kind of problem?"

The kettle began to whistle, and Ellie turned the burner off. "Bob and I are fine," she said, selecting a bag of jasmine from the tea canister.

"Are you pregnant?"

Ellie splashed water into her cup. "You've been watching too many soap operas, Mom. Strange as it may seem, I'm still a virgin."

Mrs. Greenfield leaned back in her chair. "Maybe you have mono. I'll make an appointment with Dr. Levin."

"If you want." Ellie sipped her tea. "I don't think he'll find anything in particular. It's just nerves. I'll be okay after exams."

Sooner than that.

Eat your breakfast, Johanna.

I have pain, Ellie. I cannot eat.

Again, Ellie felt the beads of the rosary passing through her fingers, and she glanced at her empty hand, curled it into a fist. Johanna's voice might be reciting the Ave Marias and the Pater Nosters, but her mind was crying out to God for release. Ellie concentrated on the cup of tea, the heat flowing down her throat, the sweetness of sugar, and the sound of her mother's questions.

"Why don't we take a week off in Florida, sweetheart? Just the two of us?"

"I can't leave school, Mom."

"We did it when you were in high school."

"College is different. I can't afford to lose a single day. Things move too fast."

"We could even take Bob along if you want."

Ellie shook her head. "He couldn't go either. Please, Mom—there's nothing to worry about. You'll realize that when you see my grades."

"Grades don't mean a thing if you're a physical wreck."

"I'll make it." She yawned elaborately, stretching her arms above her head. "I think I'll go back to bed.

Here is Paula with the needle.

Ellie looked at the kitchen clock. *Isn't it a little early?*

I have pain.

"Good night, Mom."

"Good night, honey. Sleep well."

You must sleep, Ellie.

If you promise no more nightmares.

I don't think I will sleep any more today.

The shot will make you tired.

I don't think so. I hope the priest comes again this afternoon. I would like to talk to him.

As Ellie climbed the stairs to her room, Johanna fancied she was climbing the hill to the cemetery. The headstones bore familiar names, the names of her kin and her neighbors, Peters, Koos, Sonnen—inhabitants of the village of Erdorf since time immemorial. There, beside her beloved Georg, under the sign of peace, she would lie.

You're still young. You should remarry. Ellie closed her eyes and curled into fetal position beneath her electric blanket.

I wish the pain would go.

Try to relax. The shot will help.

Sleep, child.

Sleep, Johanna.

Five uneventful hours later, Ellie gobbled a bagel with cream cheese as she ran to her car. She found a parking space a block from class, rushed into the exam only two minutes late. *Wish me luck.*

You never need it.

Spasibo. Russian exam: Ellie translated as fast as she could write, finished before any of her classmates, then went back to the beginning and checked the whole paper through.

I'm proud of you, child; you are a true linguist.

That comes of early practice.

You learn Russian as easily as you learned German.

I hardly think so, but thank you for the compliment. You're not bad yourself.

After so many years of constant practice, I know English well enough, but you have left me far behind in Russian.

We'll speak it together more often.

There won't be time, Ellie.

Johanna, I must study. On the second floor of the library, she found an empty armchair, opened a book, and examined the chemical transformations she would have to perform later in the day.

In Germany, a woman dozed, reliving wordless memories twenty years old: a soft humming in the ears, a feeling of warmth, as if she were immersed in a freshly-drawn bath—Johanna had lain down and waited for the sensations to pass. She considered seeing a doctor, but there was little money in the bag tucked under the mattress. Paula looked in to ask why she was resting in the middle of the day. "Just a little tired, dear," Johanna said, and she rose and went back to scrubbing the floor.

Weeks later, the humming and the warmth were still with her, though she had pushed them to the back of her mind and no longer consciously recognized them. She was asleep between a thick pair of featherbeds when her dreams of Georg and the old good days before the war were interrupted by a sudden pressure enveloping her whole body, squeezing the breath from her lungs. She woke, clawing at air, tossing off the light covers, jumping out of bed to stand, shivering in the darkness of the room she shared with Marie. Beneath her bare feet, the floor was cold. Through the windows, pale moonlight splashed the room. The pressure was gone.

Johanna dressed quietly and went to the kitchen for a cup of tea. She checked the stove for coal embers, added a few sticks of wood to build a blaze for the kettle. She was stirring a bit of honey into her tea when the pressure returned.

It was a tenuous thing this time, a distant echo of the first—a ghostly cocoon, contracting and expanding in slowly accelerating rhythm. Awake, breathing with conscious regularity, she could almost push it away, as if it were a spiderweb in the garden, momentarily blocking her path. But at the limits of her perception, it remained, a mere shadow, but undeniably present. She was frightened and intrigued; there was no pain, no dizziness, no physical impairment of any sort. There was only a shadow.

Johanna prayed silently till Paula woke up at six.

"Good morning, Mama."

"I am ill, Paula. You must go down to the train station and call a taxi."

But by the time she saw a doctor, the sensations had ended in a final more powerful pulse and a brief feeling of intense cold that made her want to cry out. The doctor found no physical malady but prescribed a few days of bed rest.

Later I realized that was the night you were born.

You're giving me a taste of my own medicine these days. That big black monster—ugh.

We are most vulnerable when we sleep. Do you ever feel the pain in your dreams?

Sometimes, a little.

You wake from it.

Yes, and then it fades quickly.

You need more sleep.

Not you, too!

You're losing weight, Ellie.

Stop it, Johanna. I can barely take it from my mother.

It's my fault.

Don't be silly.

I will kill myself, and then you won't suffer from my nightmares and my pains any more.

Johanna!

I know it's a terrible thing, but our case is special—surely God will forgive me for ending your suffering.

I'm not suffering, Johanna.

You can't lie to me.

There's no point in discussing this any further. I have to meet Bob for lunch.

I am ruining your studies as well.

You're drowning in self-pity, that's what you're doing. My studies are fine; I aced that exam and I'm going to make the Dean's list.

You have the endurance of youth. My sister Marta is almost ill herself from the strain of looking after me . . . and knowing. But Paula is young and taking it well. Oh, why is God testing us all like this?

Ellie sighed. Rapport with Johanna had early imbued her with a Catholic belief in God, but later training and thinking had weaned her away, first to the nebulous Judaism of her family and then to atheism. She loved Johanna, but they could no longer discuss religion in a rational manner, and Ellie shied away when the subject came up.

Bob was waiting in the Coffee Shop, and he hugged her. "I thought you'd be later."

"I got tired of studying. I know it as well as I ever will."

"Doesn't look too hard. Sugarman going to use you as the class example like he promised?"

"I haven't heard a word since Wednesday. He's probably forgotten."

"Not him." He took a large bite out of his sandwich and talked around it. "Say, they're showing *War of the Worlds* at B-J Friday night. Want to see it?"

"I hear it's pretty scratched."

"Just the first reel, according to Jerry."

"Okay then."

"And we're having a party afterwards."

"At the house?"

He nodded.

Don't go, Ellie.

You're too conservative. Of course I'll go.

You're alone with him too often.

I'm never alone, Johanna.

You want to wear white at your wedding.

I haven't decided yet.

Ellie, I love you like my own Paula.

Johanna, stop worrying about me! With you around I could never do anything without thinking three times about it first!

Don't be angry, Ellie.

I'm not angry. Yes, I am angry, but not very much. Let me run my own life. "What time does the movie start?"

"I'll pick you up at seven."

Ellie glanced at her watch. "I'd better get going."

"I'll walk with you."

They linked hands and strolled out to the quadrangle.

He only wants one thing, child.

I think I'll get birth control pills next week.

I know God will forgive you these thoughts.

Johanna, sometimes you wear my patience very thin.

Ellie kissed Bob goodbye in front of Rosenwald Hall and ran up the steps to her history class. She sat in the back of the room, as usual, looking down on the instructor who stood in the well at the blackboard. Her pen worked almost automatically as her mind roamed. Johanna was looking into the past again at a kaleidescope of disjointed memories that Ellie readily recognized: Georg's farewell hug as he boarded the train that carried him to the Eastern Front and death; the tolling of church bells on the Sunday after surrender; the smell of ripening strawberries from the garden, purchased by the kilogram by G. I. wives from the nearby airbase; the taste of hamburger, spiced and savory, reserved for special meals. To Ellie, Johanna's memories and experiences both waking and sleeping existed as a constant hum in the back of her mind, just below the threshold of consciousness; like the television set that her parents left on all day and deep into the night, they were there if she cared to concentrate on them, but they were easy to ignore.

Except during sleep.

They shared dreams in their overlapping periods of slumber—especially when Ellie was very young and napped during her daytime. Later, if one slept while the other went about her daily routine, the dreamer's imaginary experiences were influenced by the waker's real ones. Ellie's parents had often remarked on the ease of her sleep and the rarity of her nightmares; only once, when Johanna's placid life was interrupted by a narrow miss by a speeding Volkswagen, did Ellie—then six years old—wake screaming. Sally Greenfield was disturbed enough to mention the unusual event to her daughter's psychiatrist.

Dr. Berger had been called upon for help when Ellie's parents noticed that she had an imaginary playmate named Johanna, a lady who lived in an old house with a vast garden and a backyard full of cows. At an early age, Ellie had insisted that her own name was Johanna, and the Greenfields, amused at first, sometimes called her that. By the time she was five, she had differentiated Johanna from herself, spoke to her almost constantly and seemed not to understand that her parents could not perceive the woman.

Dr. Berger had a number of long talks with Ellie, none of which uncovered any deep-rooted problems. Eventually, Ellie realized that Johanna's existence was the source of his concern and that he would never stop badgering her—and her parents would never be satisfied—until she admitted that Johanna did not exist. To bring peace to the Greenfield home, she admitted it.

How can you blame them, Ellie? I heard your silent voice, and I could not believe, either. I thought I was losing my mind. I prayed, how I prayed! And you were always there, listening to my prayers. For a time I thought you were an angel. I was hearing voices, like Joan of Arc. Me, Johanna Peters. It was absurd. I confessed to the priest, and he suggested I see a psychiatrist. But there was no money, and the psychiatrist was far away. I resolved to ignore you. As if that were possible!

When did you decide I was another human being?

When I received your letter.

Not till then?

Not till then.

Ellie had learned how to act, and she had also learned that other people did not share dreams, hear voices, see, smell, and feel the shadows of sights, odors, and touches. She was a solitary child out of choice, preferring books to games and Johanna's friendship to that of children her own age. Johanna's life was different from hers, and fascinating: milking cows, picking beans and berries, building a coal and wood fire beneath a copper cauldron of bath water, riding trains and buses through farmland and woodland—these were not activities that her parents offered. Ellie could sit in a quiet corner of her room and follow Johanna's life as if she were watching television: the reception was dim and fuzzy, but it was there whenever she wanted it and could be tuned a trifle sharper with concentration.

I don't think I would recognize your mother on the street, Ellie.

I don't think I would recognize you, Johanna, if it weren't for the photo you sent me. Your self-image is dim. But I would know Georg.

A few strong things are clear . . . my love for George. Your birth. My death.

Johanna, no!

We won't meet, Ellie.

Just another year, Johanna. Most of the money for the trip is already in my bank account.

I wish it could be. But you won't even be able to attend my funeral. Lay a wreath, Ellie, when you come to Erdorf. A wreath for me and Georg. I wish you could have known him.

In the fourth grade, Ellie had found Germany in the atlas of the Encyclopedia Britannica, but Erdorf, a hamlet of a hundred and fifty houses, was not marked. Bitburg, where Johanna shopped, was there—not far from the Luxembourg border. The distance from Chicago was great—five thousand miles, seven time zones. In the fourth grade, Ellie could not conceive of such spaces, but she estimated that at her best speed, she could walk to Johanna's house in fifty-two days if she didn't stop to eat or sleep.

Even at the age of nine, that seemed excessive, especially since part of the route would be over water.

She was irked by Johanna's disbelief. On the surface, Johanna readily agreed that Ellie was real, but underneath, doubt was a bottomless pit, and only her rosary could keep her safely on the brink. On her side, Ellie never had any doubts about Johanna's reality.

That was because you were born in rapport with me, but I lived the first thirty years of my life without you.

I should have sent the letter air mail. You were so nervous during those six weeks it was at sea . . .

I was afraid to greet the postman as he walked up the hill. I was afraid he would have a letter from America, and I was afraid he would not have a letter from America.

Ellie had executed the message in her childish script, just a few words: "I am real. I love you. Love, Eleanor Greenfield." She copied the address from Johanna's dictation, carefully printing both "Germany" and "Deutschland" on the bottom of the envelope. Then she went to the post office and paid for the postage in pennies that would otherwise be spent on comic books or candy.

I have the letter still. I tore it trying to open the envelope. My hands were shaking.

History class broke, and Ellie gathered up her books and papers slowly. The instructor was German—she wondered how he would react if she went up to him and began to speak in Johanna's native tongue. He was from Bremen, in the north, where they spoke a staccato sort of High German, very hard and precise, much the same language textbooks offered. Johanna, from a more southern, rural community, usually spoke a variety of Low German, an easy, slurring language denigrated by teachers and educated speakers, as well as by Johanna's daughter Paula, who had finished high school. Ellie's parents had mistaken her fluent Low German for Yiddish—a closely related tongue—when she was a small child, assuming that she had picked it up from her grandparents during Sunday afternoon visiting.

Later, when Johanna made an effort to speak—and think—only the High German her daughter was learning in school, Ellie discovered the difference between the two; she sorted them out more easily than did Johanna herself, and she found library books to read in High German—there were none in Low.

German, now Russian . . . when you come to Europe, you'll be mistaken for a native.

Better that than for an American.

You'll say you're from Erdorf.

You bet I will. Ellie glanced at her watch. She was running late again, due in the laboratory in less than a minute.

My fault, dear. I'm distracting you.

Never mind.

You've been a great comfort to me, Ellie, in these latter years. I wish we could have met.

Ellie sprinted across the quadrangle. The wind was cold, off the lake, and the sky promised rain. A few students hurried past her. *Is there anyone else like us in the world, Johanna? Maybe on this very campus, hiding. . . ?*

God has singled us out for a miracle. I often wonder why.

The laws of chance . . .

To compensate me for the loss of Georg . . .

I'll run another ad in the Tribune next week. Maybe this time someone sane will answer. She levered open the heavy door of the Chemistry Building and dashed up the stairs three at a time. Bob was waiting by her locker, holding out her lab coat. She handed him her books to be locked away.

"You're it," he said. "I just got the sign from the boss."

"The boss is going to find out just what kind of a slob I am."

The priest is here, Ellie.

"You're limping. Did you hurt your leg? You shouldn't rush up the stairs like that; Al Harris broke his leg that way."

"No, it's just a stitch in my side." Ellie prodded her waist with stiff fingers. The pain was Johanna's, she knew it from her dreams, but it had never before struck during her waking hours.

Johanna?

Father forgive me, for I have sinned.

It was a ghost pain that did not respond to kneading or exercise. Ellie willed it away, focussing her attention on setting up the apparatus for the demonstration. Johanna had confessed her sins almost every day for the past three weeks, and Ellie tried not to bother her at those times.

I have associated with an atheist, loved her as my own child and accepted her denial of God without argument.

Ellie felt indignant. *Johanna, there's no need to confess that.*

I have prayed for death and considered suicide.

Ellie picked up a thistle tube but felt the rosary beads. The pain in her side seemed to obstruct her breathing, and she began to pant. She worked the end of the tube into a two-holed rubber stopper, focussing her whole attention on that one procedure.

"Hey, you're going to break it if you keep up like that," said Bob.

"Huh?"

He took the thistle tube from her hands. "This stopper's too small."

He looked into her face, his eyebrows pinching together. "Are you feeling all right? You're pale . . ."

And I have accepted gifts of powdered coffee from the American soldiers, though I knew it was against the law.

Ellie leaned on the lab bench, gasping and clutching at the deep, all-pervading ache that spread from her side. She smiled wanly, for Bob and the woman in Germany. *Johanna, that's such a petty thing to confess.*

Bob held her arm. "Ellie, sit down somewhere."

She felt rather than saw it, black as a stormwave, mountainous, inexorable. It blanked her eyes, crushed her body, thundered in her ears. She screamed Johanna's name aloud and sank to the hard laboratory floor. The Leviathan flowed over her, and she twisted and turned and thrashed, seeking air. *Johanna, Johanna!*

A wordless shriek answered her cry. And then the great black evil melted to mist and vanished.

Ellie lay limp and exhausted, her mouth sagging open, her eyes unfocussed in the bright fluorescent light. Someone covered her with a lab coat. Someone raised her feet, propping them up with a stack of books. Some chafed her wrists and touched her forehead and cheeks in search of fever. Someone spoke to her in a low voice, calling her name over and over again.

Johanna, what was it? You were wide awake.

On every side, classmates babbled excitedly, unintelligibly. But that one silent voice made no reply.

She covered her ears with her hands, closed her eyes, shut out the palpable world of noise and brightness and delved for the echoes of five thousand miles away. She found nothing, not a rosary bead, not a misty view of the autumn-colored leaves that enfolded Erdorf, not a whisper of the soundless sound of sleep. Her mind, save for her own hollow thoughts, was empty.

Johanna!

She opened her eyes and stared up into an anxious face: Bob.

"They've sent for an ambulance, Ellie. We'll take you over to Billings, and I'll call your folks from there. You'll be all right."

She hardly heard him. She closed her eyes and ears again, searching, searching . . . But the echoes and the shadows that had been with her since before birth were gone. For the first time in memory, Ellie Greenfield was alone.

She began to tremble.

Dreaming the Sky Down

Barbara Burford

Barbara Burford (born 1944) is a medical researcher, poet, and fiction writer who lives in London. Her work is included in the British anthology A Danger-ous Knowing: Four Black Women Poets *(1985). Her first book is a collec-tion of short stories,* The Threshing Floor *(1988), from which is taken this powerful and deceptively simple-seeming fantasy, "Dreaming the Sky Down."*

Flight, and the ability to fly, is a common desire of childhood, and a common experience in dreams. It is, as well, the artist's perfect symbol of freedom, of specialness, of beauty unrecognized by others. Burford's story uses this one fantasy image and invests it with multiple meanings, resulting in a richly textured story of great depth.

"Dreaming the Sky Down" captures both the particular experience of a black girl in a racist society and the nearly universal experience of alienation, uncer-tainty, and individuality. In addition to issues of racism, this delicately structured story looks at what has come to be called "fat oppression," though in a way that is not polemical; it will resonate with the truth of personal experience for any reader who has ever suffered for being too large, too small, bespectacled, too smart, too slow, too independent, or in any manner different from what is deemed the acceptable norm.

She woke bumping gently against the ceiling, like a fairground-bought helium filled balloon. Even while she knew it was another waking dream, Donna gloried in the feeling, the light as airiness of her twelve stones drifting way above her bed.

Donna remembered to look especially at her bed this time. No, she was not there. She drifted down closer in the darkness. No, definitely not. She'd have to remember to tell shit-face Dawn Sullivan, that *she* was not having some kind of "primitive spiritualist experience", she *was* dreaming.

She arched her back and did a slow elegant backward roll, skimming the carpet, avoiding the knob on the wardrobe with a skilled half-twist of her swiftly ascending torso.

"Yah!" she whispered triumphantly to her gym teacher, wherever the hell she was. "Eat your heart out, Miss Howe!" Always going on about how elegant Black athletes were, and how much stamina and natural rhythm they had.

"You must be the exception that proves the rule, Donna!" Hah! Bloody Hah! And everybody else falling about laughing at her.

Yeah, but they should see me now, she thought, as she skimmed the long diagonal of the ceiling, leaving the blue fringes on the lampshade adrift on the wind of her speed. She pushed off from the topmost corner of the room the way the swimmers did it on TV and coasted past her enemy, the mirror, rolling slowly over in order to catch a glimpse of herself as she slipped by.

In the dim glow that was all that the curtains let in from the street lamp in the road outside, she saw herself slide by, as elegant as a dolphin. "A dolphin that wears pyjamas!" she giggled, and drifted back to hang upside down and grin at herself.

I can see my reflection, so at least I'm not a vampire.

She made fangs at herself in the mirror, but had to get up close before she could catch the gleam of her teeth in the glass. She arced over to the light switch, but putting pressure on the toggle ricocheted her backwards towards the ceiling; and only an adroit twist saved her from cannoning off that, flat splat into the wardrobe. She grabbed at her duvet, and when that started to lift, managed to snatch hold of the rail at the bottom of her bed.

She hung there, like a balloon tied to a kid's pushchair, while the racing of her heart steadied. Gradually she remembered how it worked, had always worked in these dreams, and slowly her feet drifted down till she was no longer upended, but resting lightly at the very top of the pile on the carpet. Very carefully, holding onto the fitted bottom sheet, she got into bed, and pulled the duvet over her. There was still a tendency for her body to bounce gently if she made any sudden movements, so she lay carefully still, eyes wide open, waiting to wake up.

★ ★ ★

Donna was walking Ben to school before she remembered her dream. She looked down at her younger brother, watching the blue bobble on his knitted hat bounce, as he trotted along beside her. She wondered if Ben dreamed of flying. She couldn't remember dreaming that way until she was nearly thirteen, just after her periods started, in fact. But maybe she had just forgotten, the way she had forgotten the house they lived in when she was younger.

Ben spotted one of his friends, and after checking for traffic, Donna let him tow her across the road, and then charge off along the pavement. But he waited for her at his school gate, and gave her a hug, before he ran to join the playground melée.

Donna liked Ben. The others all complained about their brothers, but despite the fact that she couldn't hang around to chat after school because she had to pick him up, and couldn't have a peaceful laze in the bath without him climbing in *and* bringing his flotilla of empty shampoo bottles, Donna enjoyed having him around.

Gurpreet, Zoe, and Tina were going round to Dawn's house after school to listen to her new *Articulated Donut* LP. Donna pretended nonchalance, insulted their new sex object, the lead singer, by saying he sounded like a frog with one testicle; and set off to collect Ben.

"Frogs don't *have* testicles, Big Bum!" Zoe shouted after her.

"That explains the way he walks then!" Donna got in the last word, before she turned the corner.

At home, she gave Ben his tea, put the TV on for him, and settled down to do her homework before the table was needed for dinner. If she didn't get it done before, she couldn't watch any TV after dinner till it *was* done. And it wasn't any good lying, her mother always checked.

God, what a life! she thought, trying to dredge up what she knew about the Equatorial Forests of Brazil. Everyone else had parents who let them watch TV till all hours, even videos, yet she had to go to bed at nine. According to the others, the discos didn't even start till then. And as for letting her go out with boys, no chance! Not, she reminded herself grumpily, that any had ever expressed an interest in taking her out. And they certainly wouldn't, now that the story of her flooring Zoe's brother at Tina's birthday party was all round the school.

Yeuk! She'd do it again, Donna thought, *"Act like a girl!"* he'd kept saying, pinning her against the wall in the passage, squeezing her breasts till they hurt, all the time trying to shove his horrible wet tongue into her mouth.

Her mother came home just before six, and brought her a cup of tea while she was finishing off her english. Donna wished that she looked like her mother, well not exactly like her, she was old after all: Nearly forty! But Donna wished that she too was slim, and could walk without her breasts bouncing. Even in her highest heels, nothing bounced on her mother when she walked. Yet, she wouldn't let Donna diet, talking about puppy fat.

If I had a puppy that fat, Donna thought sourly, and fourteen years old, I'd shoot it.

Then her dad came in from work and started to chase Ben round the place, so that he could tickle him. Donna, knowing that her dad had only to wriggle his fingers at her, to have her giggling helplessly, removed herself.

Oh, my God! Donna thought, taking refuge in the downstairs toilet. Don't parents ever grow? And, I wish he'd get another job, so he wouldn't come home on the bus in his railway uniform. It's so *embarrassing* meeting him at the top of the road when he was on early shift.

After she had turned out the light that night, Donna got out of bed and opened the curtains. She did not know if the light streaming in from the sodium street lamp would last into a dream, but it was worth a try. After all, in all her flying dreams, her room was always exactly as it was when she went to sleep.

Donna woke, but knew she was dreaming. She was still under the duvet, and the room was the colour of her mother's amber earrings. Wanting did it, she knew, and gradually she drifted up out of bed, the duvet sliding down her tilting body. She arched her toes, bent backwards from the waist, and turned gently over and over, lifting slowly till her hand brushed the ceiling. She hung suspended turning slowly to look down at her room. It was the same as when she had gone to sleep: her clothes ready for tomorrow over the chair, the book she had been reading in bed, on the bedside table. And the curtains were open!

Donna pushed off from the ceiling, and hung, legs drifting up behind her, one hand clinging to the rim of the sash window. Outside the street was deserted, the leaves on the plane tree across the way rustling secrets at her.

What would it be like, she wondered, to be out there? To drift hand over light hand up the branches of the tree, till she sat in the swaying tufts at the very top? But perhaps it would be scary. Perhaps only the ceiling of her bedroom kept her from floating off the world, and out in the open she would begin to fall up off the earth. Even in a dream, that would be scary, Donna decided, and slid away from the window.

For a long time, Donna disported herself in the air of her bedroom, the light from the window gilding her mirrored reflection. She spent ten laughing tumbling minutes trying to get out of her pyjamas in mid-air, before she tethered herself with a foot under her bed rail, and watched her clothes flop to the carpet. They did not float, even in a dream. The phenomenon interested her, and she went down after them, and taking them up to ceiling height, released them. They dropped just as they would have done if she'd tossed them out the window. She tried several other things. Her pillow was easier to lift than her dictionary; and what's more the book made a sharp noise as it hit the floor.

Donna froze, but there was no response from her parents' room, and soon she was doing lazy naked pinwheels in front of her mirror, trying to see if she could keep the reflected shadow of her navel always in the middle of the glass, while the rest of her moved around her centre.

In the weeks following, despite the occasional snide joking inquiry from the others, Donna no longer wanted to talk about her flying dreams, and the subject was dropped. At home she went to bed promptly, without any of her vast repertoire of procrastinating tactics. Yet, nowadays she seemed extra tired in the mornings, reluctant to get out of bed.

Her mother said it was because she had put on another growing spurt. And indeed she seemed to be growing: upward this time—and despite her increased appetite—not outward; muscles fining out, gaining definition, where once there were just rounded limbs.

Despite this, Miss Howe, once having cast Donna in the role of gymnastic buffoon, still singled her out for ridicule.

"Donna Hamilton!" as Donna clung with a sudden attack of vertigo, unable to tell up from down, to the top of the gym bars. "You're an absolute disgrace! Have you no pride, girl?"

"Donna Hamilton!" she said today when on dinner duty in the refectory. "If you put as much energy into moving the rest of you, as you put into moving your mouth to eat, you wouldn't have all that blubber."

That night, for the first time, Donna's room could not contain her—her angry energy batting her backwards and forwards between the furniture, the floor, and the ceiling. Finally she gripped the sash of her window to steady her body, through which storm winds blared, and gazed hungrily out at the space outside.

She tried to turn the knurled knob of the window lock, and turned herself instead. Gradually she added weight to her body, letting her feet sink to the floor, till she could gain purchase on the knob without her body shifting. Quietly, cautiously, she lifted the sash, then lightened until she could swing her body through.

She hung there, at first floor level, one hand clinging to the window frame, then she let go. She bobbed gently, controlling her weight, then with a now skilled flick of her body, she pushed off from the sill in a long shallow dive, lifting as she went. Her reaching hands grasped a handful of summer-dusty plane leaves, and she propelled herself gently, hand over careful hand, along the branch towards the centre of the tree. She added enough weight to let her rest on the branch, and one hand grasping a knobbly outgrowth of the tree trunk, looked down.

Beneath her bare feet, the leaves shifted, green as angelica; restored to springtime translucency by the lamp directly below her. She lightened and drifted carefully up the inner space of the tree, halting once to whisper, in response to startled bird cheeps: "It's okay! I'm dreaming."

There was more wind at the top of the tree, and Donna clung to the dipping swaying crown branch, her body curving gently this way and that like a lazy banner. She let go, drifted up, then added weight in a panic, and found herself chin deep in scratchy twigs and leaves, her feet foundering for a hold. Just then, Miss Howe's face, with that sarcastic twist to the lips, flashed across her mind, and Donna let go.

One fisted hand crooked above her head, she exploded up into the night, her breath escaping in a soundless scream of helpless rage. Then, up where the night wind snapped and pulled at her pyjamas, she slowed, limbs pulling inwards as if on strings, curling in on herself, as she began to tumble slowly, then faster, back towards the skein of orange diamonds that marked the road.

Gradually she regained control, shedding weight, till she stopped with a bob, and began to drift. She was in the open space directly above the road, with nothing to push off from, and her open window away from the direction of the light wind. She lifted, then sent herself in a long sliding slanted glide, her body rolling, turning gently as she added weight to first one side and then other, beginning to smile, then laugh, the wind of her going cold against her teeth and lips.

With a flick of her wrist, she pulled herself neatly under the sash into her room, remembering to add weight before she slid down the window and thumbed the screw lock fast.

"How on earth did you manage to get those scratches under your chin?" her mother's question at breakfast, sent Donna hurtling to the mirror in the kitchen.

"I'm sure they weren't there last night," her mother came after her. "You must have done it in your sleep." She took one of Donna's hands in hers, inspecting her nails. "You used to do that when you were a baby; scratch yourself. I'll have to make you sleep in mittens again." But she smiled and gave her a hug.

Donna desperately wanted to go up to her room before she left the house, but her mother was buttoning Ben into his coat, and they always left with her. At the corner, her mother straightened from hugging Ben, and caught Donna gently exploring the scratches with unbelieving fingers.

"Better leave them alone, Donna, or you'll get them infected." She tilted Donna's chin and looked at the scratches, shaking her head. "I can't imagine how you got them. We'd better remake your bed tonight, just in case there's a pin or a hairclip in it."

At school there was assembly, then double maths, before Donna could shut herself in a cubicle in the toilets. She touched the scratches with wondering fingers, then looked carefully at her short cut nails, her smile growing. She closed her eyes, shedding weight gently, lifting until her head was level with the partition. Grinning, she patted herself about the tiny space, promising herself the whole of the night sky.

"For chrissake, Donna!" Tina shouted, banging the outer door open. Donna added weight and sunk to the floor so rapidly that she turned her ankle. "We'll be late, and you know how Miss Howe loves you."

Miss Howe looked as if she had had iron filings for breakfast, and her response to Donna's request that she be excused gym because of a turned ankle, was to turn her around brusquely by the shoulders, and inspect the ankle like a farrier with a horse, before shoving her towards the changing room. All without a word in response.

Donna changed and went in with her commiserating friends. Her heart sank as she saw the range of equipment laid out like an assault course; it was going to be one of *those* sessions.

The first part of the gym session, consisting of gentle stretching exercises, was not too bad, but at the end Donna's ankle was puffing out over her plimsoll rim. She watched the others line up and begin their first run at the vaulting horse, with a sinking heart.

She'd hurt herself, she knew she would, she thought, listening to the thumps of their landings.

"Come along, Donna!" Miss Howe was waiting impatiently by the horse.

"I can't!" Donna said. "My ankle's really hurting now, *and* it's swollen."

"Nonsense! Come along!"

"No!" Donna took a step backwards, her hands fisting by her sides.

Miss Howe marched over. "I can't see any swelling or inflammation," she barely flicked a glance at Donna's ankle. "You'll use any excuse, won't you?" she sneered.

Donna looked steadily back at her. Just because I'm not pink and white, and bruise like a rainbow; you won't see, will you? But she said nothing.

"Very well. I'm giving you an hour's detention this evening, now go and—"

"But, you can't!" Donna gasped. "I have to collect my brother from school!"

"You should have thought of that before you were so insolent, shouldn't you? Report to me outside the staffroom at three-thirty." She turned away.

Donna left school premises during the lunch break, praying that no one would catch her, and tried to get through to Ben's school, but the phone was busy, no matter how many times she dialled. Directory inquiries did not have another number listed for the school, and after several fruitless tries, Donna gave up and snuck dispiritedly back into school. She spent the rest of the day worrying about Ben, and what her parents would say when they found out.

The afternoon lessons dragged, and it was a miracle that she did not collect any more detention orders because of her lack of attention. Her mum would kill her. And Ben . . . Just the thought of how worried and frightened he would be when she did not turn up to collect him on time made Donna want to burst into tears.

At the end of the afternoon, she waited outside the staffroom, and eventually Miss Howe came along. Donna had considered pleading with her, but one look at that cold antagonistic face stilled the words.

"What is your home room?" Miss Howe contrived to speak at her without looking at her.

"Room Three Twelve, Miss Howe," Donna filtered any emotion out of her voice.

"Very well. Go to your home room and draw me up a day by day list of everything that you've eaten for the last week. I'll be along presently." She vanished into the staffroom.

Misery overcoming her rage, Donna climbed slowly back to the third floor, and her empty home room. She had just put her name and the date on a sheet of paper, when a prefect stuck her head round the door.

"Donna Hamilton? Miss Howe says you can go."

Donna hurtled along the corridor to the staircase at the end, pushing open the swing doors with such force that they swung back and caught her bad ankle. She limped down the first flight of stairs, weak tears welling. Instinctively favouring her bad leg she must have shed weight for she found herself bouncing slightly.

She looked quickly over the banisters; the stairwell was empty. She lifted and slid over the rail and let the weight of her school bag take her purposefully down the well between the flights of stairs. She found she had to hug the bag to her bosom in order not to be dragged head first, and her uniform skirt soon ballooned out, further obstructing her view downwards.

Mary Poppins never has this trouble, she thought aggrievedly, trying to count the flights of stairs as they slid swiftly by.

Miss Howe was standing open-mouthed at the top of the first flight of stairs, hands gripping the banisters, the knuckles gleaming bone white. She made a sudden ineffectual grab at Donna as she slid past, then covered her eyes with both hands, her shoulders cowering up round her ears.

Donna touched down gently, and brushed her skirt down and headed for the outer doors.

"Oh, my God!" Miss Howe's hoarse shout echoed in the stairwell. "Help! Somebody help! She fell . . ." Her feet pounded down the stairs and she halted suddenly, horror-struck eyes raking the concrete floor, then lifting, widening, as Donna walked back towards her.

Miss Howe backed, hands going out in a warding gesture. "I came to tell her that her brother's school phoned . . . and she fell!" And all the time her eyes turned from Donna to the empty concrete floor.

"Who fell, Miss Howe?"

"Donna Hamilton . . . *You* fell! I saw you!"

"But you couldn't have," Donna said reasonably, and left to collect Ben.

Ben was waiting forlornly by the locked school gates, when Donna ran breathlessly up. She had shed weight in empty streets, moving in long leaping bounds when there was no one in sight. The schoolkeeper arrived, keys jangling, to let Ben out, and to read Donna a lecture on the "irresponsible kids nowadays". Donna didn't listen, stooping to hug Ben tightly.

When her mother came home that night, Donna immediately told her about being late for Ben.

"Well," her mother said, fixing her with a stern look. "It's a good thing you've owned up. One of your teachers phoned me at work, a Miss Howe, she sounded very worried about you. Something about hurting your ankle and getting detention and falling down the stairs, . . . I couldn't quite understand her. Then the headmistress took over the phone and said that you were going to be a bit late collecting Ben, through your own fault. And that Miss Howe was just upset because she hadn't realized when she gave you detention, quite justifiably that you had to pick up your younger brother."

Donna felt her heels begin to lift slightly off the floor, and grounded herself so hard that she winced.

"I'll put a compress on your ankle," her mother guided her into a chair. "But, first thing tomorrow, you are going to go to the staffroom, and apologize to that teacher." Her hand lifted Donna's chin, and the stern look was bent on her. "Do you hear me?"

"Yes, Mum."

Next morning, Donna waited outside the staffroom while the teachers were arriving. They all ignored her, intent it seemed on gaining the sanctuary of the staffroom. Mrs. Pullen, her form mistress, came along eventually. "Donna?" she paused, looking down at one of her better pupils. "Is there something wrong?"

"I'm waiting for Miss Howe, Mrs. Pullen."

Mrs. Pullen looked at the clock above Donna's head. "She's usually in by now. Did you knock?"

"No, Mrs. Pullen." Donna shifted her satchel, wishing she was anywhere else in the world.

Mrs. Pullen went in, and a minute later Miss Howe came out, carefully closing the door behind her. Donna felt her cold stare like a battering ram, and with an effort met her eyes.

"My mother says I'm to apologize for being rude to you," she said through stiff lips, and waited to be dismissed.

"Well?"

Donna shouldered her satchel, and at her movement Miss Howe took a step back.

"Well, I'm waiting."

"Can I go now, Miss?"

Miss Howe's face whitened with anger. "Do you consider that an apology, girl?"

"I apologize, Miss Howe," Donna said at the point of her shoulder.

"And I do not accept your apology. Now get out of my sight."

Donna turned abruptly away, feeling eyes like sharp splinters of ice drilling through her back. Her heels lifted slightly, as if to get her out of range as fast as possible. Donna grounded herself, pouring weight on, so that she felt as if she was trying to walk through the polished concrete of the floor.

"Donna!" The voice was cold but insistent. "What country do you come from?"

Donna turned, meeting those glacial eyes, limpidly, with all the strength of her waking reality.

"Battersea, Miss Howe," she replied, and walked away.

★ ★ ★

High in the night sky, with the multicoloured fairy lights of Battersea Bridge directly below her, the cobweb fantasy of Chelsea Bridge beyond that, and the dark squatting bulk of the power station brooding over the oily glisten of the Thames; Donna spoke into the wind:

"Not from outer space, Miss Howe! Not from some strange foreign place, Miss Howe! Battersea, Miss Howe!"

The Sixth Canvasser

⫯⫯⫯

Inez Haynes Irwin

Inez Haynes Gillmore Irwin was born in Rio de Janeiro in 1873 and died three years short of being a centenarian, in 1970. Of New England heritage and educated at Radcliffe, she was intensely involved with the National Women's Party, the radical wing of U.S. feminism prior to the passage of the Women's Suffrage Act.

In 1904, after several years at the forefront of women's politics, Irwin began contributing short stories to the leading magazines of the day: Lady's Home Journal, Everybody's, Every Week, Collier's, Liberty, Metropolitan, McCall's, *the* Chicago Tribune's *Sunday magazine,* Harper's Bazar, Hearst's International, The Delineator, *and many more. Very little of that work has ever been reprinted. After twenty years of producing noteworthy short fiction, she was belatedly awarded first place for the O. Henry Prize (1924), although by then her best work was behind her. Irwin's short novel* Angel Island *(1913), a Swiftian fantasy with radical feminist twists, has recently been reprinted after a long and undeserved period of obscurity.*

Her later career was spent on a series of children's novels. She also wrote a handful of competent murder mysteries with strong women characters, and these would stand well beside much that appears in paperback today from mystery publishers. For the most part, however, she produced little of merit after 1933, when her nonfiction Angels and Amazons: A Hundred Years of American Women *was published.*

"The Sixth Canvasser" is reprinted here from The Century *of June 1916.*

Included in critic Edward J. O'Brien's list of the fifty best short stories of its year, this endearing tale of birth and death and social and technological change was described by O'Brien as "a gently related story of the supernatural which unfolds in an atmosphere of dream."

||||

Mrs. Blaisdell sat in the shade of the elm-tree while her son Tom and his wife Ada wandered about the place, surveying present growths and making plans for future ones. She followed them with her eyes and she tried to concentrate on their movements, but her thoughts kept beating away from their activities.

The Blaisdell place included an acre of lawn, carefully cultivated, running to the street, and many acres of land, premeditately unculti-vated, running to the sound. The ground sloped both ways from the big, pleasant colonial house. In front, the slope drew after it a train of lawn that was like emerald plush. That plush was broken by haphazard growths, the product of a century and a half of care, that offered pri-vacy here, shade there, pleasing combinations of color and form every-where. The tall wine-glass elm, the huge, bulbous smoke-bush, two powdered fir-trees, the trio of slim, closely furled cypresses, the group of white birches that shivered in their filmy spring draperies—all had disposed themselves at the right distances. Here and there were flower-plots, squares and circles of freshly spaded earth.

A robin, just a few feet away, utterly unawed by the still figure in the invalid's chair, seized the wriggling end of a fat worm, tugged at it so hard that, after stretching to an extraordinary exiguity, it broke, and he fell ignominiously backward. An automobile chugged along the road, dropping a mellow-horn gurgle as it went. The electric car, which came every quarter of an hour, jingled past, crowded with people.

Mrs. Blaisdell made herself think of that motor and that car filled with people. They were all going to the beach; the heat had driven them there. Years ago she had dreaded almost equally the appearance in Wraymouth of the automobile and the electric car; they had come almost simultaneously. At first she had vowed to put a hedge between her and their clamor; but she never did that. She came to accept them first as conveniences, then as comforts, as companions. With a car pass-ing the door every fifteen minutes, she could call frequently on friends whom previously she had seen only at long intervals; and of course they called as frequently on her. Almost always somebody waved from the car as it ambled past. It was the same with many other things—the electric light, for instance. When they placed one near the left-hand corner of the place, it seemed to her that she could not endure its vulgar intrusion; and yet she had grown to look upon that as a kind of companion, too. She even admired the gush of purple-silver light that poured from it upon the fluttering white birches, giving in winter a veil to their slim nudity and in the summer an additional glitter to their gleaming draperies. She really thought the effect of the electric light more beautiful than moonlight, especially in these early days of spring; but she had never told anybody this.

Changes came all the time—she had lived long enough to expect that and not to care—but some things remained constant. Every spring, with the appearance of the spade, the robins came to pull worms from the steaming flower-beds; and every summer, as punctual as the honey-suckle itself, humming-birds appeared, little, vibrating films of iridescence stabbing with their slender, dart-like bills into the hearts of the blossoms.

Yes, changes came; and now the great change was coming to her. The great change! She must not think of that. She *must not* think of it; and yet she could not seem to prevent it.

This was the first day she had been able to sit out of doors, and she hoped that the beauty and freshness of the spring world would melt that weight that pressed so torturingly on her consciousness. Every day in the last five days she had gone over again and again that snatch of overheard conversation. If she had only not listened! If she had only not happened to go into the grape-arbor that day! How had it happened, for ordinarily she did not sit there? She had wandered in, attracted by the lucent arch that the big grape-leaves made, with the sun shining through them. But once there, she had caught a whiff of Tom's conversation with Dr. Morris. Their talk came through the open window. Tom, of course, had taken the doctor into the dining-room to get away from her. Even when she caught her own name, she had no conscious intention of eavesdropping. Something inside held her clamped to the ground.

"It may happen in Mrs. Blaisdell's case at any time," Dr. Morris was saying as she stepped into the arbor. "I can't give her more than a month, but it may come tomorrow."

Tom did not speak for an interval. When his voice came, it was husky, a little choked.

"Will she suffer much, Doctor?"

"Not long," Dr. Morris answered, and paused.

Then in one word came the spurt of Tom's grief.

"God!" he said. "God!" Then after another interval, "I'd better write George and the girls at once."

"At once," Dr. Morris assented. "It's useless for George to attempt to get here, but the girls may."

There came a brief interval of dull silence; then Dr. Morris rose, murmuring sympathy. Mrs. Blaisdell pulled herself up from the spot where she had taken root, retreated back of the house. Five minutes later Tom, very white and shaky, found her seated on the rustic seat that overlooked the sound. "Lord, Mother,"—he accounted for his panic—"you frightened me almost to death, disappearing like this! I couldn't think where you'd gone."

That night Tom wrote three letters. Mrs. Blaisdell, apparently much engrossed with a magazine, knew exactly how long those letters were and guessed their exact destination. She conjectured that telegrams also went. The next day came a telegram from Ruth, whose marriage had borne her to Pennsylvania, saying that she was coming to Wraymouth for the summer; that she would start as soon as little Tisdale had recovered from an operation for adenoids. She would arrive Tuesday. Later came a telegram from Molly, in California, saying that she was starting east immediately, also for the summer, and that she was bringing little Anna. It would be a long time before they would hear from George, whose peripatetic address was somewhere in the Philippines. Mrs. Blaisdell's heart yearned unspeakably for her two absent daughters, her one absent son, her three absent grandchildren; and yet with all the comfort that their presence would bring, there was one terror that it could not allay, one horror that it could not mitigate—the moment of death!

The moment of death! She dreaded that moment with an almost uncontrollable sense of fright. the thought of it waked her up half a dozen times, gasping, choking, sticky-wet. She was afraid it would come in the darkness of the night, when she was alone and too weak to cry out. She dreaded everything about it—the gasp of mortal agony, the tearing, searing pain, the choking as the breath left, the faintness lapsing to ultimate unconsciousness. True, under the pretext of wanting cooler sleeping-quarters, Tom had moved into the little bedroom opposite hers; he insisted on keeping her door and his door open. But she knew how impenetrable was Tom's sound sleep. Would he hear her? In all her vigorous young womanhood, in all her vigorous middle age, in all her vigorous old age, she had never known a terror like this.

It was ponderable, like an actual weight. It stayed with her day and night. She had stopped reading the papers; for the world, in the grip of conflict, titanic, bloody, riddled with cruelty, and saturated with hate, was filled with death and talk about death. And yet because the habit of sparing her young unnecessary pain still persisted, she could not speak of this horror to her children. It was the final gift of her mother's self-sacrifice. They must never know that she had suffered. She must go alone. She must face the going alone. The moment of death! The moment of death!

Nobody looking at her would have guessed this struggle. Her sickness had made her white, her sleeplessness had turned her wan; but the impression she gave, as always, was of a sweet-faced old lady whose features, a little long and pointed, had never lost their good lines, and whose silvery hair, parted and waved over the temples, still showed a youthful abundance. She wore a black skirt and a short dressing-sack of challis, cream-colored, with a little lilac figure, and pinned with a big cameo-pin. Over her head and about her shoulders lay a light, fleecy, white-worsted shawl. From under her skirt protruded her unworn shoes, square-toed and flat-heeled. On her right hand, old, crinkle-skinned, and freckled, her thin, tight wedding-ring puffed the flesh in mounds.

"The dahlias are up, Mother," Tom called cheerily.

"And the four-o'clocks," Ada added.

Mrs. Blaisdell waved her hand feebly in answer. She did not speak. It seemed to take too much effort to project her voice through the little space between them.

It would have been hard to say whether it was a day in late spring or early summer, for it had all the freshness of the one and all the lusciousness of the other. The sky was a June blue, not a May blue, and the clouds that crowded it were of a midsummer thickness and whiteness. The air had in it a little—was it moisture, honey-green, or mere light dusty-gold? Whatever it was, it served to give the atmosphere body; it seemed actually to take color from the things in it. The Baker apple-orchard on the opposite side of the way was an enormous, cushiony plane of blossom; about it the air held a rose-colored glow. The lilac-hedges that separated the Blaisdell place from the rest of the world were spiky with bloom; about them the air turned to gauzes faintly purple. The perfume of the apple-blossoms and the lilacs came to Mrs. Blaisdell on little breezes that were warmer than the air itself. Warm earth smells came to her from the smoking, turned-over flower-beds. All kinds of sounds crowded the odors in the air. From back of the house came the hoarse caw of a crow. From one side, the Mallons's new-born calf gave vent to pessimistic impressions of a new world in long blarts of remonstrance. Through the lilac-hedge she could hear little Peggy May's stuttery chatter. Opposite, she could see Virginia Small's slim, virginal figure making its way from dresser to closet and back again in one of the big front chambers of the Small house. Through two thicknesses of curtain, Mrs. Blaisdell could translate all her motions; she was doing her hair different ways, trying on belts, brooches, rings, shoes, and hats. Now that she was "going with" Ed Howes, it took Virginia precisely two hours to dress. And next door Ed, who was obviously waiting for her, had begun, all dressed as he was, to tinker with his automobile. Mrs. Blaisdell tried to fix her thoughts on each of these things in turn; but despite her best effort, the horror seeped back, the weight grew heavier. The moment of death! The moment of death!

"There are the canvassers again, Mother," Ada called. "I guess they'll get to us today."

For three days a group of six young people had been canvassing Wraymouth for signatures to a petition for equal suffrage. Mrs. Blaisdell had watched them at work all yesterday afternoon. At moments they had actually made her forget.

Situated in a rumpled stretch of land that ran from the street to the sound, the Blaisdell place faced an inclined plane, cut by many streets, that ran up to Wraymouth Heights. That tilted plane bared a big expanse of neighborhood to her inspection; for the lines of trees could not obscure the streets, nor the shrubbery and orchards the gardens. Mrs. Blaisdell, who had watched most of these houses grow, knew just the spaces that offered opportunities for inspection. Through these green alleys she followed the work of the suffrage canvassers.

There were six of them, three young girls, three young men. One reason why, despite her mental turmoil, Mrs. Blaisdell had been able to concentrate on their movements was that they were all comely and all gay. Not all gay, indeed. The sixth canvasser was very serious, and he might not, like the rest, have been comely; for Mrs. Blaisdell had not yet caught a glimpse of his face. It was apparent that he took his work very hard. The others walked straight up to the house that happened to be the point of attack with all the dazzling buoyancy and all the superb effrontery of youth. Up the walk—Mrs. Blaisdell could almost hear their quick footsteps—on to the piazza—she could almost hear their high, shrill ring—and then a long parley. Sometimes they would emerge gleeful with success, at other times a little defiant with failure. But the sixth canvasser was not like that at all. In the first place, he was a mere boy; also, it was quite obvious he was shy. He would walk up and down before a house for a long while, not even looking at it directly, but peering sidewise. Sometimes he would not go in at all; he would pass on to the next house. When he did enter, he never went to the front door; he would sidle slowly round to the back, peering up at the windows, reappearing, still sidling, on the other side. Sometimes when he had made half the circuit of the place, he would retreat, as though his courage had suddenly left him.

Today they were out again in force. Over there was the one Mrs. Blaisdell described to herself as the "tall, red-headed girl," who advanced proudly on a house as though it were a citadel that she could take single-handed. Here was the "roly-poly, dark one," who gathered a whole household about her on the piazza and made them laugh. Yonder was the "thin school-teacher one," who was quick and efficient at her work. Beyond was the "big, strong-looking boy," who was unmistakably in love with the "roly-poly, dark one," talking with "the-one-who-wore-a-gray-shirt," who was so unmistakably jealous of him. And, yes, there was the sixth canvasser staring up at the old Edgemore house. He stopped at the gate, as beautiful as a bit of carved ivory, and peered through its interstices. Suddenly he pushed the gate open and made a hesitating step up the path; but then inexplicably he turned back, his head bowed in dejection. Once outside on the sidewalk, he stopped abruptly, as though girding his courage to another effort. Then with a soft dash he entered again, flitted silently through the garden to the back. It would do him little good, Mrs. Blaisdell reflected, to ask Mattie and Laura Edgemore to sign the petition. How those women had changed! They had been so gay and open-hearted once! When Mrs. Blaisdell's children were young, they used to go to children's parties on the Edgemore place. As plainly as though it were yesterday, she could see Edgar's dark little head flitting between the high stalks of fire-colored phlox and wine-colored hollyhocks.

Edgar! Must she leave Edgar behind, or would she find him *there?* Oh, she must not think of *that;* she must not!

Mrs. Blaisdell meant to sign the petition. She had always believed in what she still called "woman suffrage." When she was a girl, she had heard Susan B. Anthony speak. She had never had to hear anybody else.

Tom came strolling over to her chair, stood beside her, smoking. Mrs. Blaisdell noticed how graceful his hand was, lightly fingering the little pipe, which seemed to cling close to the bold, graceful curve of his chin. She had always taken pride in Tom's beautiful hands because she considered that her own were ugly. She was glad, too, that he had inherited his father's fine, strong, muscular figure. Tom was handsome, regular-featured, aristocratic-looking.

"The place is looking fine this year, Mother," Tom said.

"Yes," Mrs. Blaisdell said; "so much rain has been good for everything. This is a beautiful day. I think we're going to have settled weather now."

"I hope so," Tom said. "I think probably I'll be home more this summer than I've ever been since I went on the road. Instead of taking two weeks' vacation in October, I'm going to take a day here and there. There are some things I'd like to do myself on this place this summer."

"That'll be fine, Tom," Mrs. Blaisdell said.

"And with the girls coming on," Tom went on, "of course I want to be home as much as possible. Isn't it great they're both to be here?

If only George could get back, we could have a complete family reunion."

"Except Edgar," his mother interpolated. "Don't forget Edgar, Tom. I never do."

Edgar was Mrs. Blaisdell's second son. He came between George and Molly. Over thirty years before, when he was seventeen, Edgar had gone to sea. His first voyage had been a short one, but filled with storms. Mrs. Blaisdell had hoped that he would come home cured of all desire to go again. But he had left, when he was still a slender lad, on a second trip. His ship, the *Eliza Shoreby,* stopped at Liverpool. Edgar went ashore at nine o'clock one morning; he had never been seen or heard from since. Everybody else had given him up for dead years ago, but Mrs. Blaisdell had never lost faith that he would come back to her. Whenever the gate clicked unexpectedly, whenever a strange man of middle-aged aspect appeared on the walk, Mrs. Blaisdell's heart always gave a thick flutter.

"You know, Tom," she said, a faint tone of reproach in her voice, "I have never given up expecting Edgar. I never will."

"It would be a wonderful thing if he did come back," Tom said. "Of course I was such a little shaver at the time that it didn't make much impression on me."

"You do remember him, though," Mrs. Blaisdell pleaded.

"Oh, sure!" Tom said in an offhand way. He went on to talk about his and Ada's plans for the place. They were going to throw out a piazza at the back of the dining-room, screen it in so that they could eat out of doors; they would cover it with rambler roses. They were going to get rid of the little flower-beds on the lawn. They were going to put wide flower-beds in front of the lilac-hedges, and stand phlox and hollyhocks up against them; Tom had always loved that combination. He remembered it from a boy, when he played in the Edgemore place. They were going to place wide borders of sweet alyssum about those beds.

Mrs. Blaisdell listened carefully, approved gently; but inside she was torn and bleeding again. It hurt her unspeakably that Tom did not remember Edgar as clearly as she did. She examined with a passionate fondness that picture that hung, virilely limned, vividly colored, in her mind's gallery. It was curious that, of them all, Edgar had been the throwback in the family. She would have expected it sooner of huge, powerful George or tall, muscular Tom. But perhaps George's activities as a teacher in the Philippines was one modern satisfaction of the ancient seafaring impulse in the blood, and Tom's as a traveling salesman another. Although he was strong, Edgar was pale and frail-looking. He was also soft-haired and soft-eyed. He was a "mother's boy."

"Lord! this is a beautiful day!" Tom exclaimed. "I'm glad I'm going to be home so much. I'll have this place in tiptop shape for Molly and Ruth."

He was making many references to his being at home, and many excuses for it; but, "Yes, it is a lovely day," was all Mrs. Blaisdell said.

The sky was putting on, though it was mid-morning, its noon blue. The hot-looking, white clouds—it was as though there were a little sun shining behind each of them—thinned and silvered, frayed at the edges, and melted into the dazzling atmosphere. Birds flew in and out of the Baker orchard, and constantly a pink-petaled shower shifted noiselessly to the green. The crow continued to caw, the calf to blart; robins came and went, burning a crimson hole through the air. Still Peggy May kept up her lispy chatter, and still Virginia Small fussed about her room, trying on things. An automobile glided with a nervous softness to the Baker gate, stopped noiselessly.

"Dr. Morris!" Mrs. Blaisdell and Tom said simultaneously.

"I forgot to tell you," Tom explained, "Annie told Rose this morning that Mrs. Baker wasn't feeling well. Morris came once in the night. Ada went over to ask if there was anything she could do. The nurse said she'd raise the curtain a little when the baby was born."

"I'll watch for it," Mrs. Blaisdell promised. "Oh, I hope it won't be bad this time!"

"Now, don't let it excite or worry you, Mother!" Tom said, a nervous furrow playing in his forehead.

"No, Tom, I won't," Mrs. Blaisdell said. "Besides, when you get to my time of life, you realize that births are happy things. It's only marriages and funerals that are unhappy. Why, to a mother that moment of birth—"

A sharp pang tore her. The moment of birth! The moment of death!

"How many are there of those suffrage-canvassers?" Tom changed the subject abruptly. "I make out five, three girls and two men."

"No, six," Mrs. Blaisdell corrected him. "Three young men, too. There's one you probably haven't noticed. He doesn't seem to be very successful."

"I don't know what their system is," Tom commented, "but it seems to be kind of hit or miss. They all seem to hang together about the same neighborhood instead of dividing the town up. Perhaps, though, they all take a hand at any house where there's difficulty. They say they're volunteers, college girls and boys. I suppose you're going to sign their petition, Mother?"

"Oh, yes," Mrs. Blaisdell answered; "I always have."

"I will," Tom promised, "and Ada, too."

"That'll be nice," Mrs. Blaisdell approved.

"Well, I guess I'll go over and help Ada tie up those vines." Tom strolled over to his wife's side. They stood before the clematis-trellis and talked.

Mrs. Blaisdell knew that they were talking about her, and she thought she also knew what they were saying; but she did not care. She had a sudden heart-sick yearning for George, who could not possibly get home from the Philippines in time. And she wondered with a sudden sharp sense of terror if Molly or Ruth would be too late. But again she told herself she must not think these thoughts. Resolutely she looked over to the Baker house. A little new baby, how wonderful it was! Nobody but a mother could possibly know. Dr. Morris had not come out; he was going to stay this time. About the house appeared signs of activity; windows opened, doors shut. A maid who had been sweeping off the back porch disappeared abruptly, as though in answer to a sudden call.

Mrs. Blaisdell's eyes strayed again over the surrounding neighborhood. The "tall, red-headed girl" had gathered a group about her in front of the fire-house; Mrs. Blaisdell could see the firemen tilted back in their chairs, grinning as they craned to get her talk. The "one who wore a gray shirt" had gone into the garage. Mrs. Blaisdell could just make out the dusky-white spots in the gloom that were faces clustered about him. The sixth canvasser had emerged from the Edgemore place. He had undoubtedly again been unsuccessful, for he drooped with dejection. He passed the Sawyer place, the Seaman place, the Mittinger place, three handsome modern mansions, with scarcely a look. Next came the fine old Murray place, built at the same time as the Blaisdell house and almost its twin, except that the former was painted yellow and white, and the latter slate-gray and green. Also, Mrs. Blaisdell often reflected proudly, her house had kept its big airy lookout, relic of those seafaring days when the women of Wraymouth watched the returning whalers from the house-tops. As the sixth canvasser caught sight of the Murray place, he stopped—stopped short as though something electric had caught him. The dejection seemed to pour out of him; obviously new hope flowed in. That new hope raised his head and cocked his shoulders. He studied the house again with his strange, furtive, peering glance, as though he was trying to remember something. He approached it once or twice with his hesitant, sidling step. Then suddenly he slipped, eel-quick and shadow-soft, through the entrance. The gate swung to, concealed him temporarily.

"Mrs. Blaisdell! Mrs. Blaisdell!"

It was a child's voice that called, and a child's slender body, wriggling through a crevice in the lilac-hedge, followed the call. "I b'inged you somesing."

"Good morning, Peggy," Mrs. Blaisdell answered. "Now, what are you 'b'inging' me?" "B'inging," as Mrs. Blaisdell very well knew, was Peggy patois for "bringing."

Peggy did not answer. She ran to Mrs. Blaisdell's chair, threw herself against Mrs. Blaisdell's knees, and dropped her basket into Mrs. Blaisdell's lap. In the basket were three new-born kittens.

Peggy was exactly Mrs. Blaisdell's idea of what a little girl should be, much as Molly had looked, although not half so pretty: floss-fine golden hair worn in long curls, sky-blue eyes starred by long lashes; pretty, tiny features; slender, dimpled body.

"What beautiful kittens!" Mrs. Blaisdell said. She reached into the basket with her trembling hands and smoothed the little creatures, which were peeping like young birds. "Their eyes aren't open yet, are they? See what funny little tails they've got. When did Fuzzy bring them to you?"

"Mother finded them in the closet. Fuzzy b'inged them in the night. Mother said I could b'ing them to you. They can't stay long." Peggy shook her head violently. "No, Fuzzy kies if I take them. Fuzzy dudn't like her kitties to go. I b'inged you some tortors." "Tortors" was Peggy's patois for flowers.

The "tortors" were some gone-to-seed dandelions, very short-stemmed, and much the worse for the close clutching of a moist little hand. Peggy handed them to Mrs. Blaisdell. "Kitties go 'way now," Peggy said decisively. She seized the basket and scampered back through the hedge.

Mrs. Blaisdell was sorry that Peggy had gone. Between her and the little girl had sprung up one of those sympathetic understandings possible only between old age and infancy. Peggy came to see her every day. It was true that she thought little of that overheard conversation when Peggy was with her. The moment of death!

"Are you keeping the shawl tight about you, Mother?" Ada called. She left Tom's side and came strolling over to Mrs. Blaisdell's chair. Ada was not a pretty woman, but she would have been much prettier if she had not had to wear glasses. She had a wholesome matronly figure, with a round, firm bust and strong-looking arms and a wholesome matronly face with big, clear eyes and big, strong-looking teeth. She leaned over Mrs. Blaisdell and pulled the shawl closer. "These spring days are so treacherous sometimes. Isn't it nice that Tom is going to be with us so much this summer?"

"Oh, yes," Mrs. Blaisdell answered; "I'm taking a lot of comfort out of that."

"And the girls," Ada went on. "It will be lovely to have them both here. I hope they won't think I've made too many changes."

"I know they'll be delighted with everything. You haven't done anything that hasn't improved the place, Ada," Mrs. Blaisdell approved warmly.

This was true. Just as the interior workings of the house had become at Ada's touch a perfect machine, so the outside growths had taken under her care a new impetus.

Ada still fingered Mrs. Blaisdell's shawl, drawing it closer here, pulling it into soft folds there.

"You look sweet, Mother," she said. "Are you feeling all right this morning?"

"Splendid," Mrs. Blaisdell replied. "Anybody'd ought to feel good this morning weather."

"Well, I guess I'll run back to Tom," Ada said. "We're making plans for those two flower-beds."

Mrs. Blaisdell's preoccupied gaze followed Ada's figure as she sped to her husband's side. Together Tom and Ada moved over to the corner where the birches dropped their shimmering green fountain. In their shade grew lilies of the valley. They knelt to examine them. The moment of death! The moment of death!

The Baker house was very quiet. Once Mrs. Blaisdell saw the nurse pass the window. Outside among the apple-blossoms the birds still whirled the air with a miniature rose-tinted snow-storm. The robins still made swift, fire-hot journeys from tree to tree. The sun rose higher and higher. The clouds had thinned now until they were faint silver strays filming the deep zenith blue. The little hot breezes that came from the lilacs were even more densely packed with perfume; the little hot breezes that touched the flower-beds were more heavily weighted with damp earth smells. From Peggy's direction came a sudden series of squawks as the kittens protested against Peggy's treatment. From the Mallon barn came a prolonged blart from the still-unreconciled calf. Virginia Small, arrayed at last as dewy as a rose in her pink smock and her pink, flower-covered hat, emerged from the Small house. Simultaneously Ed Howes shot from the Howes garage. They met at the front gate, and talking busily, their eyes glued to each other, they moved down the street. Mrs. Blaisdell smiled at this picture of young love. They were expecting to get the news of that engagement any day. Then suddenly her smile caught, crystallized, changed to violent contraction. The moment of death!

Nobody could help her now, not Tom or George or Molly or Ruth or Edgar—Edgar, for whom all the others had no memory and for whom her mother's heart would always yearn.

The suffrage-canvassers were still busy. The "dark, roly-poly girl" had stopped the postman. The "tall, strong-looking blond lad" was talking to the iceman. The sixth canvasser had emerged from the Murray place. Again every line of him drooped. He hadn't succeeded anywhere, Mrs. Blaisdell concluded. He shouldn't have tried to do this sort of thing. He wasn't the type for it. Now, Tom, for instance, would have been a great success at getting signatures; he was a very successful salesman. Mrs. Blaisdell watched the slim figure, still peering into front yards, turn down Mason Street. Only the empty school was there. That would bring him to their corner. She hoped that he would come to them because then he would get three signatures.

The electric car jingled past the house. Mrs. Blaisdell sat quiet, her hand to her forehead. The moment of death!

The gate clicked, opened. Mrs. Blaisdell glanced up. It was the sixth canvasser. He entered and stood, quiet and still, looking at her.

For the length of an eye-wink Mrs. Blaisdell, too, sat quiet and still, looking at him. And in that time the torturing weight on her consciousness melted, drifted away. She grew well—yes, *well*.

"O Edgar, my son!" she said at last. "You've come back!"

"Yes, Mother," Edgar answered. He smiled. Mrs. Blaisdell smiled, too. "I've come back. I've been a long time finding you. I couldn't remember. I must go away soon. I'll take you with me this time, though."

Mrs. Blaisdell clasped her hands.

"Oh, take me, Edgar!" she breathed.

"I think we'd better go now," Edgar suggested. He still smiled.

Mrs. Blaisdell arose, took a step. Not even in her youth had she known such lightness as this; her foot did not even turn the grass-blades.

"Edgar, take me away from the moment of—"

Then suddenly she understood.

"O Edgar," she said, "I didn't think it was ever like this!"

"It's always like this, Mother," Edgar answered.

He moved toward her, she moved toward him; they took each other's hands, they gazed into each other's eyes, they passed through the gateway, they floated down the street.

Something attracted Mrs. Blaisdell's eyes over at the Baker house: the nurse was raising the curtain.

Something attracted her gaze back to her own place: under the elm Tom and Ada were bending over a very old lady whose white face had sagged sidewise upon her shoulder.

An Unborn Visitant

ıllı

Vita Sackville-West

Victoria Mary (Vita) Sackville-West (1892–1962), daughter of the third baron Sackville, was born at Knole Castle, which later inspired the setting for much of Virginia Woolf's fantasy novel Orlando *(1928). The protagonist of that novel, a dual-gendered immortal, was modeled on Sackville-West herself. She was a member of the famed Bloomsbury Group, of which Woolf was one of the most famous members; their friendship has been the subject of many popular studies and volumes of Sackville-West's letters have recently been best sellers. Very likely, as with George Sand, more people have read about her life than have read her works.*

Sackville-West's novels include Challenge *(1923), a thinly disguised account of her affair with Violet Keppel with herself cast in a male role, for many years suppressed in England; her recognized classic* The Edwardians *(1930), about a young duke's struggle against his own heritage; a novel of the supernatural,* Dark Island *(1934); and an "alternative history" science fiction novel,* Grand Canyon *(1942). Her nonfiction works include the biographies* Aphra Behn *(1927), about England's first professional woman writer;* Joan of Arc *(1936); and* Pepita *(1937), about her maternal grandmother, a Spanish gypsy.*

Her short stories are found in The Heir and Other Stories *(1922) and* Thirty Clocks Strike the Hour *(1932). The latter includes "Gottfried Künstler," a beautiful, tragic love story set in a time of the persecution of witches, and "An Unborn Visitant." This supernatural story contrasts a time-travelling flapper with a conservative Edwardian woman and offers reflections on marriage and motherhood and a denouement that is wonderfully hopeful about the relationships of mothers and daughters.*

ılılı

All her friends agreed that Elsa Branksome was a hopelessly ordinary woman. They had said it so often that it was a wonder they had not tired of saying it. It was still more of a wonder that they had not tired of including so ordinary a woman in their parties. Human persistence, in some respects, would seem to be incalculable. Wherever there was a party, there Elsa Branksome was sure to be; and wherever there was a party, there was a knot of people getting into a corner and saying how hopelessly ordinary poor Elsa was.

One wag even went so far as to describe Elsa Branksome as the "woman in the street" at last typified. She never failed to say exactly what was expected of her. Her response to everything could be foreseen. But even while such response to anticipation exasperated some people, there was something reassuring about it. It confirmed a comforting sense of the endurance of certain values.

Perhaps that was why people continued to include Elsa Branksome as an element in their parties. She was not inspiring. She was never illuminating. But she was emollient.

Needless to say, Elsa Branksome had never married. No romance, no scandal had ever brushed across her name. She was Society's old maid; well on the way to becoming legendary in that rôle. Her age was undefined: thirty-five? forty? and the more kindly-disposed struck a happy mean at thirty-eight. No one could be really ill-disposed towards Elsa Branksome. She was too inoffensive for that; she was nobody's rival and everybody's confidante.

Moreover, rare quality in a confidante, she was discreet. She never made mischief. No storm centre she, whether of her own storms or anybody else's. She was essentially a non-explosive. Therefore the astonishment, and indeed the indignation, of her friends may well be imagined when the attractive and hitherto unapproachable Evan Sinclair was observed to pay her what is known as marked attention.

Even Elsa herself, humble though she was (humble almost by profession), could not fail to observe it. Evan Sinclair was always at her side. She had known him, of course, for years—they moved in the same set—but their acquaintance had never advanced beyond a mere social familiarity. And now, suddenly, there he was; always there; tactful but insistent; saying, "Let me fetch your wrap," or, "You oughtn't to sit on that damp grass." Assuming proprietary airs towards her.

At first Elsa couldn't understand it. And then her friends began to tease, and she was forced to understand. She felt the scratch beneath their teasing—it wasn't likely that her friends would relinquish Evan without a scratch—but at the same time she felt that their respect for her was enhanced. She had ceased to be dear old Elsa and had become a woman, with a woman's claims and woman's danger.

The experience was novel, terrifying, and exquisite. For the first time in her starved existence she apprehended the emotions which ordinary people regard as their birthright. She, Society's old maid, had secured a man—and what a man!—for herself.

She was bewildered. Over and over again, every night, in fact, she told herself that she must keep her head. But she knew very well that she had already lost it, and her heart to boot. Evan Sinclair was the most attractive man that she, or any of her friends, had ever known. He was good-looking—like a Gainsborough, they said, with his gray hair brushed back—athletic, scornful, socially charming, but inwardly, and incorrigibly, reserved. Of impeccable manners, he was said to reveal his real self to none.

Women petted him, and he gave nothing but his charm in return. He laughed, and joked, and slipped away. And now Elsa Branksome—dear old Elsa—poor old Elsa—such a dear, but rather a bore, rather an old cup of tea—nice old Elsa—Elsa of all people had caught him. Elsa Branksome, that ordinary woman!

She sat before her mirror, taking down her hair. (The year, it must be said, was nineteen hundred and eight, when women still allowed their hair to grow to its natural length, and paid the penalty in a nightly brushing-out of long, luxuriant tresses.) She sat, then, before her mirror, taking down her hair.

She laid at least one pound of the stout hairpins upon her dressing table, and at least another pound of pads which had puffed out her coiffure in the necessary shape. But she did these things mechanically. She was thinking neither of hairpins nor of pads, nor even of the *bigoudis* with which she prepared the curls for the succeeding day. Her gestures were purely automatic. She was thinking of Evan Sinclair—thinking of him with an ecstasy that amounted to an agony. An agony of bewilderment and love.

The teasing of her friends had at last crystallized into a certainty. That teasing, which for so long she had tried to dismiss with a deprecatory laugh. "Evan? but how absurd of you! We've always been very good friends. You know as well as I do that Evan has never been serious about anything in his life."

And now, it seemed, Evan was serious. His elusive, charming manner had changed to intensity. That evening, after the children's Christmas tree (they were both staying at the same house for Christmas), he had caught her alone in the library. His handsome Gainsborough face had pleaded with her; he had knelt beside her chair. She had been terribly afraid that someone would come in.

But what had he said? Words that she had long since ceased hoping to hear. Words, indecent almost, in their urgency. "Marry me, Elsa—marry me. I want you so much for my own."

And she, what had she said? She could hardly remember, so great was her amazement, as she mechanically laid stout hairpin after stout hairpin upon the dressing table, taking down her hair. Was it possible that she had kept her head? Yes, she had kept it. She had pushed him away gently. She had just had time to tell him that she would give him her answer to-morrow, and then somebody had come in. . . .

She stuck a pin into the cushion on her dressing table, through the wire of a pin-curl; and with accustomed fingers began to roll up the curl around the greasy leather of the *bigoudi,* but all the while she thought of Evan as one in a trance.

"Evan—Evan," she said to herself, she who had never called him anything but Mr. Sinclair, according to the stilted fashion of her day—for she was nothing if not correct in her behaviour; but now she felt she might whisper "Evan" to herself, in the secrecy of her bedroom, a bedroom which he would soon have the right to share.

She shivered at the daring thought; and the *bigoudi* went crooked, so that she had to disentangle it and roll it up again. "Evan!" she whispered, stealing a fearful look at herself in the glass; and she seemed to see that lean, attractive face looking over her shoulder into the glass at her own reflection. The transfixed pin-curl in the foreground was not a very romantic adjunct; and, having successfully screwed it up into its *bigoudi,* mixture of lead and leather, she stuffed it away hastily into the drawer of the dressing table.

At that moment she heard a voice behind her saying, in drawling tones unfamiliar to her ear, "How you can put up with all that hot, false hair on your head beats me."

Elsa turned; she saw the slim figure of a girl perched on the back of the sofa behind her. The girl had an impudent little face; short wavy hair; she perched on the sofa clad in a jacket and trousers of rose-red silk; her legs were crossed, and from the corner of her mouth dangled a cigarette.

Every line of her garment advertised the charms of her young body; yet she seemed completely unaware. She perched there, quite at her ease, surveying Elsa with disingenuous interest and curiosity. "And what a bore having to brush it out every night."

So convincing was her presence, though so improbable her appearance, that Elsa must perforce take her for granted. This was no ghost. Ghosts manifested themselves always in stomachers or crinolines; such was Elsa's training. This apparition reverted in no way to the past, as portrayed either by Holbein or Winterhalter. Lely and Vandyke were equally out of the running.

This, therefore, was no ghost. There remained only one thing for Elsa to say; and, true to her character, she said it; "And who," she said, "are you?"

"Me?" replied the apparition, easily, uncrossing and recrossing her silken legs; "why, of course, I'm your daughter."

"My daughter?" said Elsa. She passed her hand with a worried gesture across her forehead, forgetful that that forehead was now denuded of its fringe, a condition in which she never allowed anybody to see her. Then she made another obvious remark for which she was perhaps scarcely to be blamed. "But," she said, "I haven't got a daughter."

The apparition was unperturbed by this denial of its existence. "Oh, not yet, naturally," it replied, blowing a thread of smoke, "but you soon will have. You'll be engaged to Evan to-morrow."

At this cool intrusion into her most secret thoughts, Miss Branksome, outraged, revolted.

"Evan? I don't know who you mean."

She said this triumphantly, as though she had settled the matter and expected the girl to vanish up the chimney. Instead of which, the girl laughed in the tolerant way reserved by the young for the elderly, and condescended to an elucidation. "Evan Sinclair—my father. He proposed to you this evening, didn't he? A nice man, I'm glad you chose him. But please do buck up about it, because I'm in a terrible hurry to get born. When I've finished talking to you, I'll run along to his room and give him the same message. Which room is he in, do you know?"

Elsa, to her own consternation, found herself answering as though she were carrying on an ordinary dialogue.

"I most certainly don't know where Mr. Sinclair's room is"—("No," said the apparition with a sigh, "I suppose you wouldn't")—"and in any case," Elsa added severely, "if Mr. Sinclair is really your father, you have no business to speak of him by his Christian name. Where have you been brought up? And smoking too! You seem to be a most extraordinary young person. I don't understand in the least."

"No?" said the apparition sympathetically. "Well, perhaps it is a little difficult. But I'm not really extraordinary—we're all the same, everybody, I mean, of my age. You see I'm living in a different year from you, that's all. It's quite simple. I'm living in nineteen-thirty-two. You're in nineteen-eight, aren't you? That's right. I'm just twenty-three at present—*my* present. If only you knew about Einstein, you'd understand."

"Einstein?" said poor Miss Branksome.

"Oh," said the apparition with some impatience, "I can't stop to tell you about Einstein now. You'll find out about him all in good time. For the moment I can only tell you that I'm living in the fourth dimension—so are you, for that matter—but you won't understand that either. So you must just take it from me, on trust. By the way, my name's Daphne."

"Daphne? Daphne what?"

The apparition stared. "Well, Daphne Sinclair, of course—what else? You didn't think I was married, did you? Not me. You won't get me to marry in a hurry, my dear old thing. Marriage is *too* bogus. You won't catch me marrying till I'm well over thirty, if then. I shan't be thirty till nineteen-thirty-nine, shall I, if I'm born next year?"

"Oh," said Miss Branksome, pressing her hands to her head. "I *can't* do these sums."

"Never mind, I think that's right. But now tell me," said Daphne, jumping off the sofa and coming up to Elsa, who shrank miserably away, "what do you think of me? D'you like me or not? Take a good look. It isn't everybody, you know, who's privileged to see their daughter as she will be twenty-four years hence."

Elsa gazed at the rose-red figure poised before her, so gay, so boyish; and the virus of a horrified disapproval entered into her veins. Never, she thought, had she beheld so outrageously impudent a creature, with its mop of short brown hair and the cigarette dangling from its mouth.

The creature seemed sexless, too; it might have been a girl, but equally it might have been a mediæval page. Elsa stared; she was trying to think of the most crushing thing she could possibly say.

"Tell me," she said at last, very slowly and deliberately, "are you supposed to be a lady?"

Daphne flung back her head and uttered peal after peal of laughter.

"Oh, you dear priceless old thing," she cried when at last she could speak, "what is it you don't like about me? My pyjamas? My hair? But we all look like this, you know. You can hardly tell us apart. It's the post-war type."

"Post-war?" said Miss Branksome.

"Oh, sorry, I forgot you didn't know about that either. I won't en-lighten you—no good giving people disagreeable anticipation. But, as I was saying, we all look like this. We don't go in for voluptuous curves nowadays. We like everything—how shall I say?—pared away. As little fuss as possible, whether in clothes or figure or manners."

"Or morals either, I should say," observed Miss Branksome tartly. She was rather pleased with that. She felt she had scored a point.

Daphne shrugged. "Oh, well, as to that! Perhaps you're right. It saves a lot of trouble. Nobody minds, you see."

An Unborn Visitant/119

She suddenly dropped to the ground at Miss Branksome's feet and sat there, hugging her knees and staring up at her hostess.

"Funny, isn't it," she observed, "to think you're going to be my mother? Do let's go on talking. I can't stay long, so let's make the most of it. Haven't you any curiosity? About what you call the future? About me? After all, I *am* your child, and though of course *we* don't believe in maternal instinct and all that nonsense, I expect you still do. Ask any questions you like; I'll answer."

She waited expectantly, and taking a cigarette case from the pocket of her pyjama jacket, she lighted another cigarette from the stub of the last one.

"Chain smoker, I'm afraid," she remarked, throwing the stub into the fire. "Bad habit. Can't break myself of it. Nerves. That's the worst of my generation—nerves. I'd give anything for a cocktail, but I suppose you don't deal in such things. Lord, what dull lives you must lead! But I'm doing all the talking. It's your turn now."

Miss Branksome, however, had nothing to say. If the truth must be told, she was struggling against a feeling of the most violent antipathy she had ever experienced, and which confusedly she felt to be wrong, since this creature was after all (apparently) her child, and, according to Miss Branksome's standards, one ought to love one's children, whatever they might be like. She felt that she ought to gather this child to her arms, suffused meanwhile with an emotion of pure heavenly bliss.

Far from any such impulse, she remained appalled by the completed spectacle of the being for whose existence she was to be responsible. Horrible! She shuddered. The vulgarity, the shamelessness of the creature!—for it must be remembered that Miss Branksome, despite her social activities, was a highly correct spinster in an age which prided itself upon its good breeding, and valued manners far above candour.

As though Daphne divined what was passing in her mother's mind, she broke the silence by saying, "I see, you don't like me. Well, I don't blame you, though it's a pity. Perhaps by the time I really am my age—if you follow what I mean—I shall have educated you up to looking at me with rather less of a shock. Perhaps I've been too sudden for you, offering you so to speak the finished article before you'd seen it through its various stages. There really is a big jump between you and me, isn't there? Much bigger than you'd think from the mere years that separate us. I wonder why? It can't be entirely due to the war." ("What is this war," thought Elsa, "that she keeps talking about?") "It must be a difference in our tempo"—and this, again, was a term unfamiliar to Elsa Branksome.

"That's it!" cried Daphne, as though she had made a discovery; "you're slow-motion, you see, and I'm speeded up. I've got it now.

You like things to be slow and thorough; I like things to be quick and shallow. I haven't time to be ponderous. Love, now—I daresay you think you'll stick to Evan all your life?"

It was on the tip of Miss Branksome's tongue to reprove Daphne again for alluding to her father by his Christian name; but, realizing that she must concentrate her forces upon coping with this extraordinary situation and upon deciding what steps (preventive) she could take about the future, she remained silent. Daphne chattered on.

"I rather envy you, you know. There's something left in me which rather likes your old-fashioned sentiment. Of course, that's a thing I could only say to you—my own friends would simply hoot at me. It's rather for me to tell you what I really think—we spend such a lot of time in telling each other what we think we ought to think in my generation. And we're so bright that we positively dazzle ourselves and each other with our own brightness. It's a funny sort of relief," said Daphne, swinging herself round and leaning confidentially against her mother's knee, "to prattle away to a dear pre-historic old thing like yourself."

Miss Branksome looked down on the boyish head. She disliked Daphne's vocabulary, she disliked it intensely, but she discovered suddenly that she did not dislike Daphne nearly so much as she had started by disliking her. She felt a queer and sudden interest in this troubled, nervous, intelligent freak. She went so far as to lay her hand upon the head, and a curious thrill ran through her at the contact of her fingers with the soft, wavy hair.

"My dear child," she said, and was astonished to hear her own voice saying it, "you're much too analytical."

Daphne jumped round. She sat on her haunches and stared eagerly up into her mother's face. "But of course! How bright of you. We all are. Not one of us takes things as they come, but we want to know why, why, why? Freud, you know—but no, of course you don't know. Sorry. But you see we've got this passion for what we call honesty. Knowing ourselves. Motives, instincts, complexes."

Miss Branksome was puzzled again. But she let it pass. She just said softly, "You've forgotten the charm of mystery."

Daphne thought over that. She blew rings of smoke and vaguely speared them with her finger. It was obvious to her that her mother was talking a different language, and she doubted whether her mother and herself would become quite intelligible to one another, but she was in the mood to be lenient. It was necessary, perhaps, for the generations to go their own way; to develop along their own lines.

"Oh, well," she said, "I daresay we shall worry along all right, you and I, if we avoid too much argument."

An Unborn Visitant/121

They were each making concessions.

"You know," said Miss Branksome, after a pause, "this is very queer."

"Yes, it is rather odd, isn't it? But it seems quite natural, somehow—not shaming in the least—that I should be sitting here talking to you. Shall we remember it, do you think? I mean, shall we be able to talk about it in the future, when I'm really there? What fun! I say, you'll hurry up with that marriage, won't you? It *is* such a bore, waiting about."

"At any rate," said Miss Branksome, rather wryly, "you seem to have plenty of appetite for life."

"Oh, yes, we've all got that. You see, you don't know yet how exciting life is going to become. Lord, how I could puzzle you if I liked! You wouldn't think, would you, that people in Australia could hear a concert in London? Or that people could fly at three hundred miles an hour? Or that you'll hardly see a horse in the London streets?"

"Daphne, dear," said Miss Branksome, and her voice was the voice of a mother reproving her little girl in the schoolroom, kind but firm, "don't say such exaggerated things. It's silly."

Daphne was delighted. "All right. Wait and see. I'll remind you of this conversation—some day. On Christmas Day, nineteen thirty-two. I'll remind you of it. And I daresay we'll be able to do a great deal for each other, if only we're sensible. Christmas Day, nineteen thirty-two, remember. It's an assignation.—I say, look at the time."

Miss Branksome turned obediently, and looking at the clock on the mantelpiece she saw that it was exactly midnight. At that moment the bells rang out from the village church.

It was Christmas Day. She turned again to Daphne with both hands held out; but Daphne was no longer there.

"Well, I never," said Miss Branksome. She stared heavily at the various objects on her dressing table—the false curls, the hairpins.

She even touched them gingerly, as though doubtful of reality. She looked at the rug beneath her feet, where Daphne had been sitting, but no trace remained; even the gray splotches of ash, where Daphne had flicked her cigarette onto the carpet, had disappeared.

This fact disconcerted Elsa even more, for some reason, than Daphne's disappearance. She had fully expected Daphne to vanish, but she had not expected Daphne's little traces to vanish with her. Had she imagined it all? But she was most certainly not asleep.

"Daphne," she said aloud, tentatively, timidly.

And then she thought, "Heavens! she has gone to see Evan."

A girl in a man's room at midnight. Ought she to go in pursuit? Then she remembered that Evan was Daphne's father. "Oh, dear," said poor Elsa, sitting down in despair, "I'm getting so dreadfully muddled." She continued to sit, staring, thinking. Did she want Daphne? Could she actually cheat Daphne out of her future if she really wanted to?

Which was uppermost, the hostility she had felt towards Daphne, or the queer, shy tenderness which had crept over her as the girl so artlessly revealed herself?

With these questions revolving in her mind, she continued mechanically to prepare herself for bed.

She was almost unconscious of the process of her thought. But as she climbed into bed and blew out the candle she surprised herself whispering, "I wonder how quickly one can get a licence for a registrar's office?"

Tamar

ıllıı

Lady Eleanor Smith

Lady Eleanor Furneaux Smith (1902–1945) was the daughter of the first earl of Birkenhead and sister of the second. Educated by a French governess and brilliant from an early age, she composed her first autobiography at the age of eight and a rather more complete one when she was 37. A circus buff, she worked briefly as a publicist for a circus, occasionally venturing into the ring on horseback. She began her first novel, Red Wagon *(1930), at the age of 19.*

Proud of her bit of gypsy blood inherited from her father's grandmother, though otherwise of French and Cornish descent, Smith learned the Romany language and became expert in the folkways of the gypsies. This and her interest in Russian ballet are reflected in such novels as Ballerina *(1932) and* Romany *(1934; Tzigare in Britain). Among her other novels are* Portrait of a Lady *(1936),* Man in Gray *(1941), and a time-travel story,* Lovers' Meeting *(1940). Her fiction reveals an easy acceptance of society's outcasts, from gypsies to actors to homosexuals.*

The title character of "Tamar" might well be interpreted as one of those embodiments of pure evil who, when they recur in sexist tales—too dark, too intelligent, too powerful—are usually destined to a much-deserved and horrible doom. But Smith has taken a liking to the archetype, so that Tamar is not doomed, but is menacing and powerful and is not forced to pay retribution for her rebellious nature. More clever than the devil, she is a female version of an anti-hero type who almost always is portrayed as male.

This text is reprinted from Smith's only collection, Satan's Circus, *published in 1932.*

ılıl

Tamar, the gipsy, was left alone in the camping-place. This was by her own desire; had she wished she could have accompanied members of her tribe, who were known as the Bear People, to the Christmas fair held in a village not ten miles distant from the camp. But she had not wished; she was in a bad mood, and preferred to brood in solitude. She had watched the others depart with their huge lumbering Carpathian bears, their tambourines, their violins and guitars, and the sleepy pythons that they would afterward charm in the market-place while the peasants stood by to gape in awe. They had gone trailing away down the hill, singing and whooping and fiddling, their ragged rainbow clothes very bright against the snow that lay spread white and smooth as icing sugar.

It was bitterly cold in the camp. There the snow had been heaped into a sheltering wall; it was frozen and looked like thick green glass. The tents and wagons were huddled together to form a barrier, but the wind whistled between them, and the donkeys stood about dejectedly, with hanging heads. Behind the tents, hollowed like a low tunnel into a huge flank of rock, was hidden a cave, the dwelling-place of the Bar, or chief of the tribe. This cave was empty, since the chief had gone with his bear and his entire family to the *fiesta,* and Tamar had every intention of sleeping inside it.

She stood for an instant near her tent, scowling at the bleak and desolate scene around her. The ravine was a sheet of ice; the mountains lay buried deep in snow and against a sky like hard blue steel a grove of black fir trees appeared more sinister than a group of witches. Far away in the mountains a wolf howled faintly and the donkeys pricked their ears, suddenly nervous. And then the east wind struck the ravine like a sword of ice, and the gipsy, shrugging her shoulders in disgust, went inside the cave.

In the darkness burned a crimson glow of fire, and, groping, she found a candle which she lighted, then knelt to warm her hands. It was still dark, and she did not hesitate to light another candle. Then she stood up and looked around her, contemptuous, her arms folded. The cave was big and roomy. She noticed a heap of fire-wood piled on the hearth, near the kettle and pot; on the floor were spread blankets and cured skins and soft rugs. In a corner she observed, with some satisfaction, a basket of bottles containing *swika,* a fiery spirit of which she was exceedingly fond. And from the ceiling hung a fine ham. She smiled; she could make herself comfortable for one night in the Bar's cave, and before dawn she would be on the road for Braila. She was tired to death of the Bear People, and in Braila there was a café where she could dance whenever she pleased, for the proprietor of the café was in love with her.

She rolled herself a cigarette, sat down cross-legged before the fire, and began to tell her fortune with a pack of greasy cards produced from the pocket of her dress. The first card shuffled was the King of Spades.

The gipsy was a young woman of not more than twenty, but she appeared at least ten years older. She would have seemed handsome had she been less sullen. She was as tawny as a tigress, with coal-black hair that hung in snaky locks about her face and brilliant, oblique, wicked eyes. She wore baggy Turkish trousers of raspberry-pink, a yellow sash, and a ragged Roumanian bodice that left her bosom half-naked. She wore silver rings on all her fingers, gold coins in her ears, and gilt anklets. She was barbaric, insolent and gaunt. She cared for no one, and submitted to no laws, not even to those laws imposed by the chief of her tribe. Whenever she quarreled with him, which was often, she tramped away from the Bear People to Braila or Kustendje or Galatz or Jassy, and remained away sometimes for many months. No one knew what she did or how she lived during these periods, but it was considered probable that on more than one occasion she had found herself in jail.

When she wished she was expert both at telling fortunes and at dancing the wild, wicked, leaping *tanana* of the Roumanian gipsy people, but if she did not feel inclined for sorcery or for dancing she would remain obstinately idle. Therefore she was more often poor than prosperous.

But every day she told her own fortune.

Squatting before the fire, absorbed, reflective, she now considered the King of Spades. He had appeared during the last few days with a strange significance in her *dukkeripen,* or fortune, and she had as yet no idea what part he was destined to play in her life. That he was a lover seemed improbable. A lover was usually represented by the King of Hearts. No. The King of Spades, she thought resentfully, was far more likely to appear to her in the guise of a spying, insolent policeman, or some revengeful farmer determined to punish her for having filched away his wife's savings.

"What do I care?" she thought, but her ill humor increased, and she spat at the image of the King of Spades.

She then decided, for it was still bitterly cold in the cave, to refresh herself at the Bar's expense. It is uncommon for gipsies to thieve from other gipsies, but Tamar did so whenever she felt inclined. She went across to the farthest corner of the cave, opened a bottle and poured herself out a glass of *swika*. The drink ran down her throat like fire.

"That's better."

She wiped her mouth with her hand, and was about to put down the glass when suddenly she started, stood for a moment as though transfixed, then slipped away like a ghost into the shadows by the entrance of the cave. Outside she had heard something move; for a moment she was not quite sure, and then, as she listened she became perfectly sure. What she had heard was the crunch of footsteps on the frozen ground outside. Some one was approaching the cave.

"Why don't the dogs bark?" she wondered, and then one of them howled, and she was still uncertain. The visitor could be nobody they knew, no gipsy, that is, and yet they were strangely apathetic. She crept closer, peering forth unseen. Outside the cave, very dark against the snow-blanched desolation of the ravine, stood the figure of a man. She had never seen this man before; he was no doubt the King of Spades. He called out:

"Is there anybody there?"

She did not hesitate. This was no policeman, no stupid furious peasant. She strolled slowly forward, arms akimbo, flaunting herself, insolent and assured, typical daughter of Egypt.

"What do you want?"

"I am cold," he said, "and lost in the mountains. Can I take shelter?"

She lighted a cigarette, looking him up and down, puffing the smoke into his face. Then she shrugged her shoulders.

"Yes. You can come in."

He followed her toward the fire, and she noticed that he limped.

"A fine night," she said, "for a lame man to lose himself in the mountains."

"A fine night," he agreed, adding, "but a confoundedly cold one."

The gipsy flung some more wood on the fire. As the flames blazed up she glanced curiously at the stranger. He was tall, and was wrapped in a dark cape. He was young, with a white beautiful face, a vivid mouth that looked as though it had been painted, and eyes that seemed immense and black, perhaps because they were so deeply shadowed. His face was like a mask; he was unlike any man she had ever before seen.

"You have been telling your fortune?" and he looked at the cards scattered on the floor.

"Yes." And she laughed. *"You* are in my fortune. You are the King of Spades."

"I know," said he, and sighed.

"Are you going to drink with me?" asked the gipsy.

"I don't drink," said the stranger.

"Then you miss more than you know," she retorted. She poured out a glass of *swika*.

"You were lucky," she said when she had finished drinking, "to find this encampment. More lucky than you know."

"But I was looking for you," said the stranger.

She became immediately suspicious; her eyes narrowed and grew watchful, like the eyes of a snake. She told him positively:

"I have never seen you before."

"But I have seen you," he said gently, almost in a deprecating tone of voice.

"Where?"

"Many times, in many different places."

"That's a lie," the gipsy said roughly.

The stranger was silent.

"Well?" she challenged him.

"The last time, if you really want to know," he confided, "was in Jassy, where you were telling fortunes and picking pockets. You stole, that evening, if I remember aright, two purses, three watches, a gold cigarette-case, and a five hundred *lei* bank-note."

"You're a police spy," she cried, her voice shaking with anger.

"No. Only an observer."

There was a pause.

"One must live," the gipsy at length grumbled, rolling a cigarette with her thin brown fingers.

"Naturally. But I have seen you on a number of other occasions."

"When?"

"Once," he told her, "was in Galatz. Outside a church, just before dawn. There was a man with you who loved you. You made him break into the church and steal for you an ikon of gold, studded with precious stones. You sold the ikon the next day to a Jew, but your lover was put in prison. I expect that he is still in prison."

"He was not my lover!" she protested furiously. "I'm a gipsy—do you suppose I mix with *gajo* men?"

The stranger shrugged his shoulders.

"What about the young officer you used to drive with in Bucharest? Do you remember—the one who always filled your carriage with flowers? The one you drugged one evening—and robbed. Have you forgotten him?"

"I had," she said sulkily. "How do you know all this?"

"I know much more," he told her, smiling. "I know, for instance, that you were never faithful to your gipsy husband."

"My *rom?* What do you mean? He's dead, my *rom.*"

"Yes, he was hanged at Braila, wasn't he, for stabbing another man in the back. The man he stabbed was your lover, and it was you who screamed for the police. But when the police came you were gone. You hid yourself in the forest, then, for months. Until your child was born."

The gipsy's face turned gray beneath its olive tan. Her cigarette fell from her fingers.

"Oh, I know all about that," the stranger informed her easily. "You abandoned the child, which is now dead, and went as wet-nurse to the family of a great Boyar in Transylvania. You put a spell about the Boyar so that he could not forget you. He gave you his wife's jewels and then cut his throat because of your cruelty. You ran away, but that time you were caught, the jewels were taken from you, and you went to prison. When you came out you had no money, and so you sold yourself, in the streets. And then a man became too fond of you. You grew tired of him, and you gave him gipsy poison. When he was dying, he still cried out for you. But you were far away, and very drunk, dancing the *tanana* for some young officers in a café not far from Bucharest."

The gipsy pulled herself together and tried to smile. She said, defiantly:

"All those matters, my fine gentleman, are what we call 'affairs of Egypt,' and as such don't concern you at all. You have found out, somehow, things that are not good for you to know. You had better go, before I turn you out."

But the stranger drew nearer, and thrust the white beautiful mask of his face close to hers.

"You can't," he said, "be rid of me so easily. I told you just now that I came here in search of you. Now that I have found you, do you really suppose that I shall let you go?"

The gipsy, who had very frequently had occasion to find herself in more desperate situations, remained perfectly silent and composed. But her mind worked quickly. She was alone with one who knew all her dark and shameful secrets, one as sinister as he was beautiful. She thought that he must hate her and had come to kill her, and yet of this she was not sure, for the Ace of Spades had not appeared in her fortune, and the Ace of Spades, not the King, meant death. Perhaps, then, since she was not to die herself, she was destined to kill her companion before the night was over. She threw away her cigarette.

"Let me tell your fortune?" she suggested in a wheedling tone of voice.

He laughed.

"What use would that be? I know my fortune, and yours too. They are bound together."

"Who says so?"

"The Fates say so."

"Listen to the wind!" she cried suddenly, and shivered; "there will be a blizzard to-night, and whatever happens I must be on the road to Braila before dawn."

"We will travel together," he told her calmly.

"Not I," she retorted. "I don't saddle myself with cripples when I must travel fast."

She glanced at him suddenly, curiously.

"Why are you lame? What's the matter with your feet?"

He shrugged his shoulders.

"Nothing much. A slight malformation. It's no handicap to me."

At that moment a terrible thought occurred to the gipsy, and she shuddered once more, although she was now crouched close to the fire.

"Who are you?" she cried suddenly.

He laughed. "I thought you had guessed," he said. "I am the Devil, my dear."

She trembled once more, but she said, trying to laugh: "The Devil's old and ugly. I should know him anywhere. You aren't the Devil."

"The Devil is a fallen angel, don't forget that. Angels are beautiful, even when they are fallen."

Fascinated, the gipsy held a candle above her head and stared at her companion as though for the first time. His hair was coal-black and curled thickly; the denseness of the curls could not altogether conceal the sprouting of two hard-looking conical lumps that gave to him rather the air of a dissipated faun. He was the Devil; she could see his horns. He watched her ironically.

"Are you convinced, or would you care to see my cloven feet?"

She shook her head.

"No. You are certainly the Devil."

And quite suddenly her angry terror left her; she merely felt dejected and indifferent to her danger.

"What do you want of me?" she asked.

"That's easily explained," he told her. "For a long time now I have been searching for you. You are the most wicked woman I know. When you were a child you were already corrupt. In all your life your heart has never once been touched; you have never done one kind deed; you have never had one innocent thought."

"I said, what do you want of me?"

"Hell," explained the Devil, "is incomplete without your presence, and I have come for you. I shall marry you. I have always wanted a wife."

"Have you known me a long time?" the gipsy inquired.

"Yes, a very long time," replied the Devil. "I have followed you everywhere and been near to you more often than you know. I have always realized that the queen of Hell would probably be a gipsy, but I assure you that you are the only existing gipsy wicked enough to satisfy my exacting taste. You are without one single redeeming characteristic. You are admirable. And so I have come for you."

The gipsy got up from the floor. Her bangles tinkled as she walked across to the farthest corner of the cave.

"What are you looking for?" he asked her.

"The *swika,*" she replied over her shoulder. "After what you have told me don't you imagine I have need of a drink?"

She returned with a new bottle and two clean glasses.

"It's a pity, isn't it," observed the Devil agreeably, "that drink should be one of the few pleasures which hold for me no temptation whatsoever?"

"A great pity," she agreed, but all the same she filled two brimming glasses, and a curious insinuating smile curled her lips as she looked across at her companion.

"Tell me about Hell," she entreated.

"You will soon see it for yourself," the Devil replied. "There are some beautiful women there, but their names would mean nothing to you, and you are more interesting than any of them, so let us not waste time talking about such matters."

"Very well, as you wish," agreed the gipsy.

She remained intent upon her glass for a moment, and then suddenly asked in a humble tone of voice:

"Will you do me a favor?"

"Perhaps," replied the Devil cautiously. "What is it?"

"Oh, nothing of any importance . . . only, you must understand that it is not every day the Fiend comes for one . . . it is something of an occasion, something that will only happen once in the life of a poor gipsy like myself. . . ."

"Well?"

The Devil's voice seemed to have grown harder.

"It's nothing of importance," repeated the gipsy, smiling upon him and still speaking in a cajoling voice, "but at the same time something that would give me great pleasure. . . . Prince, I know you do not drink, but I ask you as a favor to raise your glass just once, to wish your bride good fortune. If you are taking me to Hell with you, you can do no less than grant that one small request."

The Devil appeared to consider.

"One toast in Romany," begged the gipsy insinuatingly. She glided closer, offering him the glass. Her great eyes, fixed full upon him, seemed to blaze with an unholy light, brighter even than his own. They were like cat's eyes, in the darkness of the cave.

The Devil felt quite at home, and smiled back at her, showing his teeth.

"Please . . ." whispered the gipsy, pressing the glass against his hand. Her eyes became suddenly cozening and innocent, like the eyes of a very young girl.

"You are more wicked even than I thought," said the Devil softly.

"Then that should enchant you! Please will you drink to me?"

The Devil burst out laughing. "Very well! To please my future wife! Give me the glass."

She handed it to him.

"To the bride of Satan," said he, draining it off.

"*Aukka tu pios adrey Romanés,*" replied the gipsy dreamily, in her own language. She smiled at him again.

The Devil made a wry face and threw his glass away. It crashed to pieces against the wall.

"Your *swika* is very bad," he observed.

"It's not mine," the gipsy answered indifferently, "the *swika* I drink is always paid for by others."

"And very strong," the Devil added, still grimacing.

She laughed. "That's as it should be."

She stretched out her hand to pick up a guitar that was lying near the fireplace.

"As a reward for having drunk my health," she said, "I'll play you a gipsy song."

The Devil had risen slowly to his feet and now stood facing her, his face pale as death itself in the dusky glow of the firelight. He opened his mouth to speak, but she at once began to strum the guitar. She burst out laughing.

"Here's a song for you, my gipsy husband, my dear husband, my beautiful husband from Hell. . . ."

And she chanted:

"Two horns has my Ro;
Two hoofs for prancing;
I gave him drao
To set him dancing. . . ."

The Devil seemed to stagger, as though he had stumbled in his lameness, and he flung his hand against the wall to steady himself, and cried out gasping:

"*Drao?* What do you mean? What have you given me?"

The gipsy laughed so much that she almost dropped her guitar.

"Oh, my poor husband! You are not so clever as I thought! How can you expect to marry a gipsy woman when you don't know what *drao* means? . . . Yes, I've given you *drao,* Prince, and *drao* is gipsy poison that will grip your entrails until I'm away from you—far away on the road to Braila!"

And she continued to laugh immoderately, while the Devil, cursing, fell upon his knees before her to writhe and groan as though he were himself suffering the torments of those damned spirits he ruled in his own kingdom. She picked up a candle the better to observe him and saw with delight that the white mask of his face was distorted now, no longer beautiful, but frankly hideous in its agony. He had ceased to look like Lucifer, the fallen angel, and was now the Fiend, most frightful to behold.

Yet the gipsy, when she had once recovered from her mirth, appeared more inquisitive than terrified. She bent over her companion with an air of the greatest interest, clapped her hands, as though well pleased with her ruse, and poured herself out another glass of *swika.*

The Romany *drao,* a coarse white powder contained in a tiny bag of leather, she replaced at once in the pocket of her dress. There was plenty left for another time, and she was a woman of frugal habits wherever her own possessions were concerned. She was by this time a little drunk, and she once more began to play the guitar. Her voice rang out, wild and strange, amid the deepest shadows of the cave:

"Two horns has my Ro;
Two hoofs for prancing;
I gave him drao
To set him dancing. . . ."

The guitar, throbbing beneath her fingers, seemed to chuckle with an impish glee.

"Do you hear what I said to you, my dear husband? I told you to dance."

And she continued to sing, with a false and mocking tenderness:

"Dance, then my chavé
Thy limbs are lazy!
Dilo, dilo, the world's gone crazy!"

She threw away her guitar and advanced once more to examine the writhing semi-conscious form of her companion.

"The world has indeed gone crazy," she jeered, "when the Prince of Darkness allows himself to be outwitted by a poor strolling gipsy with scarcely a rag to her back! Yes, Prince, you were right to call me the most wicked woman in the world. I am so wicked that I can even make a fool of the Devil himself. Another time beware of me and of my spells!"

The Devil groaned, but the gipsy had turned her head toward the mouth of the cave, through which a pale shaft of light crept like a ghost to glimmer faintly upon her bangles and her sequins.

"Ah-ha!" she cried, "the dawn at last! Farewell, Prince, until our next meeting—in a few hours from now you will no doubt have recovered from my *drao* . . ."

She picked up her bundle from the ground and laughed once more, dragging it behind her, shaking her wild locks over her eyes.

"Farewell," she called again, "I leave you my cave and my *swika*—at least let us call them mine—but not my soul, for, between you and me, I don't believe that I possess such a thing."

And without one backward glance she walked out of the cave and down the snowy hillside, past the tents and the wagons, until she found herself upon the frozen road. And then she slung her bundle over her shoulder, and began to stride out swiftly, for she was in a hurry to reach Braila before dusk.

As she walked she occasionally laughed out loud, and hummed once more the words of her song:

"Two horns has my Ro;
Two hoofs for prancing . . ."

"It seems to me," she reflected, "that men can always be deceived by the gipsies—yes, all men, even the Devil himself. . . . What a fool he is, to be sure!"

She increased her pace, gliding like a bright shadow along the frost-blanched road, and when peasants passed her on their way to the next village, they drew back fearfully and crossed themselves. It was not the wildness of her aspect that disconcerted these simple people so much as the fact that she seemed to them accompanied by a swift, dark, limping shape that, gaining on her, drew ever closer to her shoulder.

But Tamar the gipsy saw nothing unusual.

She thought only of reaching Braila before dusk.

There and Here

ıllıı

Alice Brown

Alice Brown (1857–1948) made her lasting mark as a writer with Meadow Grass *(1895), a collection of classic New England stories, and with the equally renowned* Tiverton Tales *(1899). These two volumes have maintained her reputation to this day, alongside the work of two other great New England local colorists, Sarah Orne Jewett and Mary E. Wilkins Freeman.*

Like Jewett and Freeman, Brown was a regionalist who occasionally wrote stories of horror and the supernatural. Elements of fantasy, however, pervade all her work to lesser or greater degrees, whether as nature mysticism, Tolstoian psychological irony approaching the uncanny, or actual occultism. Specifically fantastic works are found among her novels, especially The Wind Between the Worlds *(1920); her plays, notably the poetic dialogue* Marriage Feast *(1931); tales for children,* The One-Footed Fairy *(1911), and the three-act fairy play* Golden Ball *(1929); poetry, such as the long "Pan" in* Harper's Monthly, *November 1894; allegories, including unpublished ones housed in the Yale University rare manuscripts collection; and in her short stories. A complete collection of her supernatural stories,* The Empire of Death and Other Weird Tales, *will be issued soon.*

In the 1890s Brown was deeply involved with women's rights and prison reform movements and was a key member of a Boston group of radical young artists, poets, authors, and activists. She travelled with an equally Bohemian companion, the poet Louise Imogen Guiney, and wrote about their journeys. Her tale of strange reunion, "There and Here," first published in Harper's Monthly,

November 1897, and reprinted here from High Noon *(1904), foreshadowed the eventual parting of Guiney and Brown. Guiney eventually moved to England (although not to wed, as in the case of Rosamond in "There and Here"; Rosamond is a name that recurs in Brown's fiction) to pursue Anglophile interests while Brown remained in Boston.*

"There and Here" shares several thematic focuses with Elizabeth Stuart Phelps's "Since I Died," including the central relationship between two women. Brown even includes a bedroom scene, albeit a very wholesome if symbolically weighty one, to complete her portrait of the relationship. Lesbian relationships were known at the time as "New England marriages" and "Boston marriages," and were not at all uncommon. "There and Here" is an enduring and very touching ghost story. It is also an accurate reflection of Brown's own heart. Neither she nor Lou Guiney ever married.

Perhaps Ruth Hollis was no more conscious at one time than another of her loneliness and heart-hunger for Rosamond Ware, the friend of her childhood, and indeed her entire life. It was an ever-present pain— not poignant now, but grown into that emptiness of loss which attends a broken kinship. Ruth had lived for her thirty-one years in the standstill, colonial-flavored town of Devonport. Rosamond, on the death of her father, mother and two brothers, in the space of a week, had gone to Italy to be with an older brother, a man with a jangled body and a tempered artist soul. That had not been altogether desirable, for the very fineness of his nature imposed its limitations, and he exacted much, even while he gave. She had been there eight years, from month to month prophesying her return, but never being quite able to effect it. Her unwilling feet would not drag themselves back to America. She longed for it, she brooded over shivered associations with a passionate regret; but when the moment came for clasping the lax link again, cowardice shot up in her and cried off. Her grief was poignant enough already; when she thought of voluntarily sharpening its edge, the apprehensive nerves rebelled. The house at Devonport had been given her by will, and now it was standing exactly as the family tragedy had left it. The unworn garments in the closets could hardly fall more absolute prey to mice and moth; they were in ruins already. But daily the dust and mildew of time wrote a sadder record on the blurring page, and the inexorable master of all spurred himself to show what havoc he could compass, left to his own will. Again and again Ruth wrote her friend, begging her to have the house opened, aired, and cleaned: not for the sake of thrift only, she urged, but because the place was dear to both of them. There they had played together at mimic living, and loved and dreamed after living began. It was her home too, according to spiritual tenure, and she had a right to speak. But Rosamond always answered, "Not yet!" Time had rent her web of life, and she was still too selfish to enlarge the rift made in the nature of things.

One late twilight, in an ice-bound spring, Ruth was wandering about the rooms of her own home, setting them in order by an observant touch here and there, and making ready to close the house for the night. The rest of the family had gone, on sudden summons, to spend a day or two with an uncle, twenty miles away, whose prodigal son had come home, and who thus bade all his accessible kin to the rejoicing. Ruth, for no tangible reason, had been disinclined to go; as the day drew nearer, her unwillingness increased, and at the very last she refused entirely, promising to spend the night and the next day with Aunt Barnard, a mile's distance out of the town. The two maids, having been given holiday, had already fastened their domain and departed. Ruth meant every minute to follow them; but the house so wooed her in its simmering afternoon warmth that she still lingered and dallied with her purpose. The fires were dying safely down, but there was a red glow in every room. The scented geraniums were sweet from the windows, and the stillness seemed benignant. At length, unable to conjure up more excuses for idling, she did get on her hat and cloak, and stood fastening the last button before the front window, where the snow lay dead white, and the great chestnut-tree stretched gaunt arms against the darkening blue. She stopped, with an arrested motion, in putting on her gloves. Some one was coming. It was a woman, walking very fast yet lightly, with a buoyant motion Ruth seemed to know. She wore a flowing cloak, and a great hat with a long feather. Ruth watched her with a tightening at her throat and a straining of the eyes. She came nearer, stopped, and waved her hand. It was growing dark so fast that a tangible veil seemed falling between them; but Ruth was sure she smiled.

"Rose!" she called wildly from the window. "Rosamond! Rosamond!"

The woman nodded. Ruth tore out of the front door, dropping her gloves behind her, and ran down the path. Now the newcomer was laughing, and Ruth felt a sudden passionate relief at the sweet familiarity of the sound. She began to see, in that instant, what her loneliness had been. She sobbed a little.

"I don't believe it," she whispered. "You are not really *you!*"

"That's your impudence," said Rosamond. "As if I'd take the trouble to be anybody else!"

They were walking into the house together, side by side and hand in hand. Ruth never knew whether they had kissed or not. It was quite likely they had not, for Rosamond was an elusive creature, who held that there are few moments when the soul is the better for the body's sacrament. Inside, the dark had fallen thick.

"Let me get a lamp," said Ruth, again with a little sob of joy completed. "I want to see you."

"No, Grandmother Wolf, not to-night. You're going over to the house with me."

Ruth turned back from the table and let her match burn out.

"Not to-night, dear," she entreated. "It's cold. It's—awful. You would break your heart."

"Ah, say yes!" coaxed Rosamond, in her old spoiled fashion. "Just to step inside and see whether we want to stay. Just to peep in. Why, Ruth, it's *home!*"

But while she spoke she was at the door, and Ruth was following her, saying martyrwise:—

"You'll have your way, of course. It's to be expected; but I do wish you wouldn't. Wait till morning, Rose. Only till the fires are built."

Rosamond laughed lightly and happily.

"Not an hour. Not a minute. Come, shut that door, and race me to the stump. No letters in it now."

The door banged behind them, and they ran together down the frozen drive. Rose was mad with glee. She sped like a stream of darkness, softly, glidingly. She was first at the stump, and she stayed there till Ruth came up, panting.

"Over the crust now," she laughed, in a bright exhilaration. "Come! come!"

But though she ran in little dashes, and waited between, Ruth, making what shift she could to follow, crashed through and gave it up.

"Come back!" she called. "You're a fay. I'm a good twenty pounds heavier. That's according to precedent. Don't you see it won't bear?"

But Rosamond skimmed back like a leaf, and then they went on soberly, side by side again. Ruth kept turning to look at her.

"You certainly are changed," said she; "but, oh, you're so pretty! You've got a radiance. You seem to shine. Are you my old chum?"

"Your old chum, your pal in vulgar moments, your Rose to keep."

"Then don't you wither!"

Rosamond laughed again, with that thrilling undercurrent more significant than mirth.

"I may be transplanted," said she, "but wither, no! See the little twigs pricking through the crust! Hear the tips of the pine trees talking! Oh, what a world! what a world!"

"How you enjoy! Exactly like your old apostrophes, 'hot and hot'! You're the most universal lover I know. You're the moon that looks on many brooks. Berries? How ever do you manage to see them in this light? But then, you always were cat-footed and owl-eyed."

It was only a short stretch of road to the Ware homestead, and then a long driveway wound up through the grounds. There the thick evergreens, untrimmed for many years, so encroached upon the way that they half sheltered it from snow, and made it still accessible. Rosamond kept darting into the fir woods, to return laden with news.

"Do you remember how we used to gather cones and burn them on the Anvil Rock? The pines are full. And the hollow locust where we found the squirrel's nest? Nobody has touched it since that day, and his greatest-great-grandson lives there now. Do you remember how we used to do up nuts in our hair, and sit under the tree to let him pull them out? The hepaticas on the bank are in such a temper—you can't think! They're waked up and ready to sprout, and there's no encouragement."

"That's according to the light of the spirit. Even you can't see under the snow, Sharp Eyes!" Ruth spoke from the dreamy acquiescence born of full content. She knew quite well that they ought not to be going by night into a deserted house, but Rosamond's assurance had lulled her will to sleep. She was penetrated by the wonder of seeing this dearest creature in the world, whom she had pictured broken and desolate, so lightsome and free of care.

The last sweep of the driveway brought them out in front of the old house, spacious and still imposing, though so evidently the subject of a lingering death. Ruth paused an instant, not daring to look into her friend's face, and only guessing what grief must be painted there. But Rosamond dropped her arm and ran up the steps alone.

"Welcome home!" she called blithely. "Welcome! Why do you wait?"

Ruth had stopped now in a detaining afterthought. "We're simpletons," said she. "The key is at the Daytons', where you left it. That's a sign we're not to go in. Come back, dear, and wait till morning."

But Rosamond held her place. "Come up here, doubter," cried she. "When was anything lost by trying? The oracle appears because you have previously besieged the shrine. Come on! There, now. Shall I lift the latch? Shall I?"

It yielded with the old familiar click, and the great door swung open. Ruth gave a joyous cry.

"You witch, you've got the key already!" She put a hand on Rosamond's cloak, in gentle suasion. "Let me go in first. Please! I can't bear to have you feel how cold it is, with no one to welcome you. Why, it's light!" An airy intangibility of warmth and fragrance poured out upon them like a river delayed and eager. The odors were familiar—a mystic alembic made of the breath of flowers, but so fused that you could never say which was heliotrope and which the spice of pinks. They made up a sweetness bewildering to the sense. "Oh!" she cried again; "enchantress! Merlin and Ariel in one!"

Rosamond shut the door behind them. The spirit of a delicate witchery was playing on her face while she led the way into the front room on one side of the hall; this had been the family meeting-place and talking-place in days gone by. It lay there smiling, in happy renewal of the past. A fire flickered on the hearth with the burgeoning of new flame above old embers. The tall clock ticked in measureless content. The firelight seemed to fill the room. Ruth drew a long breath of rapturous recognition.

"How like you!" she murmured. "You came days ago, weeks ago. You put it all in order—for me. But the intention isn't all. Somebody else might have thought of it, but nobody could have done it."

"You like it? Then I'm glad."

Two chairs were ready before the blaze. They threw off their wraps, and sank into the accustomed places. They sat for a time in silence, while the clock ticked.

"Do you remember"—began Ruth.

"Yes; that was the last time we were here together. I was telling you, over and over again, that the lonesome house would kill me. I behaved like a child—an ignorant, untrained child."

"I won't hear you blamed. You were beside yourself."

"I was a child," repeated Rosamond conclusively. "I can't imagine any one so ignorant, so pathetic in her ignorance. I told you death denied the laws of life. I could only think of my mother in her coffin. I was a savage."

Ruth turned and looked at her in the firelight. Her face lay soft and lovely under a happy seriousness. She seemed absolutely serene, with the well-being of outdoor things, the pine trees, and the snow.

"Rosamond," said her friend impulsively, "have you got religion?"

Rosamond laughed out. "You are so droll!" she answered. "I might as well ask, have you got air in your lungs? Have you?"

"But you're so changed, and for the better. You've grown."

"I had to grow," said Rosamond whimsically. "Part of it at a jump! But let's not talk about finalities. There's one thing I meant to write you about. I made my will, two months ago, and left this house for a home for tired women. It's to be called the Margaret Home—for my own mother, you know. It's to be for middle-aged, tired women: their very own, so that they can come here from the cities and rest. I have named you executor, but I wanted to speak about it, too. There's nothing in particular to say, for you would always know how I should like things; still, I thought it would be well to mention it."

Ruth drew nearer, in sudden fear; but the firelight, playing over Rosamond's face, only brought out the wholesome tints of ruddy cheek and clear gray eye.

"You're not going to die?" She spoke with that keen alarm hid ever "in the heart of love." Rosamond smiled straight into her eyes, and her strength and beauty seemed to diffuse a certain power like beams of light. Her voice thrilled through the ear to the heart:

"I'm not going to die. I am safe, contented, happy."

"I've often thought," began Ruth hesitatingly—"I have hoped you would marry. I never expected you to be serene, a lone stick like me. You have such an appetite for joy! How could you be contented with that one thing left out?"

Rosamond did not answer at once, but the peace of her presence still made itself felt, and Ruth was sure she had not probed her too far.

"That is one of the things I meant to tell you to-night," she began slowly, as if she had some difficulty in making her phrases fit. "It was not left out. Three years ago I met some one in Italy. He died, and so if I— In any case, I should never have married." Her voice was still musical and unmoved, and Ruth looked at her in amazement. There seemed to be nothing to say. Rosamond went on, broodingly: "You will be glad to know how perfect it was. We understood each other from the first. Whatever it may mean to say, 'I am yours—you are mine," was true for us. It was when that feeling came that I began to understand life a little better. It was my alphabet. I never spoke about it to you because he died so soon after we found each other. And I didn't take it well. Then, too, I was a child." For the first time some sadness crept into her voice—regret for an obedience missed. Ruth could not answer; she was beginning not to understand. Her friend seemed to speak from the state of one charged with a knowledge not to be fully shared.

"However," continued Rosamond, rousing herself and calling back her former lightness, "it's absurd to wish we had been better and braver and sweeter. What's done is done, and now—'the winter is past, the rain is over and gone.' "

Ruth dared probe her no further; she felt invisible barriers.

"Is this another of your witch ways?" she asked, with a groping return to the tangible. "Flowers everywhere? I've been speerin' through the dark and naming them. That's goldenrod in the big jar at my feet: asters, too. Those are columbines on the mantel, and you've put mignonette and heliotrope on the table, just where they used to stand. Do you carry the magic lamp? In my day florists never brought the seasons quite together, like righteousness and peace."

Rosamond put on a merry disdain.

"Magic lamp!" quoth she—"a kitchen cupboard full. You might as well learn now that lamps seem magical only when they're out of place. Come, old lady, isn't it your bedtime? Do you still go when it's dark under the table?"

"Yes, but not to-night. Still, I suppose we ought to be getting home. I hate to leave this fire. At least, let's take some of the flowers with us."

"With us, forsooth! We're going to stay here."

"No, child: not in mildewed beds. I draw my line at that."

Rosamond took both her hands and drew her up from the chair.

"Come and see!" she said. "The ocular proof! I scorn to argue." She led the way out into the hall, and up the broad worn stairs. Ruth followed, like a child.

"I'm a coward, and you know it," said she. "But to-night I'm not afraid. I wouldn't have believed I could be induced to stay till this hour in a deserted house with only sweet you to guard me. But here I am, and here 'I means to stick,' if you say so."

The hall above was peopled with playing lights and moving shadows. The clock on the landing ticked with ancient peace. The firelight came smiling and beckoning from the two opposite rooms at the head of the stairs. Ruth, speechless, stepped into one chamber and then the other. The fires blazed opulently; the beds were ready, turned down in the V shape both girls had learned from their mothers; it seemed to belong to their dual childhood.

"Are we truly going to stay here?" Ruth cried. "Here together? Why, it's like Christmas! It's like heaven!"

"Into bed with you! I'm going down, but I'll come back again presently and tuck you up. And—if you lie still, like a good little lady, I'll tell you a story."

Ruth began throwing off her clothes in haste.

"Rosamond," she called blithely after her, "cover up the sitting-room fire. We forgot the fender."

So much of life is a barren gleaning after the true harvest! Little broken impressions, scintillæ of feeling, stay floating about in the memory, and happy is he who can fit them into some sort of a patchwork when days are bare again. Ruth was never so happy, so well content, she remembered afterwards, as when, with an absorbing delight in physical well-being, and a charming sense of the new and absolutely desirable, she made ready for bed, stopping here and there, as she moved about the room, to greet some ancient treasure with a murmur of delight. There was the red cow with one horn; they had milked her daily in other times. There were the wax flowers they had tried to imitate; but, alas! poor little handmaids, because they worked surreptitiously, with the curious secretiveness of childhood, they had no instruction, and no material save the beeswax in their mothers' work-baskets, chewed into wads by their patient teeth. There, oh joy! was Miranda, the oldest doll of all, with her abbreviated skirt and long pantalets, sitting woodenly in a corner, quite unmoved by this strange, bright resurrection. Ruth gave her a kiss in passing—a passionate kiss for the sake of former days. She took a handful of sweet-pease from the bunch on the mantel, and dropped them in Miranda's lap. Joy was cheap enough to share. Then she slipped into bed and waited. Rosamond came. She placed a chair by the bedside, and seating herself, drew Ruth's hand into hers.

"Once upon a time" —she began.

"Did you cover up the fire?"

"It's all right. Once upon a time there was a little Child, and he was always crying because he didn't know the difference between Here and There. He was always hating to be Here, and longing to be There. So one day a Strong One came and said to him, 'Come, you Silly Thing, you may go There if you want to.' And he set him on a feather of one of his wings, and took him There. And There was a place you couldn't imagine if I should describe it to you. The best I can do is to say it was all flowers, and living odors, and pine trees, and clear sunlight, and sweet winds. It's a place where everybody can be tucked up at night"—

"What makes you have any night?" asked Ruth, from her doze. "Have it all day."

"Leave out the stars, the night dews, the counsel of the leaves? No; we must have night There. But There black is just as lovely as white; so it's all one. And the Child was happy at once, but the Strong One smiled, and said to him, 'It is always so. They are all happy at once, and they might have been before, if they had had eyes to see that Here is There and There is Here.' And the Child said"—But Ruth was soft asleep and breathing peacefully, and Rosamond smiled with great tenderness. Ruth remembered afterwards that Rosamond bent over her once to kiss her on the eyelids, but only to check herself and to draw back among the shadows.

The late moon was regnant in the chamber when she came broad awake. Rosamond was standing over her, one hand on hers.

"Oh, what made you wake me? what made you?" she cried, quite querulous in her loss. "I was dreaming such a dream. I was in a place I never saw—I can't describe it—I'm forgetting it now. But they were telling me something: the one thing, you know, that explains everything." She sat up in bed, and tried to grasp at the fleeting memory.

"It's gone!" She was near crying as she said it. "I almost had the words, but they won't stay."

Rosamond paid no attention.

"Hurry!" she whispered. "Get up and dress. We are going over to your house now. Come!"

Ruth sprang out of bed, and mechanically laid hands on her clothing. She hesitated for a moment to study Rosamond's face.

"You're not frightened?" she asked. "What is it?"

"I've let you sleep too long, that's all. Don't question, dear one. Come!"

She did, indeed, look pale, but something so sweet and comforting still hung about her and the smiling room that Ruth was not afraid. It did not come to her till afterwards that somebody—an alien somebody or something—might be in the house. Rosamond gave a quick little movement of relief when the last hook was fastened. She had Ruth's hat and cloak on her arm, and she pressed them upon her in eager haste. Then she threw her own cloak about her, and drew Ruth down the stairs. Ruth forgot to step cautiously lest they be heard; she remembered afterwards how her boots clicked, and the rustling of her dress. The fire still flickered in the sitting-room, and the air of the house exhaled a summer sweetness. Rosamond threw open the front door to an icy breath; she parted her lips and caught at it in sobbing thankfulness.

"Ah," she sighed, "that's good!"

The door closed behind them, and they hurried down the path. Rosamond swept on like a shadow, her cloak billowing behind her in the wind. A picture flashed before Ruth's vision of their coming, when they had hurried in play; now their haste was tragic.

"Rosamond!" she called, with all the breath left in her, "you've forgotten your hat. You'll get your death."

"Come! come!" called Rosamond, over her shoulder. "Hurry! hurry!"

"Then give me your hand. I can't keep up with you."

"Not now!"—her voice came back, a dying sound upon the wind. "Hurry!"

They ran like fleeting clouds.

"There, you mad thing"—Ruth began, as they reached her own door, but the urgency of haste clung to her, and she could not finish. She fitted the key to the lock and stood aside.

"Go in," breathed Rosamond faintly. "Go in, dear one, dear one!"

Ruth stepped over the sill, and the door closed behind her. She turned and tugged at it with a sudden sense of loss. It would not yield. She put forth all her strength. "Rosamond," she called, "push! I can't move it!"

When the door opened, Ruth looked out on the sterile dusk of the early morning. The moon had gone down, and the earth seemed mourning her. No on was there. She bent forward into the darkness. "Rosamond," she said. "Rosamond!"

There was no answer. A rustle came from the one oak-tree in the yard. Then there was silence, for the wind had died. In the midst of her gathering alarm a strange peace, a sense of the sweetness and natural-ness of the world, fell upon her like a charm, and she smiled out into the darkness as if it were a friendly face. Then, in serenity of soul, she thought it all out. Rosamond was ever a sprite; now she was playing her a trick. She had gone into the shrubbery to hide. Call, and she would not answer; leave her unnoticed, and a moment would bring her tapping at the window. She shut the door and went in. The rooms were still warm, though the hearth fires had died; and she took a fur cloak from the hall in passing, threw it about her, and sat down by the win-dow to wait. And as she waited, the lovely content of the evening stole over her again. She closed her eyes, and to a purring sense of spiritual warmth the dream began where it had left off, and she learned the secret which explains everything. But she never could remember that dream.

She started awake with the sense of some one in the room. The fire was blazing up over new kindling; the sun lay warm on her shoulder. Her mother stood there, and the maid was bringing in wood. Ruth rubbed her eyes and worked her way out of her wraps.

"What a sleep!" she yawned. "Oh, I remember. But what made you come home?"

Her mother was looking at her sadly. She took Ruth's hand. "I had to come," said she. "We've had bad news, and I didn't want you to hear it from any one else. Ruth, you must be brave. Rosamond died yesterday. They cabled her Aunt Amy from Italy."

Ruth regarded her with straining eyes. Then she began to laugh.

"My poor child," said her mother, beginning to rub the hand she held. Ruth drew it away.

"You mustn't, mummy, you mustn't," said she. "Don't be sorry for me. It isn't sad. It's lovely, only you don't know it. There's been a queer mistake. No, I won't tell you. Just come with me and I'll give you a surprise. Here's your shawl. Put it on."

She threw it about her, found some gloves and pressed them upon her. Life seemed very dramatic since last night's prologue. She drew her mother along in merry haste; but at the door Mrs. Hollis left her for a moment to step back into the kitchen and whisper a word to Nora:—

"Watch the way we go, and tell Mr. Hollis to follow us. Tell him I can't explain, but he must come."

Then she went out where Ruth was waiting, tapping her foot impatiently, and scanning the path, the shrubbery, the road, lest she be caught herself by her own surprise. She ran an arm through her mother's, and hurried her down the walk. When they passed the stump post-office she laughed again; but her mother's look of pain recalled her.

"Poor mother!" she said, in a specious coaxing. "Wait a bit, and you'll laugh too. So Rosamond is dead?"

The tears came fast down her mother's cheeks.

"Yes, dead," she answered. "You don't realize it."

Ruth tried to be serious and demure.

"Not yet," she assented. "Just now you're realizing for two." They were rounding the curve of the drive. "But I don't see any smoke. The thriftless thing! she's let the fires go down."

They mounted the steps together, and Ruth, in happy assurance, laid her hand upon the latch. It did not yield. Her mother stood looking wildly down the drive, and praying for her husband's coming. Ruth, her self-possession inexplicably overthrown, was beating at the door.

"Rosamond!" she was calling. "Oh, Rosamond, let me in! Don't be cruel! Let me in!"

"Dear, come home," begged her mother, crying bitterly. "Come home."

Ruth knelt, and looked through the keyhole at the dark. She sprang to her feet.

"I'm going in," she said. "I will go in."

She ran around to the side piazza, on a level with the long windows, opened a blind, and broke a pane of glass. The blood dripped down on it. She turned the fastening, threw up the window, and stepped in, and her mother followed. The room was dark, save for the light from that one window, for all the other blinds were closed. She ran up to the clock and looked it in the face. It was dead and still, the impassive hands pointing stolidly to a lying hour. She laid her hands upon it, as if to shake it into life. The dust lay thick over table and chairs. She threw herself upon her knees before the fireplace and thrust her hand into the ashes. They were cold.

"Mother!" she cried out piteously—"Mother!"

"Come home, dear, come home!"

Ruth rose to her feet, sick with wonder, yet reanimated by one last hope.

"Just a minute!" she implored, and ran up the dusty stairs. The door of her own sleeping-room was closed, but she flung it open and walked shudderingly into the darkness within. The bed was unmade, with only a mildewed cover over the mattress. A mouse fled silently across the floor, a swift brown shadow. Where was the china cow? Where was Miranda? With a throb of premonitory knowledge she threw up the cover of the trunk near the bed. There lay the doll, on orderly rows of playthings packed away for doomsday; they looked as if they might have been there always.

Her mother had followed her, and Ruth turned about, trying to smile.

"I begin to understand it now," she said. "I'll go home. You mustn't think I'm crazy. I'm not."

They descended the stairs together and crossed the deserted sitting-room. At the window Mrs. Hollis paused before stepping out.

"I can't understand it," she said musingly. "The house isn't in the least musty. It's as sweet as a garden. Sweeter!"

Ruth stopped, arrested by the truth. The odors of the night were all about her, and as she stood there accepting them, great peace and the sense of security fell upon her like a mantle. She began to smile.

"And they might all be happy," she said to herself, "if they could only remember that There is just the same as Here!"

The Substitute

⑃

Georgia Wood Pangborn

Georgia Wood Pangborn (1872-1955) graduated from Smith College, married in 1894, and after the turn of the century lived on Wall Street at the center of New York City's literary establishment. Her stories were very popular with readers of such magazines as Scribner's, Bookman, Forum, Collier's, Lippincott's *and* Woman's Home Companion. *Her name was a household word at the height of her success, her stories read largely by women with a taste for the macabre. She wrote of ghostly situations that chiefly involved women or children and handled them with rare pathos, subtlety and, often enough, genuine scariness. Although she was among the best supernatural writers of her day in the United States, she fell into obscurity after she stopped writing in the mid-1920s and has been ignored by modern anthologists who tend to mine pulp magazines, missing the better part of what has been written.*

Her first story, "The Gray Collie" (1903), reversed the conservative clichés of terror tales. Such stories are commonly set in men's clubs, and feature cigar-smoking fellows telling each other frightful adventures. In Pangborn's story, a group of women lounging before a fireplace, serving up chocolate instead of brandy or cigars, tell their own kind of frightful story. "Cara" (1914) is about two children with an invisible playmate who turns out to be the mother's friend's dead daughter. A similar pair of children (undoubtedly modeled on her own children, Mary and Edgar Pangborn, themselves noted fantasists) appear in "The Substitute." Another of Pangborn's recurrent concerns was women and madness. "The Intruder" (1907), set in a mental institution, questions the definition of madness, begging comparison to Josephine Daskam Bacon's "The Miracle," written a few years earlier.

"The Substitute," reprinted here from the December 1914 issue of Harper's Monthly Magazine, *where it was first published, succeeds as a fine imagining of a ghost in ordinary earthly life. The tale centers on two women, a spinster who is professionally successful but getting a bit lonely, and a single mother who is deeply loved by her children but has worked herself quite literally into the grave. Spinster and specter demonstrate the limitations of the choices too many women have been offered.*

A modern and very belated collection of all Pangborn's ghost stories, The Wind at Midnight: Collected Uncanny Tales, *is in press.*

The day's heat, for a time made endurable by a small breeze, had been weighed down toward evening by a thunderous humidity. Only along the line of the beach it was tolerable.

Miss Marston had sat so long over her coffee that the room was now in twilight, but she had intercepted by a fretful gesture the maid who would have turned on the light. Her dining-room windows overlooked the water. Fifty feet below she could see the blurred figures of people on the beach, and could hear their voices at intervals, among them the piping staccato of Mrs. Van Duyne's convalescent children, allowed to stay up and be active in the cool of the evening to atone for the languor of the afternoon. Now and then the fretful cry of an ailing baby over-rode the other voices. But the babies that were sent to Mrs. Van Duyne always got well. That was her very wonderful business—making them well.

The heat was like a presence—a thing of definite substance that could be touched. Like a drug, too, making the senses strange, distorting distance and time. Although her eyes were upon the ocean, where the foam appeared and vanished dimly in long lines, lit only a little way out by the lights at the pier-head, it was the dark campus of her college town that Anna Marston's vision beheld, and the unsteady foam-crests of the waves were girls in white dresses, long rows of them coming and going within the obscurity of the trees.

"I am thirty-two," said Miss Marston aloud, and for that reason thought more keenly about when she was twenty-two. The same heavy air had folded in the evening of her Commencement Day, yet the girls had not seemed to mind.

"I suppose we had plenty of other things to think about," said she.

For a while she had gone about the campus with them, singing and laughing, and then, like this, had come to her window-seat to think; to decide, finally, *not* to marry Willis.

"And Mary Hannaford came in—Mary Hannaford—to show me her ring. I told her she was silly!"

Miss Marston moved restlessly.

Matters long ago forgotten will upon occasion freakishly insist upon remembrance, approaching suddenly, like the surprise of a familiar face in a crowded street. A dream plucks us by the sleeve, and we turn to see a childish countenance which has no more right than our own to inextinguishable youth. Or again, a word or a bar of music causes the barrier of years to fall as though it had never been, and we are in gardens that were dust years and years ago. Having once returned, these revenants keep us company for a while.

"I don't see why I should keep on thinking of Mary Hannaford," said Miss Marston, and went on thinking about Mary Hannaford—that perhaps she had not been silly, after all, but rather sensible to marry instead of keeping sulkily to something she called an "ideal," as Anna Marston had done.

"I wish—" said Miss Marston, vaguely, then frowned as the cry of the sick baby came up from the beach.

"Children—" said she; yet her tone, though troubled, was not exactly that of annoyance. Annoyance does not make the eyes wet.

She struck her clenched hand into her open palm, then lay back, drowsily inert in attitude, except that her underlip was caught between her teeth and her forehead was wrinkled with discontent.

She knew that the maids had slipped out for their walk on the beach. They had passed in their black-and-white, giggling, to the bluff stairs, and their squeals of joy at their release had reached her as soon as they were out of sight. She was alone, therefore. Yet she did not feel as if she were alone; not that there seemed to be another presence in the house, but the house itself had changed. Girls—so many!—went in light-footed haste through the halls. The room in which she sat was no longer a conventional dining-room. The walls, hidden in shadow, were garishly sprinkled with photographs and college pennants; the cushions of the window-seats were bright with college colors, and in a moment more Mary Hannaford would come in, wanting to talk under cover of the darkness about how happy she was, how fortunate above all other girls in the world. Mary Hannaford again!

Some one spoke her name. She sat up quickly and was aware of the indistinct pallor of a face.

It was by the voice, however, rather than by anything she saw that she recognized her visitor.

"Why, Mary Hannaford!" said she. "I haven't seen you for ten years! And I've been thinking of you all day."

The figure came forward swiftly and seated itself at the other end of the window-seat. Anna sank back, her sudden rousing having caused that odd vertigo which is common enough in times of great heat. She could not have said whether for an instant her hand touched that of her guest or not.

When the dizziness had passed, Mary was speaking. She sat with her knees drawn up and her hands clasped about them in the attitude Anna so well remembered.

"It's ever so long since I stopped being Mary Hannaford. I'm Mary Barclay, you know."

"Of course. You were the first of our set to go. How romantic we all felt about it! But you stopped writing after the babies came. All girls do. That's what turns us old maids so sour—at least, partly. But do tell me! Have you a cottage here? And how did you find me?"

Mary Barclay appeared to be looking down at the beach. She did not answer her friend's eager queries.

Anna Marston leaned forward and regarded her anxiously.

"Aren't you feeling fit? You seem so pale."

"Oh, quite!"

Anna reached toward the electric button, but Mary Barclay's hand intervened, protesting.

"We don't want lights, do we? Don't you remember how we always liked to talk in the dark like this?"

"Well," laughed Anna, "I'd just as soon you didn't see my wrinkles yet. *You* look just the same, except that you haven't any color. You had the reddest cheeks in the class."

"And you didn't marry, after all," said Mary Barclay, slowly.

"No," admitted Anna, rather fretfully. "The right man wouldn't have me."

"That is like you. You'd never make a second choice. Not that I think it's wise of you."

From the beach the baby's cry rose again, weak, fretful, insistent. Anna Marston fidgeted.

"One of Mrs. Van Duyne's patients. Of course I know the children there are all right, but sometimes I wish they weren't quite so near. That's a marasmus baby that came to-day. Its parents are very rich people. She's keeping the children on the beach late this evening for the coolness. Think," she broke out suddenly—"think what this day has been for the babies in the tenements! If it has been bad here, what must it have been there!"

"Yes," said Mary Barclay. "It is very bad in the city just now." She was looking steadily down toward the beach.

Anna waited for a moment, then asked timidly, "Aren't you going to tell me something about yourself and your family?"

Ten years is a long time in which to know nothing of a friend—time enough for tragedies which will not bear discussing.

"Calvin died three years ago," said Mary Barclay, after a silence.

"I didn't know," said Anna, softly.

"Three years ago. Benny was a year old then. There—wasn't anything. We had been living on his salary. Death—we had forgotten there was such a thing. I found work. You know I had a sort of cleverness about clothes. I found fashion work that paid pretty well, only . . . they weren't very strong babies. They had to have the best, or—or they wouldn't stay, you know. Until now—they've stayed."

"They are well now, then?"

"They are well now."

Anna rose with an exclamation and walked up and down.

"Then I envy you. What a full life! Working—and for your own children. Lucky woman! In spite of your sorrow, lucky, lucky woman! Look at me. What good am I? I started out being my father's companion and secretary. It did very well for a time. Then he married again, and I took my mother's fortune and went my own way—clubs, municipal reform, every galvanic imitation of life I could find. I've been so desperate at times—"

"I know," said Mary Barclay.

"How can you know?"

Anna halted in her pacing to stare at her friend through the obscurity.

"That was partly why I came over here," said Mary Barclay, in an odd, still voice. "I had to come, anyway, to see my babies. I had to do that," she repeated.

"Your babies? At Mrs. Van Duyne's? But you said they were well now."

"Yes," said Mary Barclay. "She knows how to keep them well. The right air and food. There is so much to know. It isn't simple. If I'd tried to keep them in the city—" She shook her head. "Calvin and I always agreed that if we could only bring them safely through the first five years they would be as strong as anybody's children. Their brains are ahead of their bodies. But they aren't weaklings! If they had been—weaklings don't get anything out of life worth staying for. I—shouldn't have been able to come here to-night if they hadn't been worth while. But, you see, I know now—better than I did before—what they are."

She broke off with a cry, yet when Anna would have drawn her arms about her she evaded her like a mist.

"Envy me," moaned Mary Barclay, "but pity me, too!"

Recovering herself quickly, she leaned forward and spoke rapidly: "What becomes of children when fathers and mothers die? Sometimes things turn out all right, I know. It isn't always the same as when parent birds are shot and the nestlings starve. But sometimes it's like that. When there are no relatives to take them, and no money has been left for their support—

"What happens when a little girl is left without a mother to tell her about growing up? And then children are always so—themselves. One child is never like another, yet people who don't know try to treat them all alike.

"My little Martha! She never tells when her heart is broken or she has a pain and is really sick. She just gets cross, and you have to guess. She is apt to be rather naughty anyway. I've had to be patient—very. And, oh, such strange big thoughts as she thinks! And she can suffer, too! And then Benny; I suppose it was his sickness that— It was too much. Mrs. Van Duyne saved him. He was dying when I took him there. She saved him, but—I didn't take care of Martha right when Benny was sick, and so she began to be sick, too. What could I do? So I've let her have them. Anything less than the best wouldn't do, you see. I sold things—all I could—and went to work to earn money to pay her. Perhaps I worked a little too hard. I thought, I suppose, that so long as I was doing it for them nothing could beat me. Well, what's done is done. They laugh and have red cheeks. But—"

She rose and looked down at her friend, then out of the window.

"The nurses are bringing them in from the beach to go to bed. They are very sweet when they are going to bed. Shall we meet them?"

They stepped from the window to the porch, Mary Barclay going lightly ahead. Her dress, of some indefinite color which mingled with that of the sand, made her almost invisible.

There was a long flight of steps leading from the bluff down to the beach. From its summit the slow footsteps of the nurses and children and their mingled voices were audible before their heads came into sight.

One rather fat and sleepy voice counted the steps incorrectly: "One, two, free, seventeen, a hundred—I got up first!"

The pioneer appeared abruptly on all-fours—something of a wounded veteran by his bandaged head, but cheerful. Terrible warfare he had been through, coming out of it with flags flying and glory rebounding to the surgeon first, but to Mrs. Van Duyne with even honor. He bore the proud title of Double Mastoid. Death had been close at his heels; Pain unspeakable had held him very tight in her terrible arms for a long time. Silence had threatened, too: no more kind voices, no music—but all those ogres had been sent to the right-about, far away now from a fat little boy. Already he was forgetting that anything had been wrong.

"I got up quicker'n anybody," he crowed.

Then appeared a white cap, somewhat awry, and strong, kerchiefed shoulders. A young face bent over a tiny sleeping creature on an air-cushion carried steadily and lightly. This was little Marasmus, the latest recruit, and his attendant.

Then came just a plain feeding-case, whose mother didn't dare take him back for fear that she and he would go and do the same wicked things over again just as soon as his Auntie Van Duyne's back was turned. He was sleeping like a cherub. Nothing whatever the matter with *him!* He was one of Mrs. Van Duyne's "Results," said to have been once the duplicate of little Marasmus, but now the kind of person that tired-eyed physicians wag their heads over gloatingly and poke in the ribs—*not* with a stethoscope—and call "Old Top" in a companion-able way, as if they respected him for having done something rather fine all on his own responsibility. He had had about a year of it, and Mrs. Van Duyne was going to hang on to him as long as she could, for she had her own opinion of mothers. Often and often they had undone her fine work just as she had everything going nicely. They never knew anything whatever of their children's inwardness; clothes and hair were as far as they could go. She had all that wonderful hidden territory mapped out. She didn't believe in raw milk very much, for one thing, and she did believe in a few other things which—well, she got results, anyway. Look at "Old Top"!

After him came two children, hand-in-hand; and these, Anna knew at once, were Mary's two. She would have known even without the long trembling sigh that breathed past her ear. The little girl looked so like Mary! She was about six, Anna judged, and her hair was twisted in a little knob on top of her head for coolness' sake—a fashion of hair-dressing for very little girls which, more than another, perhaps, brings a lump into the throat. Is it because of its sweet caricature of maturity, as though both the promise and the menace of the years were revealed in those lines? Or is it that the curve of the back of the neck shown in this way is so lovely that it has a spiritual significance, like the odor of the first grass in spring or the color of evening sky through trees?

She walked with a rather conceited air, her gait indicating a lofty scorn of the Double Mastoid's claim to be a pioneer. She made it very evident that *she* could come up one foot after another, just like all other grown-ups, and she did it with a swagger, to render as obvious as possible her superiority in age, strength, and wisdom over the little boy at her side, who could do no better than one step at a time, and even so had to touch his hand to the tread now and then.

They were thin children, but thin like elves—not with the sadness and languor of sickness. And their faces in the twilight had a lambent quality, their eyes a liquid brightness. One felt that if the whim took them they might easily thrust forth gauzy wings and suddenly sail away with other night creatures.

In their conversation there was a pleasing breadth of impossibility that showed them to be as yet little acquainted with the restrictions of mortal life.

"I'm going to be an engineer when I grow up," stated the boy, "but I'm not going to be a man. I'm going to be a mother. My name isn't Benny."

"What is your name?" the girl asked, without surprise.

"I'm Nelly."

"Well, then, I won't be Martha. I'll be Rosie, and you're my little sister." She was in a kindly mood, which might not last. Only so long as the current of her dream flowed smoothly would Martha be good. The interruption came quickly.

"No, I'm your *big* sister. I'm not little at all. Auntie Van Duyne says I'm getting bigger every day."

"All right, then; I sha'n't play with you," quoth Martha, crisply, and stalked ahead, as naughty as her mother had described. And then Anna saw Mary, who had silently left her side, stoop over and apparently whisper softly to the cross little face surmounted by its wisp of topknot. Martha stopped, finger in mouth, to kick the sand with her toe and look with sidelong friendliness at Benny as he arrived, panting. Then they went on, once more in amity, their short arms stretched about each other's waists. And the mother kept beside them, still whispering in their eyes and kissing them. Yet—they did not turn to her or answer.

"I hope mother'll bring us some paints," Martha was saying as they passed beyond hearing.

"If she does, I'll make her a picture of an engine," Benny joyfully planned.

"Mary!" called Anna. She was surprised to feel that she was trembling, not that she was in any way afraid. She could not have said what had so shaken her. No longer seeing her friend, she laughed and said aloud, "Oh, she must have gone into the house ahead of them."

A slower step was now coming up the bluff stairs, and there appeared a figure in professional white, strong and purposeful, but for the moment rather weary and thoughtful.

Miss Marston stepped forward.

"Good evening, Mrs. Van Duyne. I was coming over to see the Barclay children."

The troubled face was crossed by a flash of joyful surprise and relief.

"Oh, do you know them? I'm so thankful. I wish I'd known before. I've been nearly frantic. Of course, then, you know—"

She took a twist of yellow paper from her belt and handed it to Anna Marston, who did not open it, but trembled very much as she looked at Mrs. Van Duyne, in whose fine, wise eyes the tears glittered and brimmed over, unheeded. Tears were something which in Mrs. Van Duyne's code were a matter to be disregarded, like any other physical weakness in a person who never allowed herself to be sick.

"I haven't told them, of course. I shall put if off—as long as I possibly can. She worked herself to death—" She broke off with a burst of that kindly anger to which the very good and just are so easily stirred. "Her heart wasn't strong, and the heat finished her. The telegram came this afternoon. I can't tell you how glad I am to find out you are her friend. So far as I can make out she had no relatives. I"—she spread out her hands with a sort of desperation—"I do what I can."

Anna had heard tales enough to know that "what I can" meant an amazing amount of work without return in money, that it meant great kindliness, of which advantage was often taken by weak and selfish people. Not that Mrs. Van Duyne ever told. Nevertheless, it had got about that one of the babies had never paid its board since it was a month old, yet you could not have guessed which was the delinquent by any difference between its care and that of "Old Top" or little Marasmus, for example, whose parents came and went in limousines loaded down with all sorts of toys, whose wardrobes were all silken-fine, and who, when they grew up, would be very high and mighty folk indeed. Old Top, certainly; Marasmus, in all probability—though that was going to be pretty brisk and delicate work for a while.

"Since you are a friend," went on Mrs. Van Duyne, "perhaps you can tell me what to do. I'm not talking about the immediate present. They—well, they are here, and they are dear children, though that little Martha is certainly a handful." She half laughed through her tears. "But there is so much future. . . . What about the years and years?"

Anna Marston was still shaking as though through the heat an icy wind had blown upon her. Once more she was aware of Mary Barclay—vividly aware—but this time it was not with her physical eyes that she seemed to see her. There was no further illusion—if it had been illusion—of that indistinct figure bending above those little, unconscious heads, touching them, kissing them, enveloping them, like a bird hovering over its nest.

Instead there was, as it were, an inward vision. She and Mary Barclay were again face to face, but it was not in any way a pitiful entreaty for charity which she read in her friend's eyes. Rather it was a command.

"Dear Mrs. Van Duyne," said Anna, trying to bring her voice under control, "Mary Barclay knows that I am ready to take her place. She knows I—I want them—both of them—more than anything else in the world."

The first sigh of the coming coolness breathed past them from the sea. It was like the long breath of one who, after great restlessness, turns at last to sleep.

The Teacher

Luisa Valenzuela

Far too little of the rich literature by feminist magic realists writing in Spanish, Portuguese, and Catalan has been translated. The few recent short story collections available in English include María Luisa Bombal's New Islands *(1982), which was not translated until after her death; Clarice Lispector's* Foreign Legion Stories and Chronicles *(1986) and some of her other work; Mercè Rodereda's* My Christina and Other Stories *(1984); Lygia Fagundes Telles's* Tigrela *(1986); Silvina Ocampo's* Leopoldina's Dream *(1988); an anthology of Latin American women's fiction,* Other Fires *(1986); and the darkly fantastic works of Luisa Valenzuela.*

Valenzuela was born in Argentina in 1938, lived for several years in France and the United States, and now lives in Buenos Aires. She inherited her literary talent from her mother, also a writer, and grew up surrounded by her mother's writer friends, including Jorge Luis Borges. She wrote her first novel at the age of twenty. In 1967 her first short story collection was published. Her books in English translation include: Clara: Thirteen Short Stories and a Novel *(1976), which contains "The Teacher,"* Strange Things Happen Here: Twenty-six Short Stories and a Novel *(1979),* He Who Searches *(1982),* The Lizard's Tail *(1983),* Other Weapons *(1985), and* Open Door *(1988), titled after a lunatic asylum in Argentina.*

"The Teacher," a tale of black humor that turns to terror, uses fantasy to depict the fear, lust, and adoration men feel for women, and the contradictory

*roles of bitch, teacher, mother, and whore that those feelings impose on women.
The translation is by Hortense Carpentier and J. Jorge Castello.*

⫙

"She's going to be proud of me, yes, she is, when she learns that I faithfully followed the path she once marked out for me."

Mendizábal walked through the neighborhood of neat little houses and carefully groomed gardens, carrying along the memory of his history teacher, a memory as light and sweet as one of those passing loves that scarcely touch reality. With her hair in a bun, and low-heeled, sensible shoes on her feet, she had an austerity that removed her from time. With his diploma under his arm, Mendizábal felt he could at last face her again and discuss the great exploits of history, as he had learned to do, and praise the integrity of a past free of the foulness of more recent events.

At the wooden fence, he extended his hands to examine his perfectly manicured nails, he brushed the dandruff from his shoulders, and he arranged the point of his pale-pink handkerchief that peeked out of his breast pocket.

He opened the gate and entered, but when he got to the back-yard, instead of the mother, he found the children.

Jam was dripping from their chins, and judging by the way they were throwing bread at each other, they were angry enough to kill. He didn't realize that this was their usual diversion at teatime and that it always ended in the laughter that he mistook for shrieks of horror.

A hand holding a slice of bread paused in midair when Mendizábal appeared, and a howl was cut short by surprise, but only briefly, for these children couldn't remain still or surprised for very long.

Generously, they thought that the stranger might want to share in their games.

"Come on, come on, play war with us!"

"Let's go, let's go. . . ."

Mendizábal was alarmed and wanted to run away. She had children, of course, she adored children. If his memory wasn't playing tricks, some time back she had talked of twins, Aníbal and Augusta—that's right, pretty names with a historic ring. But, good heavens, the children facing him were animals, they didn't even look like children.

"Have a glass of milk with us. Don't stand there like a dummy."

"Shut up, stupid. He doesn't want that sissy stuff. You offer a man brandy."

"Once I drank half a bottle. . . ."

"Sure, and we had to put you to bed. And you spent the whole night

The Teacher/159

throwing up. It was a joke. Anybody can do crazy things, anybody, especially a person without a brain."

"Do you have a cigarette?"

"Stop that silly talk, or I'll punch you in the eye."

Mendizábal knew nothing of the magic world of children. He wished the ground would open up and swallow him. But a flicker of hope helped him recover his voice.

"Mrs. Ortiz? Is she your mother?"

"You've got the wrong house," he hoped they'd answer him. Or better still, "What mother? We don't know any Mrs. Ortiz. Go away."

But they stared at him with hostile eyes and said nothing. The silence became palpable, unfriendly. The children lowered their heads and nudged each other as if to hide something.

"Where's your mother?" Mendizábal persisted, looking at the oldest child.

They looked at each other out of the corners of their eyes, almost motionless. The youngest took a bread crumb and crushed it between his fingers while the others watched him covertly, stretching the spring of silence until it snapped and they all reacted at the same time. One of the boys kicked the cat that was rubbing against his legs, and the shrieks of the animal mingled with those of the children.

"What mother are you talking about? We don't have a mother. You're crazy. Get out of here, get out. We're sick and tired of you."

"Get out," they chorused, "get out!"

Mendizábal now understood that he had not been mistaken, for there they stood: identical twins with an identical lock of hair falling over their dark, hard eyes. He stood indecisively amidst that wild howling pack, staring at the shine of his shoes. Suddenly, beyond the noise of the children, he heard the creaking of the gate. The children's expressions altered with the sound, and Mendizábal knew that something was about to happen. The youngest girl jumped from her chair and ran to the house, calling, "Mama!"

The rest of the children reacted as if they shared a single impulse, colliding against the table and upsetting the milk. A few drops splattered Mendizábal's dark trousers. How could he greet her like that? He would have to wipe them clean.

Separating itself from the darkness beyond, a figure appeared in the door, clad in an enormous yellow raincoat, her head crowned by a hideous untidy bun, from which strands of hair fell, yellow and dirty like the raincoat. The figure advanced slowly toward Mendizábal, speaking in a hoarse voice.

"How are you, young man? I am Mrs. Ortiz. You probably don't remember me, which is just as well. It would be better if you didn't remember anything at all. Now you can go. I'm rushed. Forgive me."

It was Augusta, really, and Mendizábal wanted to ask her why she had disguised herself. But Augusta vanished, with the certainty of having fulfilled her duty. Before long, another strange character appeared, this time dressed in a bathrobe, with a tulle hat on her head. Now the voice was subdued.

"I am Mrs. Ortiz, of course, and I come to say good-by. I can't see you today. The truth is, I'll never be able to see you, though you may wish to try us again in a few years. With a bit of luck, you'll find us all dead, rotted, covered with flies. God bless you, my son. And good luck."

Seven Mrs. Ortizes paraded in front of Mendizábal. The last one reached only to his waist and walked entangled in a long muslin curtain. Each said good-by and asked him to leave, but his only thought was to stay long enough to discover the outcome of this madness.

At last, the real Mrs. Ortiz made her appearance. She was more grotesque than all the children's disguises put together. Her hair was short and adolescent-looking; she undulated rather than walked as she approached him with her lips ready. Mrs. Ortiz, teacher, mother, always so majestically out of his reach, how could she appear like that to him?

He thought he heard her say, "You are astonished, my dear Mendizábal. You find me changed, don't you? Well, it's to be expected, with so many young boys around. . . ."

What she really said was, "You are Mendizábal, right? With so many young boys around, I've lost track of the names by now. . . ."

"I think I was always a good student," he mumbled apologetically.

"That's why I remember your name. But now that you're grown up, I can confess to you that good students, bad students, curriculums, all that nonsense bores me."

"I've just received my history degree, like you . . ."

"Poor man. You'll see how arduous it is to live among faceless heroes that become stereotypes."

She smiled at him tenderly, and Mendizábal thought he heard what he once would have liked to hear: ". . . heroes with your face. Sometimes you were Attila, sometimes Alexander the Great. While I was conducting the class I would give their faces a mouth like yours, eyes like yours—following each of my gestures, adoring me. . . ."

But in truth she was saying: ". . . the boys who watched me with amusement in their eyes, the ones who fought in the back of the classroom, and all the things I had to do to maintain order. Now I'm free of all that, and so happy. I even look younger, right, children? I want to laugh, to have fun."

The children surrounded her, looking at her like puppies, a little afraid of their mistress's quick-changing moods. A spark of admiration escaped from their eyes and made them blush.

"Now go and play; I'll have a chat with Mendizábal, who has been so kind as to come and visit me."

There was a long silence as the sun began to set in all its sweetness, and she saw, in the pensive Mendizábal, still another child. She put her hand on his shoulder.

He jumped back in his chair and decided that he must run away and forget his old teacher, who was damned, possessed by the devil. He opened his mouth several times before he could finally shout, "I have to leave! I'm in a hurry, I have to leave. It's too late, too late."

"You always were a shy boy, but I thought age would cure you. I'll bring you a whisky. That'll calm you down."

"I must go. I must go."

She came closer and took him by the arm. "Don't be so nervous. Those thick glasses are all right in class, but you can take them off here. You look dazed."

She caressed his hair and lowered her hand to remove the glasses, but he slapped her so hard that his glasses flew off and dropped into the grass. Darkness overwhelmed him and he fell down on his knees to look for them. Suddenly, he thought he saw a woman's body moving around on all fours, wanting to rub against him, to coil her legs around his, to plant her hot, painted mouth inside his dry lips. And as he frantically searched in the grass for the glasses, his dim world filled with the shouts of children, who were coming in a group to sink him irretrievably into darkness and the heat of the woman.

He felt a tangle of legs and arms on top of him. With great effort, he extricated himself and crawled to the fence. He managed to get up and walk along the fence until he reached the gate. He opened it, then turned around to close it almost casually. He left the fiendish garden behind and moved toward salvation.

Behind him, the blows and shouts continued, as if in the confusion and anger they hadn't realized that he was far away, or as if they had all been blinded like him and were still fighting among themselves in the bushes and shrubs.

Death must be like the street, emerging from the fog constantly following him. But he was moving slowly, and life was finally able to overtake him. In a fresh uproar, the children were calling his name, destroying his peace.

"Hey, Mendizábal, come here!"

"Come here, we found your glasses."

"Your glasses, here!"

They had climbed up on top of the gate and were pushing one another, stretching out their arms to him.

"Here, here, we found them next to the orange tree."

He went toward them slowly; he felt some hands. When he put on his glasses he came back to life. Suddenly, everything returned to the quiet reality of a blue spring dusk, with no sign of the crisis he had just passed through. Mendizábal cursed the imagination that had played such nasty tricks on him. It had been a bad dream, and he thanked the trees, the clouds, and those seven blond children who were looking at him with pride while they said, "We love you a lot. We're your friends. Call us whenever you need us."

A bad dream, yes, had it not been for the silhouette of the teacher that he thought he saw behind the children's heads and beyond their laughter, trying in vain to get up from the ground.

The Ghost

⑊

Anne Sexton

Anne Harvey Sexton was born in Newton, Massachusetts, on November 9, 1928 and died of asphyxiation inside her idling automobile at the age of 45. She had spent much of her creative life chronicling personal, morbid, and frightening aspects of women's psyche.

Sexton was a student at Radcliffe College from 1961 until 1963, taught high school for one year, and taught at Boston University and Colgate University in the early 1970s. She received the Pulitzer Prize for Live or Die *(1967) and a Guggenheim Award in 1969. That same year her play* Mercy Street, *about a woman seeking safe haven across a landscape of insanity, was produced.*

She contributed to such major publications as Harper's, The New Yorker, Partisan Review, Hudson Review, The Nation, Saturday Review, *and* New World Writing. *Her volumes of poetry include* To Bedlam and Part Way Back *(1960),* The Death Notebooks *(1974), and* The Awful Rowing Toward God *(1975). Her poetry is preoccupied with death, depression, and the fantastic.* Transformations *(1971), her most fantasy-oriented and perhaps most accessible volume, is comprised of frightful revisions of once-innocent fairy tales. Not since Amy Lowell had there been a poet who could so easily wed shocking beauty with a taste for the macabre.*

Though primarily a poet, her sentiments and obsessions were perfectly suited to the supernatural horror story. Unfortunately, her regular editors rejected her best work in this vein. Three macabre stories, including "The Ghost," were published posthumously in Anne Sexton's Words for Dr. Y: Uncollected

Poems *(1978)*. *In the preface to that volume her sister stated, "Anne enjoyed writing these stories perhaps more than anything else she ever produced and was proud of the result," as indeed she should have been. The three stories are among the most gruesomely gorgeous weird tales ever written, achieving in a very few pages what* The Exorcist *required rough language and an entire novel to half way approach. To the feminist literature of madness and horror—which includes Virginia Woolf's "Lapin and Lapinova" and Charlotte Perkin Gilman's "The Yellow Wallpaper"—must be added Anne Sexton's "The Ghost."*

ılılı

I was born in Maine, Bath, Maine, Down East, in the United States of America, in the year of 1851. I was one of twelve (though only eight lasted beyond the age of three) and within the confines of that state we lived at various times in our six houses, four of which were scattered on a small island off Boothbay Harbor. They were not called houses on that island for they are summering places and thus entitled cottages. My father, at one time Governor, was actually a frustrated builder and would often say to the carpenters, "another story upwards, please." One house had five stories, and although ugly to look upon, stood almost at the edge of the rocks that the sea locked in and out of.

I was, of course, a Victorian lady, however I among my brothers and sisters was well educated and women were thought, by my father, to be as *interesting* as men, or as capable. My education culminated at Wellesley College, and I was well-versed in languages, both the ancient and unusable as well as the practical, for the years after Wellesley College I spent abroad perfecting the accent and the idiomatic twists. Later I held a job on a newspaper. But it was not entirely fulfilling and made no use of these foreign languages but only of the mother tongue. I was fortunately a maiden lady all my life, and I do say *fortunate* because it allowed me to adopt to maiden heart the nieces and nephews, the grandnieces, the grandnephews. And there was one in particular, my sister's grandchild, who was named after me. And as she wore my name, I wore hers, and at the end of my life she and her mother and an officious practical nurse stood their ground beside me as I went out. Death taking place twice. Once at sixty-four when my ears died and the most ignominious madness overtook me. Next the half-death of sixty shock treatments and then still deaf as a haddock—a half-life until seventy-seven spent in a variety of places called nursing homes. Dying on a hot day in a crib with diapers on. To die like a baby is not desirable and just barely tolerable, for there is fear spooned into you and radios playing in your head. I, the suffragette, I of the violet sachets, I who always changed my dress for dinner and kept my pride, died like a baby with my breasts bared, my corset, my camisole, tucked away, and every other covering that was my custom. I would have preferred the huntsman stalking me like a moose to that drooling away.

There is more to say of my lifetime, but my interest at this point, my main thrust, is to tell you of my life as a ghost. Life? Well, if there is action and a few high kicks, is that not similar to what is called life? At any rate, I *bother* the living, act up a bit, slip like a radio into their brains or a sharp torch-light going on suddenly to blind and then reveal myself. (With no explanation!) I can put a moan into my namesake's dog if I wish to make a point. (I have always liked to make my point!) It is *her* life I linger over, for she is wearing my name and that gives a ghost a certain right that no one knows when they present the newborn with a name. She is somewhat aware—but of course denies it as best she can—that there are any ghosts at all. However, it can be noted that she is unwilling to move into a house that is not newly made, she is unwilling to live within the walls that might whisper and tell stories of other lives. It is her ghost theory. But like many, she has made the perfect mistake; the mistake being that a ghost belongs to a house, a former room, whereas this ghost (and I can only speak for myself for we ghosts are not allowed to converse about how we go about practicing our trade) belongs to my remaining human, to bother her, to enter the human her, who once was given my name. I could surmise that there are ghosts of houses wading through the attics where once they hoarded their hoard, throwing dishes off shelves, but I am not sure of it. I think the English believe it because their castles were passed on from generation to generation. Indeed, perhaps an American ghost does something quite different, because the people of the present are very mobile, the executives are constantly thrown from city to city, dragging their families with them. But I do not know, for I haunt namesake's, and she lives in the suburbs of Boston—despite a few moves from new house to new house. I follow her as a hunting dog follows the scent, and as long as she breathes, I will peer in her window at noon and watch her sip the vodka, and if I so desire, can place one drop of an ailment into it to teach her a little lesson about such indulgence and imperfection. I gave her five years ago a broken hip. I immobilized her flat on the operating table as I peered over his shoulder, the surgeon said as he did a final x-ray before slicing in with his knife, "shattered," and there was namesake, her hip broken like a crystal goblet and later with two four-inch screws in her hip she lay in a pain that had only been an intimation of pain during the birth of two children. A longing for morphine dominated her hours and her conscience rang in her head like a bell tolling for the dead. She had at the time been committing a major sin, and I found it so abhorrent that it was necessary to make my ailment decisive and sharp. When the morphine was working, she was perfectly lucid, but as it wore off, she sipped a hint of madness and that too was an intimation of things to come. Later, I tried lingering fevers that were quite undiagnosable and then when the world became summer and the green leaves whispered, I sat upon leaf by leaf and called out with a voice of my youth and cried, "Come to us, come to us" until she finally pulled down each shade of the house to keep the leaves out of it—as best she could. Then there are the small things that I can do. I can tear the pillow from under her head at night and leave her as flat as I was when I lay dying and thus crawl into her dream and remind her of my death, lest it be her death. I do not in any way consider myself evil but rather a good presence, trying to remind her of the Yankee heritage, back to the Mayflower and William Brewster, or back to kings and queens of the Continent who married and intermarried. She is becoming altogether too modern, and when a man enters her, I am constantly standing at the bedside to observe and call forth a child to be named my name. I do not actually *watch* the copulation because it is an alien act to me, but I know full well what it should mean and have often plucked out a few of her birth control pills in hopes. But I fear it is a vain hope. She is perhaps too old to conceive, or if she should, the result might be imperfect. As I stand there at that bedside while this man enters her, I hum a little song into her head that we made up, she and I, when she was eight and we sang each year thereafter for years. We had kissed thirteen lucky times over the mistletoe that hung under a large chandelier and two door frames. This mistletoe was *our* custom and *our* act and tied the knot more surely year by year. The song that she sang haunted me in the madness of old age and now I let it enter her ear and at first she feels a strange buzzing as if a fly has been caught in her brain and then the song fills her head and I am at ease.

She senses my presence when she cooks things that are not to my liking, or drives beyond the speed limit, or makes a left turn when it says NO LEFT TURN. For I play in her head the song called "The Stanley Steamer" for Mr. Stanley's wife was my close friend and we took a memorable ride from Boston to Portland and the horses were not happy, but we disobeyed nothing and were cautious—though I must add, a bit dusty and a little worse for wear at the end of the trip.

It is unfortunate that she did not inherit my felicity with the foreign tongue. But not all can be passed on, the genes carry some but not all. As a matter of fact, it is far *more* unfortunate that she did not inherit my gift with the English language. But here I do interfere the most, for I put *my* words onto her page, and when she observes them, she wonders how it came about and calls it "a gift from the muse." Oh how sweet it is! How adorable! How the song of the mistletoe rips through the metal of death and plays on, singing from two mouths, making me a loyal ghost. Loyal though I am I have felt for a long time something missing from her life that she must experience to be whole, to be truly alive. Although one might say it be the work of the devil, I think that it is not (the devil lurks among the living and she must push him out day by day, but first he must enter her as he entered me in my years of deafness and lunacy). Thus I felt it quite proper and fitting to drop such a malady onto a slice of lemon that floated in her tea at 4 P.M. last August. It started immediately and became in the end immoderate. First the teacup became two tea-cups, then three, then four. Her cigarettes as she lit them in confusion tasted like dung and she stamped them out. Then she turned on the radio and all it would give at every station on the dial were the names and the dates of the dead. She turned it off quickly, but it would not stop playing. The dog chased her tail and then attacked the woodwork, baying at the moon as if their two bodies had gone awry. At that point, she sat very still. She kept telling herself to dial "O" for operator but could not. She shut her eyes, but they kept popping open to see the objects of the kitchen multiply, widen, stretch like rubber and their colors changing and becoming ugly and the lemon floated in the multiplying and dividing teacups like something made of neon.

When her husband returned home, she was as if frozen and could not speak, though I had put many words in her head they were like a game and were mixed and had lost their meaning. He shook her, she wobbled side to side. He spoke, he spoke. For an hour at least he tried for response then dialed the doctor, and she went into Mass. General, half carried, half walking like a drunk, feet numb as erasers, legs melting and stiffening and was given the proper modern physical and neuro-logical exams, EEG, EKG, etc., but the fly in her head still buzzed and the obituaries of the radio played on, and when they took her in an ambulance to a mental hospital, she could not sign her name on the commitment papers but spoke at last, "no name." They could not, those psychiatrists, nurses aides, diagnose exactly and most days she is not able to swallow. The tranquilizers they shot into her, variety after va-riety, have no power over *this*. I will give her a year of it, an exact to the moment year of it, and during that time, I will be constantly at her side to push the devil from her although there was no one in my time to push him from me. She is at this point enduring a great fear, but I am with her, I am holding her hand and she senses this despite her conviction that each needle is filled with Novocain, for that is the effect on her limbs and parts. Still, the slight pressure of my hand, the sound of the song of the mistletoe must comfort her. Right now they scream to her and fill her with an extraordinary terror. But somehow, I know full well she is indubitably pleased that I have not left. Nor do I plan to.

Three Dreams in a Desert

Under a Mimosa-Tree

⁂

Olive Schreiner

Anti-war radical and suffragist Olive Emilie Albertina Schreiner (1855–1920), the "mother of South African feminism," is revealed in Ruth First and Ann Scott's 1980 biography as a woman practically born with a mission. Today she is remembered mainly for the classic novel The Story of an African Farm (1883), an indictment of colonialism as gritty as Rebecca Harding Davis' Life in the Iron Mills (1861), but as stylish and with characters as unusual as Virginia Woolf at her best. Her own favorite works, however, were her allegories, which were wildly popular in the 1890s but are relatively neglected today.

Schreiner (pronounced SKRAY-ner) believed moral and political ideals were more successfully revealed in allegory than in polemics. Her "natural" method of inducing the free-flow of allegories is similar to later surrealist theories of direct contact with the subconscious; these short tales were written while in a trance-like state caused by long periods without eating or sleeping. There is a strong affinity between these stories and the surreal fables of Leonora Carrington in The Oval Woman (1975) and other volumes.

Most of the allegorical vignettes are no more than a page or two long. The best of them appear in Dreams (1890), published on four continents and in numerous editions. The rest of her allegories were collected posthumously as Dreams and Allegories (1923), equally worth obtaining. A small collection of short stories, Dream Life and Real Life (1893), is far more realistic in approach, although the title story includes a supernatural denouement in which a murdered girl saves her family from treachery.

"Three Dreams in the Desert," reprinted here from Dreams, *is one of the longer and more didactic of her poems-in-prose. It was written in the mid-1880s and read as a kind of "ABC train schedule," or guide, by militant feminists of the day in England and South Africa, who found in it a significant map to the future. Schreiner's acute belief in a sexually egalitarian future, conveyed in this tale, carried her through times of depression and disillusion.*

॥॥६

As I traveled across an African plain the sun shone down hotly. Then I drew my horse up under a mimosa-tree, and I took the saddle from him and left him to feed among the parched bushes. And all to right and to left stretched the brown earth. And I sat down under the tree, because the heat beat fiercely, and all along the horizon the air throbbed. And after a while a heavy drowsiness came over me, and I laid my head down against my saddle, and I fell asleep there. And, in my sleep, I had a curious dream.

I thought I stood on the border of a great desert, and the sand blew about everywhere. And I thought I saw two great figures like beasts of burden of the desert, and one lay upon the sand with its neck stretched out, and one stood by it. And I looked curiously at the one that lay upon the ground, for it had a great burden on its back, and the sand was thick about it, so that it seemed to have piled over it for centuries.

And I looked very curiously at it. And there stood one beside me watching. And I said to him, "What is this huge creature who lies here on the sand?"

And he said, "This is woman; she that bears men in her body."

And I said, "Why does she lie here motionless with the sand piled round her?"

And he answered, "Listen, I will tell you! Ages and ages long she has lain here, and the wind has blown over her. The oldest, oldest, oldest man living has never seen her move: the oldest, oldest book records that she lay here then, as she lies here now, with the sand about her. But listen! Older than the oldest book, older than the oldest re-corded memory of man, on the Rocks of Language, on the hard-baked clay of Ancient Customs, now crumbling to decay, are found the marks of her footsteps! Side by side with his who stands beside her you may trace them; and you know that she who now lies there once wandered free over the rocks with him."

And I said, "Why does she lie there now?"

And he said, "I take it, ages ago the Age-of-dominion-of-muscular-force found her, and when she stopped low to give suck to her young, and her back was broad, he put his burden of subjection on to it, and

Three Dreams in a Desert/171

tied it on with the broad band of Inevitable Necessity. Then she looked at the earth and the sky, and knew there was no hope for her; and she lay down on the sand with the burden she could not loosen. Ever since she has lain here. And the ages have come, and the ages have gone, but the band of Inevitable Necessity has not been cut."

And I looked and saw in her eyes the terrible patience of the centuries; the ground was wet with her tears, and her nostrils blew up the sand.

And I said, "Has she ever tried to move?"

And he said, "Sometimes a limb has quivered. But she is wise; she knows she cannot rise with the burden on her."

And I said, "Why does not he who stands by her leave her and go on?"

And he said, "He cannot. Look—"

And I saw a broad band passing along the ground from one to the other, and it bound them together.

He said, "While she lies there he must stand and look across the desert."

And I said, "Does he know why he cannot move?"

And he said, "No."

And I heard a sound of something cracking, and I looked, and I saw the band that bound the burden on to her back broken asunder; and the burden rolled on to the ground.

And I said, "What is this?"

And he said, "The Age-of-muscular-force is dead. The Age-of-nervous-force has killed him with the knife he holds in his hand; and silently and invisibly he has crept up to the woman, and with that knife of Mechanical Invention he has cut the band that bound the burden to her back. The Inevitable Necessity is broken. She might rise now."

And I saw that she still lay motionless on the sand, with her eyes open and her neck stretched out. And she seemed to look for something on the far-off border of the desert that never came. And I wondered if she were awake or asleep. And as I looked her body quivered, and a light came into her eyes, like when a sunbeam breaks into a dark room.

I said, "What is it?"

He whispered "Hush! the thought has come to her, 'Might I not rise?' "

And I looked. And she raised her head from the sand, and I saw the dent where her neck had lain so long. And she looked at the earth, and she looked at the sky, and she looked at him who stood by her: but he looked out across the desert.

And I saw her body quiver; and she pressed her front knees to the earth, and veins stood out; and I cried, "She is going to rise!"

But only her sides heaved, and she lay still where she was.

But her head she held up; she did not lay it down again. And he beside me said, "She is very weak. See, her legs have been crushed under her so long."

And I saw the creature struggle: and the drops stood out on her.

And I said, "Surely he who stands beside her will help her?"

And he beside me answered, "He cannot help her: *she must help herself.* Let her struggle till she is strong."

And I cried, "At least he will not hinder her! See, he moves farther from her, and tightens the cord between them, and he drags her down."

And he answered, "He does not understand. When she moves she draws the band that binds them, and hurts him, and he moves farther from her. The day will come when he will understand, and will know what she is doing. Let her once stagger on to her knees. In that day he will stand close to her, and look into her eyes with sympathy."

And she stretched her neck, and the drops fell from her. And the creature rose an inch from the earth and sank back.

And I cried, "Oh, she is too weak! she cannot walk! The long years have taken all her strength from her. Can she never move?"

And he answered me, "See the light in her eyes!"

And slowly the creature staggered on to its knees.

And I awoke: and all to the east and to the west stretched the barren earth, with the dry bushes on it. The ants ran up and down in the red sand, and the heat beat fiercely. I looked up through the thin branches of the tree at the blue sky overhead. I stretched myself, and I mused over the dream I had had. And I fell asleep again, with my head on my saddle. And in the fierce heat I had another dream.

I saw a desert and I saw a woman coming out of it. And she came to the bank of a dark river; and the bank was steep and high.[1] And on it an old man met her, who had a long white beard; and a stick that curled was in his hand, and on it was written Reason. And he asked her what she wanted; and she said "I am woman; and I am seeking for the land of Freedom."

And he said, "It is before you."

And she said, "I see nothing before me but a dark flowing river, and a bank steep and high, and cuttings here and there with heavy sand in them."

And he said, "And beyond that?"

She said, "I see nothing, but sometimes, when I shade my eyes with my hand, I think I see on the further bank trees and hills, and the sun shining on them!"

He said, "That is the Land of Freedom."

She said, "How am I to get there?"

He said, "There is one way, and one only. Down the banks of Labour through the water of Suffering. There is no other."

She said, "Is there no bridge?"

He answered. "None."

She said, "Is the water deep?"

He said, "Deep."

She said, "Is the floor worn?"

He said, "It is. Your foot may slip at any time, and you may be lost."

She said, "Have any crossed already?"

He said, "Some have *tried!*"

She said, "Is there a track to show where the best fording is?"

He said, "It has to be made."

She shaded her eyes with her hand; and she said, "I will go."

And he said, "You must take off the clothes you wore in the desert: they are dragged down by them who go into the water so clothed."

And she threw from her gladly the mantle of Ancient-received-opinions she wore, for it was worn full of holes. And she took the girdle from her waist that she had treasured so long, and the moths flew out of it in a cloud. And he said, "Take the shoes of dependence off your feet."

And she stood there naked, but for one white garment that clung close to her.

And he said, "That you may keep. So they wear clothes in the Land of Freedom. In the water it buoys; it always swims."

And I saw on its breast was written Truth; and it was white; the sun had not often shone on it; the other clothes had covered it up. And he said, "Take this stick; hold it fast. In that day when it slips from your hand you are lost. Put it down before you; feel your way: where it cannot find a bottom do not set your foot."

And she said, "I am ready; let me go."

And he said, "No—but stay; what is that—in your breast?"

She was silent.

He said, "Open it, and let me see."

And she opened it. And against her breast was a tiny thing, who drank from it, and the yellow curls above his forehead pressed against it; and his knees were drawn up to her, and he held her breast fast with his hands.

And Reason said, "Who is he, and what is he doing here?"

And she said, "See his little wings—"

And Reason said, "Put him down."

And she said, "He is asleep, and he is drinking! I will carry him to the Land of Freedom. He has been a child so long, so long, I have carried him. In the Land of Freedom he will be a man. We will walk together there, and his great white wings will overshadow me. He has lisped one word only to me in the desert—'Passion!' I have dreamed he might learn to say 'Friendship' in that land."

And Reason said, "Put him down!"

And she said, "I will carry him so—with one arm, and with the other I will fight the water."

He said, "Lay him down on the ground. When you are in the water you will forget to fight, you will think only of him. Lay him down." He said, "He will not die. When he finds you have left him alone he will open his wings and fly. He will be in the Land of Freedom before you. Those who reach the Land of Freedom, the first hand they see stretching down the bank to help them shall be Love's. He will be a man then, not a child. In your breast he cannot thrive; put him down that he may grow."

And she took her bosom from his mouth, and he bit her, so that the blood ran down on to the ground. And she laid him down on the earth; and she covered her wound. And she bent and stroked his wings. And I saw the hair on her forehead turned white as snow, and she had changed from youth to age.

And she stood far off on the bank of the river. And she said, "For what do I go to this far land which no one has ever reached? *Oh, I am alone! I am utterly alone!*"

And Reason, that old man, said to her, "Silence! what do you hear?"

And she listened intently, and she said, "I hear a sound of feet, a thousand times ten thousand and thousands of thousands, and they beat this way!"

He said, "They are the feet of those that shall follow you. Lead on! make a track to the water's edge! Where you stand now, the ground will be beaten flat by ten thousand times ten thousand feet." And he said, "Have you seen the locusts how they cross a stream? First one comes down to the water-edge, and it is swept away, and then another comes and then another, and then another, and at last with their bodies piled up a bridge is built and the rest pass over."

She said, "And, of those that come first, some are swept away, and are heard of no more; their bodies do not even build the bridge?"

"And are swept away, and are heard of no more—and what of that?" he said.

"And what of that—" she said.

"They make a track to the water's edge."

"They make a track to the water's edge—." And she said, "Over that bridge which shall be built with our bodies, who will pass?"

He said, *"The entire human race."*

And the woman grasped her staff.

And I saw her turn down that dark path to the river.

And I awoke; and all about me was the yellow afternoon light: the sinking sun lit up the fingers of the milk bushes; and my horse stood by me quietly feeding. And I turned on my side, and I watched the ants run by thousands in the red sand. I thought I would go on my way now—the afternoon was cooler. Then a drowsiness crept over me again, and I laid back my head and fell asleep.

And I dreamed a dream.

I dreamed I saw a land. And on the hills walked brave women and brave men, hand in hand. And they looked into each other's eyes, and they were not afraid.

And I saw the women also hold each other's hands.

And I said to him beside me, "What place is this?"

And he said, "This is heaven."

And I said, "Where is it?"

And he answered, "On earth."

And I said, "When shall these things be?"

And he answered, "IN THE FUTURE."

And I awoke, and all about me was the sunset light; and on the low hills the sun lay, and a delicious coolness had crept over everything; and the ants were going slowly home. And I walked towards my horse, who stood quietly feeding. Then the sun passed down behind the hills; but I knew that the next day he would arise again.

Note

1. The banks of an African river are sometimes a hundred feet high, and consist of deep shifting sands, through which in the course of ages the river has worn its gigantic bed.

The Fall

Armonía Somers

Armonía Somers is the nom de plume *of Armonía Etchepare de Henestrosa,
an Uruguayan author born in 1918 who is little known even in her own country.
Her fiction has been compared to that classic novel of French symbolism,* Mal-
doror *by Latreamont, considered by some to be the most "evil" document ever
concocted by the human mind and an inspiration to the modern surrealists who
fueled the development of fantasy in Canada, Mexico, South America, France,
and to a lesser extent in the United States.*

*Under her own name, Somers has published books on education. Her first
novel was published in 1950, and her collected stories were issued in 1968. "The
Fall" (1967) is one of only two of her stories available in English. By the
evidence of this story, hers is a voice unique even among feminist magic realists,
among whom such flamboyant apostasy is nearly unheard of.*

*"The Fall" is a radical revision of the character of the Virgin Mary. Legends
of the Virgin Mary are found in all nations where Catholicism has played a role,
in both modern and medieval literature. Such tales tend toward aestheticism and
the deification of woman; they commonly include no evidence of a God above,
but only of the Child, helpless in Her arms. Feminist legends of Mary include
Marguerite Yourcenar's "Our-Lady-of-the-Swallows" in* Oriental Tales
*(1985), about Her mercy toward pagan nymphs, and Selma Lagerlöf's "Sigrid
Storräde" in* From a Swedish Homestead *(1901), about a pagan Amazon's
battle with a Christian king, with Mary a gloomy power overseeing the suppres-
sion of paganism and the martyrdom of Her devotee. To some degree all such*

stories accept the common, patriarchally defined Goddess as a nurturing, melancholy virgin, but Somers's tale undoes almost two thousand years of mythologizing. Perhaps the appearance of an anti-Catholic attitude is what has made her work unpopular in Latin America. To my mind, this portrait of Mary is thoroughly liberating as She casts off the role of virgin, nurturer, and mercy-bringer.

This translation, from Other Fires: Short Fiction by Latin American Women, *is by Alberto Manguel, the editor of that collection.*

⫴

"Still raining. Damn you, Holy Virgin, damn you. Why, why is it still raining?" Too dark a thought for his black voice, for the soft saliva-tasting humble black sounds. That's why he had only imagined the words. He could never allow them to escape, into the air. And even as a thought they were something wicked, something bad for his white negro conscience. He had always prayed, spoken, differently; like a lover:

"Help me, my Lady, white Rose of the rose-bush. Help this poor nigger who killed the big brute of a white man, who did just that, today. My only Rose, please help him, my Heart of sweet almond, bring this nigger a little good luck, my bright garden Rose."

But not tonight. It was cold and it was raining. His bones were drenched to the point where the cold hurt the bone. He had lost one of his shoes walking in the mud, and his toes had come out through the other one. Every time a sharp stone lay in his path, the bare toes would hit against it violently, against that stone and not another, never against a smooth, round stone. And the blow on the toes was hardly painful compared to the savage pain that soared up the branches of his body and then fell back again, back to his toes, gripping onto them, hard, painfully hard. It was at times like these that he felt unable to understand his white, white Rose. How could She do this to him? Because the sweet Lady should have warned him that the stone was there, in his way. She should have made it stop raining so hard, so hard and cold.

The black man kept his hands stuffed into his pockets, his hat pulled down to his shoulders, the old suit buttoned up as far as the few buttons allowed. But the suit was no longer a suit; it was a rag, sodden, shining, as slippery as spit. The body was shaped under the cloth, showing perfect, harmonious black curves. And also—he kept saying to himself—She should have made night fall faster. He had needed night so much throughout the day. There was not a single hole left out there to hide this nigger's fear, in the blazing light. And only now had the white Rose sent him the gift of night.

The black man's tread was slow, persistent. Like the rain, it neither quickened nor slackened its pace. At times he and the rain seemed to know each other too well to be enemies, fighting one another, but not wounding their opponents. Also, the rain made music.

He arrived at last. How he had longed for this place! A short distance from paradise his eyes would not have shone as bright. Yes: the ramshackle house stood there alone, in the night. He had never been inside, but he had heard of it. More than once he had been told about this "safe place," but that was all.

"My rose-white Lady!"

This time he called Her with a full voice. A bolt of lightning cut out his figure, bony and long and black, against the night. Then a blast in the sky, a rough, painful blow, sharp like the one against his toes. He touched his thighs through the ripped lining of his pockets. No, he hadn't vanished into the ground. He felt suddenly happy, humbly and tenderly happy to be still alive. And the bolt had allowed him to see the house clearly. He could have sworn he had seen it move during the blast. But the house had steadied itself, like a woman recovering from a fainting spell. All around the house were ruins, where they had swept away those shacks by the river. Prostitution had made its nest there some years ago, but now all that was left was rubble, these walls left standing because of some unexplained whim. He saw it all, admiring the beautiful hovel, its lost loneliness, its locked-in silence. Now he not only saw it; he could almost touch it if he wanted to. But then, just like someone who is about to reach what he most wants, the black man felt he did not dare. He had walked so long, suffered so much to get here, that it all now seemed unreal, inviolate. The house. On both sides were bits of wall, desolate heaps of rubbish, piles of mud. With each flash of lightning the house appeared again. Everywhere he could see vertical cracks. Also a low door, and two windows, one at the front, one at the side.

The black man, with almost sacrilegious terror, knocked on the door. His fingers hurt, stiff, petrified by the cold. The rain kept falling. He knocked a second time; still no one came to open. He wanted to seek cover, but the house had no eaves, nothing hospitable on the outside. It had been different, walking under the rain. It had seemed different to brave the drifting heavens, out there. The real rain was not like this. The real rain was the one borne by the toes, the stones, all anchored things. It was only then that one could say it rained within, that the liquid world weighed down, destroyed, dissolved. For the third time he knocked with cold, stone fingers, black onyx fingers with tender yellow rose-tips. The fourth time he used his fist. And here the black man made a mistake; he thought they had come to open because he had knocked louder.

The fourth time was the number of the code established by the house. A man appeared carrying a shaded lamp.

"Master, master, let this poor nigger in."

"Go on, damn you, get in!"

He closed the door behind him and lifted the lamp, black with soot, as high as he could. The negro was tall, as if on stilts. And the other man, damn it, was short. He could see his face. It was white, wrinkled vertically, like plaster scratched with nails. From the corner of his lips to the edge of his left eyebrow ran a savage scar of unmistakable origin. The scar followed the line of the lips, the thin lips, making the whole mouth look enormous and lopsided, all the way up to the eyebrow. The eyes were piercing and small, with no lashes, and the nose was Roman. The black man snapped out of the gaze and said in a honeyed voice:

"How much, master?"

"Two prices, you choose. Quickly, nigger. Ten for the camp bed, two for the floor," came the reply, harsh, while the man shielded the lamp with his hand.

That was it. Ten cents and two. The bed, the luxury, the solitary bed lay almost always empty.

The black man looked at the floor. Full. From the bodies rose a unified snore, heaving like sounds from a midnight swamp.

"I'll take the two cents one, master," he said humbly, bending over.

The man with the scar lifted his lamp once more, and wound his way back among the bodies. The black man followed him along the twisting path, like a dog. For the time being, the white man did not care whether the visitor had money with him or not. He would find out once the negro fell asleep, even though the search was usually fruitless. Only someone who had been tricked would arrive here with money. The house was a tramp's establishment, the last refuge on a doorless night. He could not remember whether he had ever rented out the bed. Now it had become the owner's own.

"There you are. Lie down," he said at last, stopping, his voice as sharp and cold as the cut on his face. "Naked or as you are. You're lucky, you'll be between these two heaps. But if another one arrives you'll have to make room for him. This ditch is large enough for two, or three, or twenty."

The black man looked down from his height. In the broken floor, no one knew why, was a kind of valley, soft and warm like the space between two bodies.

He was about to take his clothes off. He was about to become part of the sea of heaving backs, stomachs, snores, smells, ghoulish dreams, sighs, moans. It was then, after the white man had blown out the light next to the single bed, that he discovered the image of the white Rose Herself, with a small flickering flame burning in oil, high upon a shelf on the wall he was supposed to be facing.

"Master, master!"

"Will you shut up?"

"Tell me," he asked, ignoring the order, "Do you believe in the white Lady?"

The raw laugh of the scarred man on the bed cut through the air.

"Me? Believe? You ignorant nigger! I've got Her there just in case She's in charge, eh? That way She can see to it that the roof doesn't fall down on me."

He was about to laugh again, that laugh so like his face, but he couldn't finish it. A blast of thunder that seemed to come from underneath the earth shook the house. It was different in here, thought the black man. It drummed inside his guts, deep inside him. Then the rain, the wind, whipped up again. The side window was being furiously beaten; it seemed to shake in an epileptic fit.

Above the sounds, the black man's strong smell took over. It seemed to drown them, the sounds, the other smells, as if fighting against them all.

Sleep. But how? If he kept his clothes on, it would be like sleeping in water. If he took them off, the skin on his bones would feel drenched. He chose the skin, thinking that it would somehow lend warmth to the icy puddles. And he let himself fall into the ditch, stark naked. The light of the Virgin's lamp began to turn softer, clearer, as if the shadows had fed the oil, black as the black man's skin. From the Virgin's wall to the wall opposite someone had hung a dirty gauze, flapping obsessively, swinging in the seeping wind. It was a sample of the ancient weaving that had grown within the house. Every time the wind grew stronger, the gauze's dance became more dazzling, maddening. The black man covered his ears and thought, "If I were deaf I still wouldn't be free of the wind. I'd see it, Holy Mother, in that spider's web, I'd see it, and I'd die from seeing it."

He began to shiver. He touched his forehead; it seemed on fire. At times his whole body seemed to burn. Then it would fall into ice, shaking and sweating. He wanted to wrap himself up in something, but what? No use. He'd have to brave it naked, powerless, in the ditch. How was he to stand the shivering, the sweating, the helplessness, the cold? No way of knowing. And the pain in his back was stabbing him. He tried to close his eyes, to sleep. Perhaps in sleep he'd forget it all. There was much to forget, not only his body. What he had done that day with these, his hands, now part of the pain in his flesh. . . .

But first he tried looking at the Lady. There She stood, tender, soft, white, watching over the sleepers. The man had a dark thought. How could She be there, among so many lost souls, in the midst of that dirty human mass from which a strong stench arose, a filthiness of bodies and rags, fetid breath, crimes, vices, bad dreams? He looked at the strong mixture of men, sins and lice, spread out on the floor, snoring, while She, on Her shelf, kept on quietly shining.

And he? He thought about himself, saw his own nakedness. He was the worst of the lot. The others at least didn't show their flesh to the Virgin as he did, their uncovered shame. He should hide that, not offend the Immaculate Eyes, cover it somehow. He tried. But he couldn't bring himself to do it. Cold, heat, shivers, a stab in the back, dead will, longing for sleep. He couldn't, perhaps he would never be able to, ever again. He'd lie forever in this ditch, unable to cry out that he was dying, unable to pray to the Good Lady, beg Her forgiveness for his coal-black nakedness, his jutting bones, his overpowering odour, and worse, for what his hands had done.

It was then that it happened. The white Rose began to climb down from Her shelf, very slowly. Up there She had seemed to him as small as a doll—small, compact, shapeless. But as She descended She grew—carnal, sweet, alive. The black man felt he was dying. His fear and his surprise were larger than himself, outgrew him. He tried to touch his own body, make sure of his presence, simply to believe in something. But he couldn't. Outside his pain and shivering, he felt nothing. Everything seemed impossible, faraway, like another world lost in another time. Except for this: the approaching Woman.

The white Rose wouldn't stop. Her descent was something decisive, like running water, like rising light. But the most terrible thing about it was the direction of Her movement. Could one doubt that She was coming towards him, towards *him,* the most naked and filthy of men? Now She was almost by his side. He could see Her dainty shoes of golden glazed earthenware, the rim of Her pale blue cloak.

The black man tried to get up. Useless. His terror, his trembling, his shame, had nailed him with his back to the ground. Then he heard the voice, the sweetest honey life can offer:

"Tristan. . . ."

Yes, he remembered being called that in a faraway time on the other side of that door. It was therefore true; the Lady had come down, Her earthenware feet were real, the trimming of Her cloak was true. He would have to answer or die. He would have to speak, acknowledge the arriving Flower. He tried to swallow. Thick, bitter, insufficient spit. But it helped, a little.

"You, white rose-bush Rose. . . ."

"Yes, Tristan. Can you move?"

"No, my Lady. I don't know why. Everything stays up here, in the thoughts, and won't go down to my body. I can't believe it's You, my clear Pearl, I can't believe it."

"It is true, Tristan. Don't doubt Me."

Then, incredibly, the Virgin knelt by his side. It had always been otherwise; now the Virgin humbled Herself before a black man.

"Holy Mother of God, don't do that! No, my solitary Rose on the bush, don't do that!"

"Yes, Tristan, and not only kneel, which hurts Me terribly. Other things I'll do tonight that I never dared do. And you will help Me."

"Help You, Water Lily? With these hands that will do nothing now, but that today. . . . Oh, I can't tell You, my Lady, what they've done! Rose of amber, forgive this good nigger who turned bad on this black day!"

"Give Me that hand you killed with, Tristan."

"How do You know it was a nigger who killed that man, my Lady?"

"Don't talk like an unbeliever, Tristan. Give Me your hand."

"I can't lift it. . . ."

"Then I will come to the hand," She said with a voice that seemed to grow less vague, more alive.

And now a new impossibility occurred in that descent. The Virgin pressed Her waxen lips against the hard, bony hand of the black man, and kissed it.

"Holy Mother of God, I can't resist it!"

"Yes, Tristan. I've kissed the hand you killed with. And I will tell you why. It was I who told you the words you heard inside you: *Don't stop, press harder, finish with him now, don't hesitate!*"

"You, Mother of the Child!"

"Yes, Tristan, and you have said the word. They killed my Child. They would kill Him again, were He to return. I won't go on. I want no more pearls, prayers, tears, perfume, songs. Someone had to be the first to pay; you helped Me. I've waited peacefully, but now I've understood that I must begin. My Child, my poor and sweet Child, sacrificed in vain! How I cried, how I soaked in tears His torn and mangled body! Tristan, you don't know the worst."

"What, Little Mother?"

"I could never cry after that day for His loss. Since I was made marble, wax, sculpted wood, gold, ivory, I've had no tears. I had to carry on living this way, with a lie of stupid smiles painted on My face. Tristan, I was not what they have painted. I was different, certainly less beautiful. And I have come to tell you something."

"Yes, my Lady. Tell this nigger."

"Tristan, you will be frightened by what I am about to do."

"I am dying of fright, my Lily, but I am still alive."

"Tristan," said the Virgin, Her voice more sure, almost more human. "I will lie by your side. Didn't the white man say there was room for two here in the ditch?"

"No, no, Little Mother! My tongue is fainting, I can hardly ask You any longer not to do it!"

"Tristan, do you know what you are doing? You are praying, ever since you saw Me. No one has ever prayed like this to Me before. . . ."

"I'll sing You a sweeter tune, I'll sing and cry like the reeds, but please, please don't lie by the side of this bad nigger!"

"Yes, Tristan, I am doing it. Watch Me do it!"

And the black man saw how the figure lay down by his side with a rustle of silk and necklaces, with Her smell of time and virginity mingled in Her hair.

"And now comes the most important part, Tristan. You must take these clothes off Me. Start with the shoes. They are instruments of torture, as if made of rigid iron, destroying My feet on which I must stand throughout the centuries. Take them off, Tristan, please. I can bear them no longer."

"Yes, I will free Your feet in pain with these sinner's hands. That, yes, clear Lady."

"Oh, Tristan, the relief! But you haven't finished, Tristan. See how ridiculous they look, My feet. They are made of wax: feel them, made of wax."

"Yes, my Lady of the waxen feet, they are of wax."

"But now you will learn something important, Tristan. Inside the waxen feet I have got feet of flesh and blood."

"Holy Mother, You are killing me!"

"Yes, I am flesh and blood under the wax."

"No, no, Little Mother. Go back on the shelf. This nigger doesn't want the Holy Mother of flesh to lie by his side in the dark. Go back, sweet Rose, go back to Your place of roses!"

"No, Tristan, I'm not going back. When a Virgin has left her site She can never go back to it. I want you to melt My wax. I cannot be the Immaculate; I am the true Mother of the Child they killed. I need to walk, hate, cry on this earth. I need to be of flesh, not cold and lifeless wax."

"And how can I, sweet Lady, melt the wax?"

"Touch me, Tristan, fondle Me. A moment ago your hands would not answer. Since I kissed them they are moving. You understand what your touch will do. Start now. Touch My waxen feet, you will see how the cast melts."

"Yes, my wonderful Pearl, that, yes. Your feet must be set free, in spite of stones. And I will touch them, there. And I can feel it happening, Little Mother. Look, look how the wax melts in my fingers. . . ."

"And now touch my real feet, Tristan."

"They are two live gardenias, two feet made of flowers. . . ."

"But that is not enough. Go on and free My legs."

"The Rose's legs? No, I can't, I can't go on melting. That frightens me. This nigger is very frightened."

"On, Tristan, on."

"I can feel the knee, my captive Lady. And that is all. Here I stop this savage deed, this nigger deed. . . . I swear I'll stop. Cut off my hands, sweet Mother of the Blond Child, cut them off. And make this nigger forget he ever had these hands, forget he touched the Holy Flower's stem. Cut them off, with a knife sharpened in blood."

A furious blast thundered through the night. The windows beat against their frames, shaking. The house quivered like a ship.

"Have you heard, have you seen how things are tonight? If you don't continue melting, everything will be over for Me before morning. Go on, hurry, finish melting My thighs. I need My whole legs to be Mine once again."

"Yes, soft thighs, terror of this lost nigger. Here they are, warm and silky, like lizards under a winter's sun. But no more, Little Virgin. See how I cry. These tears are my blood aching inside this nigger."

"Have you heard, Tristan, and seen? The house is shaking once more. Don't be afraid of My thighs. Go on, go on melting."

"But we are near the golden bud, my Lady. The locked garden. I can't, I shouldn't!"

"Touch it, Tristan, touch that, especially that. When the wax there melts you need go no further. Then the wax on My breasts, on My back, on My belly, will melt on their own. Do it, Tristan. I want you to do it."

"No, my Lady. Not the golden bud. That I can't."

"It will still be the same, Tristan. Do you think it will change because you've touched it?"

"But it is not only touching it. It is that one can want it so much, with one's blood, with this crazy nigger blood. Have pity, my Lady. This nigger doesn't want to lose himself forever. With tears I beg You to leave him."

"Do it. Look Me in the eyes and do it."

Then the black man lifted his eyes up to the Virgin and saw two forget-me-nots sparkling with celestial fire, like the breath of a chimera. He could no longer disobey. He felt She would consume him.

"I knew it, I knew it. Why did I do it? Why did I touch it? Now I want to enter, now I want to sink into the dampness of that garden.

Now this poor nigger can stand it no longer. Look, forbidden Lady, how this nigger's life is trembling, how his mad blood is rising to choke him. I knew I should not have touched it. Let me enter that tight ring, my captive Lady, and then kill this nigger trapped in his own disgrace."

"Tristan, you won't, you won't. You have achieved something greater. Do you know what you've done?"

"Yes, sweet Palm Tree of this nigger's dreams. Yes, I know the terrible thing I've done."

"No, you don't know all of it. You have melted a Virgin. What you now want is unimportant. It is enough for a man to know how to melt a Virgin. That is a man's true glory."

"That's too hard for this poor nigger's head. That's for the clear head of One Who comes from Heaven."

"Tristan: another thing you don't know. Tristan: you're dying."

The black man sank his head between the Woman's breasts, among the smell of blossoming flowers.

"I had forgotten, Little Mother!" he suddenly cried out, as if possessed. "It has come back to me, here, in Your Childless milk! They want to lynch me! I have touched one of their creatures! Let me go, sweet Lady, let me get away! Let me escape! Let me go, Little Mother, let me go!"

"Not so loud, Tristan, the others on the floor will wake up," said the Woman softly, as in a lullaby. "Keep quiet. Nothing can touch you now. Can you hear? The wind. This house hasn't fallen because I am here. But something worse could happen to it, even with Me under its roof. Be sure."

"What? What could that be?"

"I'll tell you. They have hunted all day. Only this place remains; they left it till the last, as usual. In a few seconds they'll be here. They will come because you killed that brute. And they won't care if you're dying naked in this hole. They will trample the others, they will fall on you. They will drag you outside by an arm or a leg."

"Little Mother, don't let them!"

"No, I won't let them. How could I? You are the one who helped Me come out of My wax. I won't forget you."

"How will You stop them from catching me alive?"

"I only have to leave by that window. Now I have feet that move; you gave them to Me," She said in a secret whisper. "They will knock. You know how many times they must knock. At the fourth knock the white man will leave his bed. They will come to get you. But I won't be there. If you were not dying I'd take you with Me, We'd jump through the window together. But in these cases Our Father can do more than I can. You cannot escape your death. All I can do is stop them catching you alive."

"And then, Holy Mother?" said the black man, kneeling up in spite of his weakness.

"You know, Tristan, what will happen without Me in this house."

"Listen.... They're knocking. That's the first time...."

"Tristan, upon the second knock We will hold each other tightly," the Woman whispered, also rising to Her knees.

The man with the scar heard the knocking and stood up. He lit the lamp.

"Now, Tristan."

The black man held the Virgin tight. He sniffed Her real hair, real woman's hair, then pressed his face against Her human cheek.

The third knock on the door. The scarred man moved among the sleepers on the floor. This was not the usual kind of knocking, the kind he recognized. This was a knocking with a full stomach, with a gun in the hand.

At that very moment the Woman opened the side window. Thin and light like a half-moon, She needed barely the slightest gap to escape. A sad, languid wind carried her away into the night.

"Mother, Mother, don't leave me! That was the fourth knock! I remember what their death is like! Any death, except theirs!"

"Shut up, you stupid nigger!" said the white man. "I bet it's because of you they're here. You swine! I thought as much!"

Then it happened. They entered like flung stones, full of eyes. They went straight towards the black man, holding their lamps ahead of them, treading, kicking the others like rotten fruit. An infernal wind followed them in. The house began to shake again, as it had done several times that night. But the Virgin was no longer in the house. There was a crack, like a skeleton snapping. Then, a world falling apart—the rumble that can be heard before something crumbles down, before a fall.

It happened. Suddenly. Over everyone, over the dead man and over the ones who had come to drag him out.

Of course the rain had stopped. The wind seemed freer, harsher and more naked, licking up the dust, the dust of annihilation.

Pandora Pandaemonia

ıllıı

Jules Faye

Jules Faye, born in 1958, lived for 11 years in San Francisco, where she was a co-owner of a women's printing company, Anarchy Press. The sadness of drug and alcohol abuse and friends dying drove her from San Francisco's Castro District, and she moved to Seattle to calm down, obtain a dreary job that barely pays the rent, and pursue her art and writing.

Her first short stories appeared in the little magazine Fantasy Macabre *and the anthology* Tales by Moonlight II *(1989). Her story "A Light from Out of Our Heart" is about a night-long sortie by a lone woman and a cat across San Francisco's preternatural slumscape; "The Cafe of the Beautiful Assassins" is an equally weird and gorgeous tale of alternative realities. "The Promenade of Misshapen Animals"—told in a manner reminiscent of South American magic realism—is the tale of a sensual and daring woman seeking to bed Death and survive the encounter.*

"Pandora Pandaemonia," published here for the first time, tears apart many patriarchal myths, symbols, and ideas, in much the same manner as Leonora Carrington's short stories and Armonía Somers's "The Fall," reconstructing them as they might have been in a more matriarchally inclined world. Whether that world is of the distant future is difficult to say. This use of the fantastic to redefine and rebuild has become common in modern feminist stories, though rarely with such perfect surrealist technique or aesthetic language.

On Thousand Shrine Island I walk in quiet awe among the spreading ruins of once sacred gardens. Peach and pomegranate groves left untamed reach out limbs across the summer wind to twist and lock in gnarled kisses. Many trees have fallen uprooted in their wilderness and from their fused embrace; bark of pomegranate enfolds withered bark of peach; new saplings rise, haloed in the infant green of newborn leaf.

Creeping stems and vines reach out to touch the hairs along my thighs and whisper homage to the women who tended these fields and woods so long ago. Thorn and thistle prick my knees and ankles, catch at my naked toes and sing histories of priestesses who walked along these same paths, priestesses who had once been honored for their fierce devotion to a great and generous Creatrix. But then had all vanished, say the weeds curling at my feet, generations ago; with their holy arts and sciences they fled into the very soil of the magnificent temple gardens.

I push away the sighing reach of fragile stems and leaves, stumbling from the woeful invitation to sink amid skeletal fingertips of seeding grass. I must tear myself from the pull to lie among the weeds mourning for this great loss of life and I stomp from density of trees into a flowered clearing.

This wing of the garden lays wide and sweet and edged with blues and lavenders of iris. A gentle breeze caresses swaying grasses. Along a subtle rise of earth lay three gigantic toppled vases, ringed and thick and beckoning like great reclining queens. I move towards the central vase like a bird, my arms stretched wide as my hands close along the black curved surface of its rim. As I step inside I am swallowed in a warm familiar darkness and am filled with such a sense of welcome, as if this were my home, my hearth, the very belly of my hungering existence.

The inner walls are fashioned with a multiplicity of intricate designs, geometrical patterns, petroglyphic symbols inlaid with ancient shards of glass, broken tile and shining bits of bone and teeth. A spiral-legged table stand before me littered with bubbling tubes and pots. Beads and stones and dice are cast amidst a spread of maps and paper charts. Thin plumes of smoke creep silently along the walls thickening the air with a pungent heat.

Working at the table is a woman, mad and wild, with burning hair and eyes like onyx, black and cold and pitiless. She stands, her eyes locking mine, and comes to me like a lover to embrace me. My flesh, my blood respond as if I've held her many times before and as I lift her in my arms, my body is sheathed in a black, black skin, hard and solid next to her airy moon-colored dresses. With her tongue she reaches

Pandora Pandaemonia/189

down the length of my longing and touches the numbed places in my body and I burn beneath her breath.

Yet, I do not know her. I set her down before me and step away, asking, begging, "Who are you?"

She lifts her robes whirling above her head to unleash the light from her breasts which pours into my blackness as she speaks.

"I am the spirit of every woman who has ever fought or loved fiercely. I am Death and the Spirit of Life in Death. My body is burdened with the things which have murdered womens' lives; my burning hair, my stone cold eyes, my dagger hands. And yet I live. I wait. I weep. I ache violently to be remembered."

Then blood is pouring from her mouth, her throat, her womb and with her claws she rents open her glowing breast, tears out her steaming heart and holds it in her palm.

"Eat this and you will know my life."

And I am deathly thirsty. I eat the heart as floods of tears flow from my eyes and carry us bound together into a great red salt sea. She carries me like a sailing ship, rocking me to sleep in her warm embrace and dreaming I begin to remember.

A red sun rises over a black sea. I stand rocking in its lap within a great warship with tattered sails and banners flapping naked in the wind. My crew of piratesses stands gripping the rails for we have found the thing we sought. The sea around the ship begins to roil and lash about; thick bubbles belch from its darkest pit. We are tossed about like bits of sand.

Then, bursting from the pitch black sea, a great beast rises. Its head is bigger than the ship, its eyes more brilliant than the sun. It whips the tip of its tongue across my chest, ripping open my left teat and cutting to the bone. Then it rises on its serpent's neck twenty feet into the air, throws back its massive head and shatters our minds with its piercing song.

As I lie deaf and bleeding on the rattling planks of my torn and beaten vessel, I cannot tear my eyes away from this enormous beast. Convinced I am looking straight into the face of either God or Devil, one, I beg of it, "Take me! Take me! Fear is nothing next to you! And Life is less than empty after having looked into your burning eye!" Then it rises up on wings that split the blood-red sky in two and from its fifty hanging teats it drenches us with sweet white rain. So that I might serve Her in the afterlife, I reach up to Her and scream, "Devour me!"

I awaken lying in the weeds of the island gardens, stretched across the path devoted to the Shrines of Deities. Above my head stands a small stone dragon with teats of inlaid mother-of-pearl and eyes of crystal sulfur. She rises angrily from a turbulent obsidian sea. I bow to the marble serpent, brush the dirt from her brow and pluck out dandelion seeds that have caught in her teeth.

Slowly I turn away to make my way back to the entrance of the gardens. I'm elated but exhausted by the dreams and visitations of the day. It has become quite late by now. The sun is setting and I still have a long journey home. I walk through drooping lilacs and lemon trees whose limbs bend almost to the ground, heavy with fruit. When I reach the island shore I turn back to gaze across the forgotten garden wilderness. I thank the island for her generosity with me, then turn to follow the white sandy beach to where I've tied my little boat.

But on the way I step onto the sharp poisoned quills of a purple sea urchin. It pierces the naked flesh of my foot and I fall paralyzed in the warm sand. The sun sets slowly coloring the sky with peach and pomegranate auras as my little red fishing boat bobs up and down at the other end of the beach. A broken thistle tumbles over my cheek tossing opal sand from its bristles into my eyes. As the sun disappears, a city of plankton lights the sea aflame with iridescent red. Then from the direction of the temple ruins I hear my name float out across the sea. Pandora Pandaemonia.

I have waked the Thousand Shrine Island from her long sleep and in return she will not let me leave; my long sleep begins. The crescent moon rises over the island and her sea; with it ride the ghosts of pestilence and courageous hope arcing into the falling night.

The Doll

Vernon Lee

Violet Paget (1856–1935) was born in France of English and Welsh parents. She travelled throughout her life and ultimately settled, for the most part, in Italy. Under the name Vernon Lee she wrote travel books, books about Italy, a collection of essays on writing, and ghost stories. Montague Summers (1880–1948), the famous fraud-priest and expert on occult fiction, considered Lee the only equal of the preeminent antiquarian ghost story writer of Britain, M. R. James, though the comparison is certainly not one of style, but quality. Despite Summers's championing of her fiction, her stories are anthologized very seldom. Her work is now falling into the public domain in England, and much of it is being reissued as a result, so we may be on the brink of a renaissance of interest in her writings.

The major collections of Lee's ghost stories are Hauntings *(1890),* Pope Jacynth and Other Fantastic Tales *(1907), and* For Maurice: Five Unlikely Tales *(1927), which includes "The Doll." She also wrote political tracts, such as* Gospels of Anarchy *(1908) and* Vital Lies *(1912), earning her the title of "the most dangerous mind in Europe." A lesbian and bluestocking, her liaisons with women were often emotionally painful. In her classic novella "Amour Dure" (in* Hauntings*) a character's love for a woman proves lethal; it is one of the scariest stories in the English language.*

Some of the same psychology is at work in "The Doll" as in "Amour Dure," and it is probably not misstepping by far to interpret "The Doll" as an exorcism of the author's feelings for women and to read the final scene as a purge of difficult love affairs in Lee's own life. Lee wanted to distance herself from the story when it was published; she states in the introduction to For Maurice *that the story actually happened to a friend of hers. The friend was a man, however, and the protagonist here is not, could not be. Lee also noted that the all-important fiery conclusion is entirely her own device.*

"The Doll" is also a bluestocking's condemnation of the artificiality of the trappings of beauty, of woman's role as ornament or "doll" in many social settings. If one reads the final scene not as a purge, it becomes, instead, the liberation of a woman's spirit from the hollowness of such trappings.

ılllı

I believe that's the last bit of *bric-à-brac* I shall ever buy in my life (she said, closing the Renaissance casket)—that and the Chinese dessert set we have just been using. The passion seems to have left me utterly. And I think I can guess why. At the same time as the plates and the little coffer I bought a thing—I scarcely know whether I ought to call it a thing—which put me out of conceit with ferreting about among dead people's properties. I have often wanted to tell you all about it, and stopped for fear of seeming an idiot. But it weighs upon me sometimes like a secret; so, silly or not silly, I think I should like to tell you the story. There, ring for some more logs, and put that screen before the lamp.

It was two years ago, in the autumn, at Foligno, in Umbria. I was alone at the inn, for you know my husband is too busy for my *bric-à-brac* journeys, and the friend who was to have met me fell ill and came on only later. Foligno isn't what people call an interesting place, but I liked it. There are a lot of picturesque little towns all round; and great savage mountains of pink stone, covered with ilex, where they roll faggots down into the torrent beds, within a drive. There's a full, rushing little river round one side of the walls, which are covered with ivy; and there are fifteenth-century frescoes, which I dare say you know all about. But, what of course I care for most, there are a number of fine old palaces, with gateways carved in that pink stone, and courts with pillars, and beautiful window gratings, mostly in good enough repair, for Foligno is a market town and a junction, and altogether a kind of metropolis down in the valley.

Also, and principally, I liked Foligno because I discovered a delightful curiosity-dealer. I don't mean a delightful curiosity shop, for he had nothing worth twenty francs to sell; but a delightful, enchanting old man. His Christian name was Orestes, and that was enough for me. He had a long white beard and such kind brown eyes, and beautiful hands; and he always carried an earthenware brazier under his cloak. He had taken to the curiosity business from a passion for beautiful things, and for the past of his native place, after having been a master mason. He knew all the old chronicles, lent me that of Matarazzo, and knew exactly where everything had happened for the last six hundred years. He spoke of the Trincis, who had been local despots, and of St. Angela, who is the local saint, and of the Baglionis and Cæsar Borgia and Julius II, as if he had known them; he showed me the place where St. Francis preached to the birds, and the place where Propertius—was it Propertius or Tibullus?—had had his farm; and when he accompanied me on my rambles in search of *bric-à-brac* he would stop at corners and under arches and say, "This, you see, is where they carried off those Nuns I told you about; that's where the Cardinal was stabbed. That's the place where they razed the palace after the massacre, and passed the plough-share through the ground and sowed salt." And all with a vague, far-off, melancholy look, as if he lived in those days and not these. Also he helped me to get that little velvet coffer with the iron clasps, which is really one of the best things we have in the house. So I was very happy at Foligno, driving and prowling about all day, reading the chronicles Orestes lent me in the evening; and I didn't mind waiting so long for my friend who never turned up. That is to say, I was perfectly happy until within three days of my departure. And now comes the story of my strange purchase.

Orestes, with considerable shrugging of shoulders, came one morning with the information that a certain noble person of Foligno wanted to sell me a set of Chinese plates. "Some of them are cracked," he said; "but at all events you will see the inside of one of our finest palaces, with all its rooms as they used to be—nothing valuable; but I know that the signora appreciates the past wherever it has been let alone."

The palace, by way of exception, was of the late seventeenth century, and looked like a barracks among the neat little carved Renaissance houses. It had immense lions' heads over all the windows, a gateway in which two coaches could have met, a yard where a hundred might have waited, and a colossal staircase with stucco virtues on the vaultings. There was a cobbler in the lodge and a soap factory on the ground floor, and at the end of the colonnaded court a garden with ragged yellow vines and dead sunflowers. "Grandiose, but very coarse—almost eighteenth-century," said Orestes as we went up the sounding, low-stepped stairs. Some of the dessert set had been placed, ready for my inspection, on a great gold console in the immense escutcheoned ante-room. I looked at it, and told them to prepare the rest for me to see the next day. The owner, a very noble person, but half ruined—I should have thought entirely ruined, judging by the state of the house—was residing in the country, and the only occupant of the palace was an old woman, just like those who raised the curtains for you at church doors.

The palace was very grand. There was a ballroom as big as a church, and a number of reception rooms, with dirty floors and eighteenth-century furniture, all tarnished and tattered, and a gala room, all yellow satin and gold, where some emperor had slept; and there were horrible racks of faded photographs on the walls, and twopenny screens, and Berlin wool cushions, attesting the existence of more modern occupants.

I let the old woman unbar one painted and gilded shutter after another, and open window after window, each filled with little greenish panes of glass, and followed her about passively, quite happy, because I was wandering among the ghosts of dead people. "There is the library at the end here," said the old woman, "if the signora does not mind passing through my room and the ironing-room; it's quicker than going back by the big hall." I nodded, and prepared to pass as quickly as possible through an untidy-looking servants' room, when I suddenly stepped back. There was a woman in 1820 costume seated opposite, quite motionless. It was a huge doll. She had a sort of Canova classic face, like the pictures of Mme. Pasta and Lady Blessington. She sat with her hands folded on her lap and stared fixedly.

"It is the first wife of the Count's grandfather," said the old woman. "We took her out of her closet this morning to give her a little dusting."

The Doll was dressed to the utmost detail. She had on open-work silk stockings, with sandal shoes, and long silk embroidered mittens. The hair was merely painted, in flat bands narrowing the forehead to a triangle. There was a big hole in the back of her head, showing it was cardboard.

"Ah," said Orestes, musingly, "the image of the beautiful countess! I had forgotten all about it. I haven't seen it since I was a lad," and he wiped some cobweb off the folded hands with his red handkerchief, infinitely gently. "She used still to be kept in her own boudoir."

"That was before my time," answered the housekeeper. "I've always seen her in the wardrobe, and I've been here thirty years. Will the signora care to see the old Count's collection of medals?"

Orestes was very pensive as he accompanied me home.

"That was a very beautiful lady," he said shyly, as we came within sight of my inn; "I mean the first wife of the grandfather of the present Count. She died after they had been married a couple of years. The old count, they say, went half crazy. He had the Doll made from a picture, and kept it in the poor lady's room, and spent several hours in it every day with her. But he ended by marrying a woman he had in the house, a laundress, by whom he had had a daughter."

"What a curious story!" I said, and thought no more about it.

But the Doll returned to my thoughts, she and her folded hands, and

wide open eyes, and the fact of her husband's having ended by marrying the laundress. And next day, when we returned to the palace to
see the complete set of old Chinese plates, I suddenly experienced an
odd wish to see the Doll once more. I took advantage of Orestes, and
the old woman, and the Count's lawyer being busy deciding whether
a certain dish cover which my maid had dropped, had or had not been
previously chipped, to slip off and make my way to the ironing-room.

The Doll was still there, sure enough, and they hadn't found time to
dust her yet. Her white satin frock, with little *ruches* at the hem, and
her short bodice, had turned grey with engrained dirt; and her black
fringed kerchief was almost red. The poor white silk mittens and white
silk stockings were, on the other hand, almost black. A newspaper had
fallen from an adjacent table on to her knees, or been thrown there by
some one, and she looked as if she were holding it. It came home to
me then that the clothes which she wore were the real clothes of her
poor dead original. And when I found on the table a dusty, unkempt
wig, with straight bands in front and an elaborate jug handle of curls
behind, I knew at once that it was made of the poor lady's real hair.

"It is very well made," I said shyly, when the old woman, of course,
came creaking after me.

She had no thought except that of humouring whatever caprice might
bring her a tip. So she smirked horribly, and, to show me that the image
was really worthy of my attention, she proceeded in a ghastly way to
bend the articulated arms, and to cross one leg over the other beneath
the white satin skirt.

"Please, please, don't do that!" I cried to the old witch. But one of
the poor feet, in its sandalled shoe, continued dangling and wagging
dreadfully.

I was afraid lest my maid should find me staring at the Doll. I felt I
couldn't stand my maid's remarks about her. So, though fascinated by
the fixed dark stare in her Canova goddess or Ingres Madonna face, I
tore myself away and returned to the inspection of the dessert set.

I don't know what that Doll had done to me; but I found that I was
thinking of her all day long. It was as if I had just made a new acquaintance of a painfully interesting kind, rushed into a sudden friendship
with a woman whose secret I had surprised, as sometimes happens, by
some mere accident. For I somehow knew everything about her, and
the first items of information which I gained from Orestes—I ought to
say that I was irresistibly impelled to talk about her with him—did not
enlighten me in the least, but merely confirmed what I was aware of.

The Doll—for I made no distinction between the portrait and the
original—had been married straight out of the convent, and, during her
brief wedded life, been kept secluded from the world by her husband's

mad love for her, so that she had remained a mere shy, proud, inexperienced child.

Had she loved him? She did not tell me that at once. But gradually I became aware that in a deep, inarticulate way she had really cared for him more than he cared for her. She did not know what answer to make to his easy, overflowing, garrulous, demonstrative affection; he could not be silent about his love for two minutes, and she could never find a word to express hers, painfully though she longed to do so. Not that he wanted it; he was a brilliant, will-less, lyrical sort of person, who knew nothing of the feelings of others and cared only to welter and dissolve in his own. In those two years of ecstatic, talkative, all-absorbing love for her he not only forswore all society and utterly neglected his affairs, but he never made an attempt to train this raw young creature into a companion, or showed any curiosity as to whether his idol might have a mind or a character of her own. This indifference she explained by her own stupid, inconceivable incapacity for expressing her feelings; how should he guess at her longing to know, to understand, when she could not even tell him how much she loved him? At last the spell seemed broken: the words and the power of saying them came; but it was on her death-bed. The poor young creature died in child-birth, scarcely more than a child herself.

There now! I know even you would think it all silliness. I know what people are—what we all are—how impossible it is ever *really* to make others feel in the same way as ourselves about anything. Do you suppose I could have ever told all this about the Doll to my husband? Yet I tell him everything about myself; and I know he would have been quite kind and respectful. It was silly of me ever to embark on the story of the Doll with any one; it ought to have remained a secret between me and Orestes. *He,* I really think, would have understood all about the poor lady's feelings, or known it already as well as I. Well, having begun, I must go on, I suppose.

I knew all about the Doll when she was alive—I mean about the lady—and I got to know, in the same way, all about her after she was dead. Only I don't think I'll tell you. *Basta:* the husband had the Doll made, and dressed it in her clothes, and placed it in her boudoir, where not a thing was moved from how it had been at the moment of her death. He allowed no one to go in, and cleaned and dusted it all himself, and spent hours every day weeping and moaning before the Doll. Then, gradually, he began to look at his collection of medals, and to resume his rides; but he never went into society, and never neglected spending an hour in the boudoir with the Doll. Then came the business with the laundress. And then he sent the Doll into a wardrobe? Oh no; he wasn't that sort of man. He was an idealizing, sentimental, feeble sort of person, and the amour with the laundress grew up quite gradually in the shadow of the inconsolable passion for the wife. He would never have married another woman of his own rank, given *her* son a stepmother (the son was sent to a distant school and went to the bad); and when he *did* marry the laundress it was almost in his dotage, and because she and the priests bullied him so fearfully about legitimating that other child. He went on paying visits to the Doll for a long time, while the laundress idyl went on quite peaceably. Then, as he grew old and lazy, he went less often; other people were sent to dust the Doll, and finally she was not dusted at all. Then he died, having quarrelled with his son and got to live like a feeble old boor, mostly in the kitchen. The son—the Doll's son—having gone to the bad, married a rich widow. It was she who refurnished the boudoir and sent the Doll away. But the daughter of the laundress, the illegitimate child, who had become a kind of housekeeper in her half-brother's palace, nourished a lingering regard for the Doll, partly because the old Count had made such a fuss about it, partly because it must have cost a lot of money, and partly because the lady had been a *real* lady. So when the boudoir was refurnished she emptied out a closet and put the Doll to live there; and she occasionally had it brought out to be dusted.

Well, while all these things were being borne in upon me there came a telegram saying my friend was not coming on to Foligno, and asking me to meet her at Perugia. The little Renaissance coffer had been sent to London; Orestes and my maid and myself had carefully packed every one of the Chinese plates and fruit dishes in baskets of hay. I had ordered a set of the "Archivio Storico" as a parting gift for dear old Orestes—I could never have dreamed of offering him money, or cravat pins, or things like that—and there was no excuse for staying one hour more at Foligno. Also I had got into low spirits of late—I suppose we poor women cannot stay alone six days in an inn, even with bric-à-brac and chronicles and devoted maids—and I knew I should not get better till I was out of the place. Still I found it difficult, nay, impossible, to go. I will confess it outright: I couldn't abandon the Doll. I couldn't leave her, with the hole in her poor cardboard head, with the Ingres Madonna features gathering dust in that filthy old woman's ironing-room. It was just impossible. Still go I must. So I sent for Orestes. I knew exactly what I wanted; but it seemed impossible, and I was afraid, somehow, of asking him. I gathered up my courage, and, as if it were the most natural thing in the world, I said—

"Dear Signor Oreste, I want you to help me to make one last purchase. I want the Count to sell me the—the portrait of his grandmother; I mean the Doll."

I had prepared a speech to the effect that Orestes would easily understand that a life-size figure so completely dressed in the original costume of a past epoch would soon possess the highest historical interest, etc. But I felt that I neither needed nor ventured to say any of it. Orestes, who was seated opposite me at table—he would only accept a glass of wine and a morsel of bread, although I had asked him to share my hotel dinner—Orestes nodded slowly, then opened his eyes out wide, and seemed to frame the whole of me in them. It wasn't surprise. He was weighing me and my offer.

"Would it be very difficult?" I asked. "I should have thought that the Count—"

"The Count," answered Orestes drily, "would sell his soul, if he had one, let alone his grandmother, for the price of a new trotting pony."

Then I understood.

"Signor Oreste," I replied, feeling like a child under the dear old man's glance, "We have not known one another long, so I cannot expect you to trust me yet in many things. Perhaps also buying furniture out of dead people's houses to stick it in one's own is not a great recommendation of one's character. But I want to tell you that I am an honest woman according to my lights, and I want you to trust me in this matter."

Orestes bowed. "I will try and induce the Count to sell you the Doll," he said.

I had her sent in a closed carriage to the house of Orestes. He had, behind his shop, a garden which extended into a little vineyard, whence you could see the circle of great Umbrian mountains; and on this I had had my eye.

"Signor Oreste," I said, "will you be very kind, and have some faggots—I have seen some beautiful faggots of myrtle and bay in your kitchen—brought out into the vineyard; and may I pluck some of your chrysanthemums?" I added.

We stacked the faggots at the end of the vineyard, and placed the Doll in the midst of them, and the chrysanthemums on her knees. She sat there in her white satin Empire frock, which, in the bright November sunshine, seemed white once more, and sparkling. Her black fixed eyes stared as in wonder on the yellow vines and reddening peach trees, the sparkling dewy grass of the vineyard, upon the blue morning sunshine, the misty blue amphitheatre of mountains all round.

Orestes struck a match and slowly lit a pine cone with it; when the cone was blazing he handed it silently to me. The dry bay and myrtle blazed up crackling, with a fresh resinous odour; the Doll was veiled in flame and smoke. In a few seconds the flame sank, the smouldering faggots crumbled. The Doll was gone. Only, where she had been, there remained in the embers something small and shiny. Orestes raked it out and handed it to me. It was a wedding ring of old-fashioned shape, which had been hidden under the silk mitten. "Keep it, signora," said Orestes; "you have put an end to her sorrows."

The Debutante

ıllıₛ

Leonora Carrington

*Leonora Carrington was born in 1917 in Lancashire, England, and as a young
expatriot in Paris became a leading participant in the surrealist movement, as
both a painter and a writer. Retrospectives of her paintings have been held in
New York City, Austin, Paris and Mexico City. Since the 1940s, she has lived
in Mexico, where she is considered something of a national treasure.*

*As a writer, Carrington has had a long career that includes novels, short fiction,
and nonfiction. Her account of the time she spent in an asylum in Spain when
she was diagnosed as incurably insane,* Down Below *(1944), was reprinted in
1983. The corrected text appears in* The House of Fear *(1988), a collection of
her early prose. Her best known work of fiction is the modern classic* The Hearing Trumpet *(1976), a novel about a group of weird and wonderful old women
who, with the aid of the occult, rise up in a libertine revolution against their
keepers in a home for the aged. This was followed into print by* The Stone
Door *(1977), a thoroughly surreal novel of a farcical quest.* The Seventh
Horse and Other Tales *(1988), contains stories in translation from French
and Spanish.*

*Her first stories, mostly published in French and in limited editions during the
height of the surrealist movement (c.1939) were eventually published in English
in the collection* The Oval Lady *(1975). The title story reclaims many mythic
images and in this regard is akin to Jules Faye's "Pandora Pandaemonia" in this
volume. "The Beloved," also in* The Oval Lady, *is about a sleeping beauty,
her devoted husband, and a young girl who wishes only to devour her stolen*

watermelon. All of Carrington's stories are darkly comic, richly symbolic, and tied closely to her "fierce and personal brand of feminism," as Marina Warner states in her introduction to The House of Fear.

"The Debutante" (1939), reprinted here from The Oval Lady, *is a gross yet elegant flight of fancy, autobiographical as are most of Carrington's works, about a girl's revolt against conventional femininity. It is, as well, a stinging satire of a society so intent on appearances, so bound by gender roles, that even a hyena, if properly clad, can pass for a debutante in it.*

This translation is by Rochelle Holt.

ıllı

When I was a debutante I often went to the zoological garden. I went so often that I was better acquainted with animals than with the young girls of my age. It was to escape from the world that I found myself each day at the zoo. The beast I knew best was a young hyena. She knew me too. She was extremely intelligent; I taught her French and in return she taught me her language. We spent many pleasant hours in this way.

For the first of May my mother had arranged a ball in my honor. For entire nights I suffered: I had always detested balls, above all those given in my own honor.

On the morning of May first, 1934, very early, I went to visit the hyena. "What a mess of shit," I told her. "I must go to my ball this evening."

"You're lucky," she said. "I would go happily. I do not know how to dance, but after all, I could engage in conversation."

"There will be many things to eat," said I. "I have seen wagons loaded entirely with food coming up to the house."

"And you complain!" replied the hyena with disgust. "As for me, I eat only once a day, and what rubbish they stick me with!"

I had a bold idea; I almost laughed. "You have only to go in my place."

"We do not look enough alike, otherwise I would gladly go," said the hyena, a little sad. "Listen," said I, "in the evening light one does not see very well. If you were disguised a little, no one would notice in the crowd. Besides, we are almost the same size. You are my only friend; I implore you."

She reflected upon this sentiment. I knew that she wanted to accept. "It is done," she said suddenly.

It was very early; not many keepers were about. Quickly I opened the cage and in a moment we were in the street. I took a taxi; at the house, everyone was in bed. In my room, I brought out the gown I was supposed to wear that evening. It was a little long, and the hyena walked with difficulty in my high-heeled shoes. I found some gloves to disguise her hands which were too hairy to resemble mine. When the sunlight entered, she strolled around the room several times— walking more or less correctly. We were so very occupied that my mother, who came to tell me good morning, almost opened the door before the hyena could hide herself under my bed. "There is a bad odor in the room," said my mother, opening the window. "Before this evening you must take a perfumed bath with my new salts."

"Agreed," said I. She did not stay long; I believe the odor was too strong for her. "Do not be late for breakfast," she said, as she left the room.

The greatest difficulty was to find a disguise for the hyena's face. For hours and hours we sought an answer: she rejected all of my proposals. At last she said, "I think I know a solution. You have a maid?"

"Yes," I said, perplexed.

"Well, that's it. You will ring for the maid and when she enters we will throw ourselves upon her and remove her face. I will wear her face this evening in place of my own."

"That's not practical," I said to her. "She will probably die when she has no more face; someone will surely find the corpse and we will go to prison."

"I am hungry enough to eat her," replied the hyena.

"And the bones?"

"Those too," she said. "Then it's settled?"

"Only if you agree to kill her before removing her face. It would be too uncomfortable otherwise."

"Good; it's all right with me."

I rang for Marie, the maid, with a certain nervousness. I would not have done it if I did not detest dances so much. When Marie entered I turned to the wall so as not to see. I admit that it was done quickly. A brief cry and it was over. While the hyena ate, I looked out the window. A few minutes later, she said: "I cannot eat anymore; the two feet are left, but if you have a little bag I will eat them later in the day."

"You will find in the wardrobe a bag embroidered with *fleurs de lys*. Remove the handkerchiefs inside it and take it." She did as I indicated.

At last she said: "Turn around now and look, because I am beautiful!" Before the mirror, the hyena admired herself in Marie's face. She had eaten very carefully all around the face so that what was left was just what was needed. "Surely, it's properly done," said I.

Toward evening, when the hyena was all dressed, she declared: "I am in a very good mood. I have the impression that I will be a great success this evening."

When the music below had been heard for some time, I said to her:

"Go now, and remember not to place yourself at my mother's side: she will surely know that it is not I. Otherwise I know no one. Good luck." I embraced her as we parted but she smelled very strong.

Night had fallen. Exhausted by the emotions of the day, I took a book and sat down by the open window. I remember that I was reading *Gulliver's Travels* by Jonathan Swift. It was perhaps an hour later that the first sign of misfortune announced itself. A bat entered through the window, emitting little cries. I am terribly afraid of bats. I hid behind the chair, my teeth chattering. Scarcely was I on my knees when the beating of the wings was drowned out by a great commotion at my door. My mother entered, pale with rage. "We were coming to seat ourselves at the table," she said, "when the thing who was in your place rose and cried: 'I smell a little strong, eh? Well, as for me, I do not eat cake.' With these words she removed her face and ate it. A great leap and she disappeared out the window."

The Readjustment

Mary Austin

Mary Hunter Austin was born in Carlinville, Illinois, in 1868. Her father died when she was young and she was mainly influenced by her activist mother. Something of a mystic but also an intellectual (and briefly overcome by Christian sentiment when she thought she was dying and went to Italy to live with the Blue Nuns), she liked for people to think of her as "that desert woman, competent, rugged, self-reliant, unconventional."

Determined to be a successful writer and to devote herself to the fight for women's rights, she pursued both goals in her work as a playwright, novelist, lecturer, poet, and author of essays, short stories, and children's books. Her novel A Woman of Genius *(1912; reprinted in 1985) expounds at length her opinions, theories, and beliefs regarding the condition and future of women, a philosophy incorporating ideas of H. G. Wells (a friend) as well as from the day's feminist movement, plus her own special brand of transcendentalism. She was a student of Native American art and folklore and dreamed of a society in the Southwest of mixed ethnicity and cross-fertilized traditions, devoted to art and happiness.*

Because of her love for nature and the desert, when she died in 1934 in New Mexico her ashes were placed in an urn in a small stone crypt in her garden. Somewhat later, friends took her ashes to the summit of Mount Picacho, New Mexico, and found for them a natural rock crypt.

"The Readjustment," reprinted here from the April 1908 issue of Harper's Monthly Magazine, *was written at a time when many women artists were*

conscious of a special unity and common cause, and much of their fiction expressed feminist concerns. This tale is not merely a touching, sad ghost story, but also an insightful investigation of men's inability, relative to women's, to express emotions, whether love or grief. A woman could be left to wonder, even beyond the grave, whether or not her husband had ever cared for her.

⫴

Emma Jossylin had been dead and buried three days. The sister who had come to the funeral had taken Emma's child away with her, and the house was swept and aired; then, when it seemed there was least occasion for it, Emma came back. The neighbor woman who had nursed her was the first to know it. It was about seven of the evening, in a mellow gloom: the neighbor woman was sitting on her own stoop with her arms wrapped in her apron, and all at once she found herself going along the street under an urgent sense that Emma needed her. She was half-way down the block before she recollected that this was impossible, for Mrs. Jossylin was dead and buried, but as soon as she came opposite the house she was aware of what had happened. It was all open to the summer air; except that it was a little neater, not otherwise than the rest of the street. It was quite dark; but the presence of Emma Jossylin streamed from it and betrayed it more than a candle. It streamed out steadily across the garden, and even as it reached her, mixed with the smell of the damp mignonette, the neighbor woman owned to herself that she had always known Emma would come back.

"A sight stranger if she wouldn't," thought the woman who had nursed her. "She wasn't ever one to throw off things easily."

Emma Jossylin had taken death, as she had taken everything in life, hard. She had met it with the same hard, bright, surface competency that she had presented to the squalor of the encompassing desertness, to the insuperable commonness of Sim Jossylin, to the affliction of her crippled child; and the intensity of her wordless struggle against it had caught the attention of the townspeople and held it in a shocked, curious awe. She was so long a-dying, lying there in the little low house, hearing the abhorred footsteps going about her house and the vulgar procedure of the community encroach upon her like the advances of the sand wastes on an unwatered field. For Emma had always wanted things different, wanted them with a fury of intentness that implied offensiveness in things as they were. And the townspeople had taken offence, the more so because she was not to be surprised in any inaptitude for their own kind of success. Do what you could, you could never catch Emma Jossylin in a wrapper after three o'clock in the afternoon. And she would never talk about the child—in a country where so little ever happened that even trouble was a godsend if it gave you something to talk about. It was reported that she did not even talk to Sim. But there the common resentment got back at her. If she had thought to effect anything with Sim Jossylin against the benumbing spirit of the place, the evasive hopefulness, the large sense of leisure that ungirt the loins, if she still hoped somehow to get away with him to some place for which by her dress, by her manner, she seemed forever and unassailably fit, it was foregone that nothing would come of it. They knew Sim Jossylin better than that. Yet so vivid had been the force of her wordless dissatisfaction that when the fever took her and she went down like a pasteboard figure in the damp, the wonder was that nothing toppled with her. And as if she too had felt herself indispensable, Emma Jossylin had come back.

The neighbor woman crossed the street, and as she passed the far corner of the gate, Jossylin spoke to her. He had been standing, she did not know how long a time, behind the syringa bush, and moved even with her along the fence until they came to the gate. She could see in the dusk that before speaking he wet his lips with his tongue.

"She's in there," he said at last.

"Emma?"

He nodded. "I been sleeping at the store since—but I thought I'd be more comfortable—as soon as I opened the door, there she was."

"Did you see her?"

"No."

"How do you know, then?"

"Don't you know?"

The neighbor felt there was nothing to say to that.

"Come in," he whispered, huskily. They slipped by the rose tree and the wistaria and sat down on the porch at the side. A door swung inward behind them. They felt the Presence in the dusk beating like a pulse.

"What do you think she wants?" said Jossylin. "Do you reckon it's the boy?"

"Like enough."

"He's better off with his aunt. There was no one here to take care of him, like his mother wanted." He raised his voice unconsciously with a note of justification, addressing the room behind.

"I am sending fifty dollars a month," he said; "he can go with the best of them." He went on at length to explain all the advantage that was to come to the boy from living at Pasadena, and the neighbor woman bore him out in it.

"He was glad to go," urged Jossylin to the room. "He said it was what his mother would have wanted."

They were silent then a long time, while the Presence seemed to swell upon them and encroached upon the garden. Finally, "I gave Zeigler the order for the monument yesterday," Jossylin threw out, appeasingly. "It's to cost three hundred and fifty." The Presence stirred. The neighbor thought she could fairly see the controlled tolerance with which Emma Jossylin threw off the evidence of Sim's ineptitude.

They sat on helplessly without talking after that, until the woman's husband came to the fence and called her.

"Don't go," begged Jossylin.

"Hush!" she said. "Do you want all the town to know? You had naught but good from Emma living, and no call to expect harm from her now. It's natural she should come back—if—if she was lonesome like—in—the place where she's gone to."

"Emma wouldn't come back to this place," Jossylin protested, "without she wanted something."

"Well, then, you've got to find out," said the neighbor woman.

All the next day she saw, whenever she passed the house, that Emma was still there. It was shut and barred, but the Presence lurked behind the folded blinds and fumbled at the doors. When it was night and the moths began in the columbine under the window, It went out and walked in the garden.

Jossylin was waiting at the gate when the neighbor woman came. He sweated with helplessness in the warm dusk, and the Presence brooded upon them like an apprehension that grows by being entertained.

"She wants something," he appealed, "but I can't make out what. Emma knows she is welcome to everything I've got. Everybody knows I've been a good provider."

The neighbor woman remembered suddenly the only time she had ever drawn close to Emma Jossylin touching the child. They had sat up with it together all one night in some childish ailment, and she had ventured a question: "What does his father think?" And Emma had turned her a white, hard face of surpassing dreariness. "I don't know," she admitted; "he never says."

"There's more than providing," suggested the neighbor woman.

"Yes. There's feeling ... but she had enough to do to put up with me. I had no call to be troubling her with such." He left off to mop his forehead, and began again.

"Feelings," he said; "there's times a man gets so wore out with feelings, he doesn't have them any more."

He talked, and presently it grew clear to the woman that he was voiding all the stuff of his life, as if he had sickened on it and was now done. It was a little soul knowing itself and not good to see. What was singular was that the Presence left off walking in the garden, came and caught like a gossamer on the ivy tree, swayed by the breath of his broken sentences. He talked, and the neighbor woman saw him for once as he saw himself and Emma, snared and floundering in an inexplicable unhappiness. He had been disappointed too. She had never relished the man he was, and it made him ashamed. That was why he had never gone away, lest he should make her ashamed among her own kind. He was her husband; he could not help that, though he was sorry for it. But he could keep the offence where least was made of it. And there was a child—she had wanted a child, but even then he had blundered—begotten a cripple upon her. He blamed himself utterly, searched out the roots of his youth for the answer to that, until the neighbor woman flinched to hear him. But the Presence stayed.

He had never talked to his wife about the child. How should he? There was the fact—the advertisement of his incompetence. And she had never talked to him. That was the one blessed and unassailable memory, that she had spread silence like a balm over his hurt. In return for it he had never gone away. He had resisted her that he might save her from showing among her own kind how poor a man he was. With every word of this ran the fact of his love for her—as he had loved her with all the stripes of clean and uncleanness. He bared himself as a child without knowing; and the Presence stayed. The talk trailed off at last to the commonplaces of consolation between the retchings of his spirit. The Presence lessened and streamed toward them on the wind of the garden. When it touched them like the warm air of noon that lies sometimes in hollow places after nightfall, the neighbor woman rose and went away.

The next night she did not wait for him. When a rod outside the town—it was a very little one—the burrowing owls *whoowhooed,* she hung up her apron and went to talk with Emma Jossylin. The Presence was there, drawn in, lying close. She found the key between the wistaria and the first pillar of the porch; but as soon as she opened the door she felt the chill that might be expected by one intruding on Emma Jossylin in her own house.

" 'The Lord is my shepherd!' " said the neighbor woman; it was the first religious phrase that occurred to her; then she said the whole of the psalm, and after that a hymn. She had come in through the door, and stood with her back to it and her hand upon the knob. Everything was just as Mrs. Jossylin had left it, with the waiting air of a room kept for company.

"Em," she said, boldly, when the chill had abated a little before the sacred words—"Em Jossylin, I've got something to say to you. And you've got to hear," she added with firmness as the white curtains stirred duskily at the window. "You wouldn't be talked to about your troubles when . . . you were here before, and we humored you. But now there is Sim to be thought of. I guess you heard what you came for last night, and got good of it. Maybe it would have been better if Sim had said things all along instead of hoarding them in his heart, but, anyway, he has said them now. And what I want to say is, if you was staying on with the hope of hearing it again, you'd be making a mistake. You was an uncommon woman, Emma Jossylin, and there didn't none of us understand you very well, nor do you justice, maybe; but Sim is only a common man, and I understand him because I'm that way myself. And if you think he'll be opening his heart to you every night, or be any different from what he's always been on account of what's happened, that's a mistake, too . . . and in a little while, if you stay, it will be as bad as it always was . . . men are like that . . . you'd better go now while there's understanding between you." She stood staring into the darkling room that seemed suddenly full of turbulence and denial. It seemed to beat upon her and take her breath, but she held on.

"You've got to go . . . Em . . . and I'm going to stay until you do," she said with finality; and then began again:

" 'The Lord is nigh unto them that are of a broken heart,' " and repeated the passage to the end. Then, as the Presence sank before it, "You better go, Emma," persuasively: and again, after an interval:

" 'He shall deliver thee in six troubles.

" 'Yea, in seven there shall no evil touch thee.' " The Presence gathered itself and was still; she could make out that it stood over against the opposite corner by the gilt easel with the crayon portrait of the child.

" 'For thou shalt forget thy misery. Thou shalt remember it as waters that are past,' " concluded the neighbor woman, as she heard Jossylin on the gravel outside. What the Presence had wrought upon him in the night was visible in his altered mien. He looked, more than anything else, to be in need of sleep. He had eaten his sorrow, and that was the end of it—as it is with men.

"I came to see if there was anything I could do for you," said the woman, neighborly, with her hand upon the door.

"I don't know as there is," said he. "I'm much obliged, but I don't know as there is."

"You see," whispered the woman, over her shoulder, "not even to me." She felt the tug of her heart as the Presence swept past her. The neighbor went out after that and walked in the ragged street, past the schoolhouse, across the creek below the town, out by the fields, over the headgate, and back by the town again. It was full nine of the clock when she passed the Jossylin house. It looked, except for being a little neater, not other than the rest of the street. The door was open and the lamp was lit; she saw Jossylin black against it. He sat reading in a book like a man at ease in his own house.

Clay-Shuttered Doors

⫼

Helen R. Hull

Helen Rose Hull (1888–1971) was born in Albion, Michigan, and educated in the midwest. She was an instructor at Wellesley College and Barnard College from 1912 to 1915, after which she taught writing at Columbia until 1956. When she first began to write, she papered one whole wall in her house with rejection slips; over time the bare "acceptance wall" also became papered.

Hull was a young radical in the years before suffrage was won, a member of the Heterodoxy Club (a group of women artists and authors fighting for the right to vote) and contributor to the leading socialist magazine The Masses. *Later, as a nationally respected novelist and a professor of creative writing, she became politically reticent, and was told by her publisher that she should avoid publicity because the fact that she was a lesbian would shock fans of her domestic novels.*

Her first novel, Quest, *was published in 1922, after a great many of her short stories had already appeared in a wide array of magazines. Some of these early stories have at long last been collected in* Last September *(1988), edited by Patricia McClelland Miller, who is also working on a biography of Hull and her lover, Mabel Louise Robinson. Islanders, Hull's third novel, first appeared in 1927, and has recently been republished with an afterword by Miller. Heat Lightning (1932) was Hull's first bestseller and can be found in the bargain bins of used bookshops to this day. In all she wrote twenty novels and more than three times as many short stories; despite restraints, she sometimes wrote about lesbian characters.*

Hull's lasting claim to fame among lovers of grim tales is her classic "Clay-

Shuttered Doors," first published in Harper's Magazine, May 1926. *Only Charlotte Perkins Gilman's "The Yellow Wallpaper" is a better known or more widely reprinted feminist shocker; both tales condemn men's perceptions of women in marriage and the devastating effects they can have on women. There is also an affinity between these stories and what is perhaps the third best known feminist shocker, May Sinclair's "The Villa Désirée" from her volume* The Intercessor and Other Stories *(1932). In Sinclair's story, male sexuality is severely treated, and a smitten woman saves herself from marriage to a man who has every outward appearance of respectability, but actually is depraved.*

Hull's story allows that a young girl may share her father's selfish egocentricity and a young boy his mother's sensitivity. Still, she has written an unwavering indictment of the nuclear family on the personal and economic levels, contrasting its destructive dynamics with the self-sufficient, unmarried narrator, a female journalist.

The supernatural event on which the story turns is itself material of high drama, but the real horror stems from something all too commonplace: the husband's selfishness. For a less condemning and more compassionate interpretation of a married couple's dynamics, try Mary Austin's "The Readjustment" in this volume.

For months I have tried not to think about Thalia Corson. Anything may invoke her, with her languorous fragility, thin wrists and throat, her elusive face with its long eyelids. I can't quite remember her mouth. When I try to visualize her sharply I get soft pale hair, the lovely curve from her temple to chin, and eyes blue and intense. Her boy, Fletcher, has eyes like hers.

To-day I came back to New York, and my taxi to an uptown hotel was held for a few minutes in Broadway traffic where the afternoon sunlight fused into a dazzle a great expanse of plate-glass and elaborate show motor cars. The "Regal Eight"—Winchester Corson's establishment. I huddled as the taxi jerked ahead, in spite of knowledge that Winchester would scarcely peer out of that elegant setting into taxi cabs. I didn't wish to see him, nor would he care to see me. But the glimpse had started the whole affair churning again, and I went through it deliberately, hoping that it might have smoothed out into some rational explanation. Sometimes things do, if you leave them alone, like logs submerged in water that float up later, encrusted thickly. This affair won't add to itself. It stays unique and smooth, sliding through the rest of life without annexing a scrap of seaweed.

I suppose, for an outsider, it all begins with the moment on Brooklyn Bridge; behind that are the years of my friendship with Thalia. Our families had summer cottages on the Cape. She was just enough older, however, so that not until I had finished college did I catch up to any intimacy with her. She had married Winchester Corson, who at that time fitted snugly into the phrase "a rising young man." During those first years, while his yeast sent up preliminary bubbles, Thalia continued to spend her summers near Boston, with Winchester coming for occasional week-ends. Fletcher was, unintentionally, born there; he began his difficult existence by arriving as a seven-month baby. Two years later Thalia had a second baby to bring down with her. Those were the summers which gave my friendship for Thalia its sturdy roots. They made me wonder, too, why she had chosen Winchester Corson. He was personable enough; tall, with prominent dark eyes and full mouth under a neat mustache, restless hands, and an uncertain disposition. He could be a charming companion, sailing the catboat with dash, managing lobster parties on the shore; or he would, unaccountably, settle into a foggy grouch, when everyone—children and females particularly—was supposed to approach only on tiptoe, bearing burnt offerings. The last time he spent a fortnight there, before he moved the family to the new Long Island estate, I had my own difficulties with him. There had always been an undertone of sex in his attitude toward me, but I had thought "that's just his male conceit." That summer he was a nuisance, coming upon me with his insistent, messy kisses, usually with Thalia in the next room. They were the insulting kind of kisses that aren't at all personal, and I could have ended them fast enough if there hadn't been the complication of Thalia and my love for her. If I made Winchester angry he'd put an end to Thalia's relation to me. I didn't, anyway, want her to know what a fool he was. Of course she did know, but I thought then that I could protect her.

There are, I have decided, two ways with love. You can hold one love, knowing that, if it is a living thing, it must develop and change. That takes maturity, and care, and a consciousness of the other person. That was Thalia's way. Or you enjoy the beginning of love and, once you're past that, you have to hunt for a new love, because the excitement seems to be gone. Men like Winchester, who use all their brains on their jobs, never grow up; they go on thinking that preliminary stir and snap is love itself. Cut flowers, that was Winchester's idea, while to Thalia love was a tree.

But I said Brooklyn Bridge was the point at which the affair had its start. It seems impossible to begin there, or anywhere, as I try to account for what happened. Ten years after the summer when Winchester made himself such a nuisance—that last summer the Corsons spent at the Cape—I went down at the end of the season for a week with Thalia and the children at the Long Island place. Winchester drove out for the week-end. The children were mournful because they didn't wish to leave the shore for school; a sharp September wind brought rain and fog down the Sound, and Winchester nourished all that Sunday a disagreeable grouch. I had seen nothing of them for most of the ten intervening years, as I had seen nothing of them for most of the ten intervening years, as I had been first in France and then in China, after feature-article stuff. The week had been pleasant: good servants, comfortable house, a half-moon of white beach below the drop of lawn; Thalia a stimulating listener, with Fletcher, a thin, eager boy of twelve, like her in his intensity of interest. Dorothy, a plump, pink child of ten, had no use for stories of French villages or Chinese temples. Nug, the wire-haired terrier, and her dolls were more immediate and convincing. Thalia was thin and noncommittal, except for her interest in what I had seen and done. I couldn't, for all my affection, establish any real contact. She spoke casually of the town house, of dinners she gave for Winchester, of his absorption in business affairs. But she was sheathed in polished aloofness and told me nothing of herself. She did say, one evening, that she was glad I was to be in New York that winter. Winchester, like his daughter Dorothy, had no interest in foreign parts once he had ascertained that I hadn't even seen the Chinese quarters of the motor company in which he was concerned. He had an amusing attitude toward me: careful indifference, no doubt calculated to put me in my place as no longer alluring. Thalia tried to coax him into listening to some of my best stories. "Tell him about the bandits, Mary"—but his sulkiness brought, after dinner, a casual explanation from her, untinged with apology. "He's working on an enormous project, a merging of several companies, and he's so soaked in it he can't come up for a breath."

In the late afternoon the maid set out high tea for us, before our departure for New York. Thalia suggested that perhaps one highball was enough if Winchester intended to drive over the wet roads. Win immediately mixed a second, asking if she had ever seen him in the least affected. "Be better for you than tea before a long damp drive, too." He clinked the ice in his glass. "Jazz you up a bit." Nug was begging for food and Thalia, bending to give him a corner of her sandwich, apparently did not hear Winchester. He looked about the room, a smug, owning look. The fire and candlelight shone in the heavy waxed rafters, made silver beads of the rain on the French windows. I watched him—heavier, more dominant, his prominent dark eyes and his lips sullen, as if the whisky banked up his temper rather than appeased it.

Then Jim, the gardener, brought the car to the door; the children scrambled in. Dorothy wanted to take Nug, but her father said not if she wanted to sit with him and drive.

"How about chains, sir?" Jim held the umbrella for Thalia.

"Too damned noisy. Don't need them." Winchester slammed the door and slid under the wheel. Thalia and I, with Fletcher between us, sat comfortably in the rear.

"I like it better when Walter drives, don't you, Mother?" said Fletcher as we slid down the drive out to the road.

"Sh—Father likes to drive. And Walter likes Sunday off, too." Thalia's voice was cautious.

"It's too dark to see anything."

"I can see lots," announced Dorothy, whereupon Fletcher promptly turned the handle that pushed up the glass between the chauffeur's seat and the rear.

The heavy car ran smoothly over the wet narrow road, with an occasional rumble and flare of headlights as some car swung past. Not till we reached the turnpike was there much traffic. There Winchester had to slacken his speed for other shiny beetles slipping along through the rain. Sometimes he cut past a car, weaving back into line in the glaring teeth of a car rushing down on him, and Fletcher would turn inquiringly toward his mother. The gleaming, wet darkness and the smooth motion made me drowsy, and I paid little heed until we slowed in a congestion of cars at the approach to the bridge. Far below on the black river, spaced red and white stars suggested slow-moving tugs, and beyond, faint lights splintered in the rain hinted at the city.

"Let's look for the cliff dwellers, Mother."

Thalia leaned forward, her fine, sharp profile dimly outlined against the shifting background of arches, and Fletcher slipped to his feet, his arm about her neck. "There!"

We were reaching the New York end of the bridge, and I had a swift glimpse of their cliff dwellers—lights in massed buildings, like ancient camp fires along a receding mountain side. Just then Winchester nosed out of the slow line, Dorothy screamed, the light from another car tunneled through our windows, the car trembled under the sudden grip of brakes, and like a crazy top spun sickeningly about, with a final thud against the stone abutment. A shatter of glass, a confusion of motor horns about us, a moment while the tautness of shock held me rigid.

Around me that periphery of turmoil—the usual recriminations, "What the hell you think you're doing?"—the shriek of a siren on an approaching motor cycle. Within the circle I tried to move across the narrow space of the car. Fletcher was crying; vaguely I knew that the door had swung open, that Thalia was crouching on her knees, the rain and the lights pouring on her head and shoulders; her hat was gone, her wide fur collar looked like a drenched and lifeless animal. "Hush, Fletcher." I managed to force movement into my stiff body. "Are you hurt? Thalia——" Then outside Winchester, with the bristling fury of panic, was trying to lift her drooping head. "Thalia! My God, you aren't hurt!" Someone focused a searchlight on the car as Winchester got his arms about her and lifted her out through the shattered door.

Over the springing line of the stone arch I saw the cliff dwellers' fires and I thought as I scrambled out to follow Winchester, "She was leaning forward, looking at those, and that terrific spin of the car must have knocked her head on the door as it lurched open."

"Lay her down, man!" An important little fellow had rushed up, a doctor evidently. "Lay her down, you fool!" Someone threw down a robe, and Winchester, as if Thalia were a drowned feather, knelt with her, laid her there on the pavement. I was down beside her and the fussy little man also. She did look drowned, drowned in that beating sea of tumult, that terrific honking of motors, unwilling to stop an instant even for—was it death? Under the white glare of headlights her lovely face had the empty shallowness, the husklikeness of death. The little doctor had his pointed beard close to her breast; he lifted one of her long eyelids. "She's just fainted, eh, doctor?" Winchester's angry voice tore at him.

The little man rose slowly. "She your wife? I'm sorry. Death must have been instantaneous. A blow to the temple."

With a kind of roar Winchester was down there beside Thalia, lifting her, her head lolling against his shoulder, his face bent over her. "Thalia! Thalia! Do you hear? Wake up!" I think he even shook her in his baffled fright and rage. "Thalia, do you hear me? I want you to open your eyes. You weren't hurt. That was nothing." And then, "Dearest, you must!" and more words, frantic, wild words, mouthed close to her empty face. I touched his shoulder, sick with pity, but he staggered up to his feet, lifting her with him. Fletcher pressed shivering against me, and I turned for an instant to the child. Then I heard Thalia's voice, blurred and queer, "You called me, Win?" and Winchester's sudden, triumphant laugh. She was standing against his shoulder, still with that husklike face, but she spoke again, "You did call me?"

"Here, let's get out of this." Winchester was again the efficient, competent man of affairs. The traffic cops were shouting, the lines of cars began to move. Winchester couldn't start his motor. Something had smashed. His card and a few words left responsibility with an officer, and even as an ambulance shrilled up, he was helping Thalia into a taxi. "You take the children, will you?" to me, and "Get her another taxi, will you?" to the officer. He had closed the taxi door after himself, and was gone, leaving us to the waning curiosity of passing cars. As we rode off in a second taxi, I had a glimpse of the little doctor, his face incredulous, his beard wagging, as he spoke to the officer.

Dorothy was, characteristically, tearfully indignant that her father had left her to me. Fletcher was silent as we bumped along under the elevated tracks, but presently he tugged at my sleeve, and I heard his faint whisper. "What is it?" I asked.

"Is my mother really dead?" he repeated.

"Of course not, Fletcher. You saw her get into the cab with your father."

"Why didn't Daddy take us too?" wailed Dorothy, and I had to turn to her, although my nerves echoed her question.

The house door swung open even as the taxi bumped the curb, and the butler hurried out with an umbrella which we were too draggled to need.

"Mr. Corson instructed me to pay the man, madam." He led us into the hall, where a waiting maid popped the children at once into the tiny elevator.

"Will you wait for the elevator, madam? The library is one flight." The butler led me up the stairs, and I dropped into a low chair near the fire, vaguely aware of the long, narrow room, with discreet gold of the walls giving back light from soft lamps. "I'll tell Mr. Corson you have come."

"Is Mrs. Corson—does she seem all right?" I asked.

"Quite, madam. It was a fortunate accident, with no one hurt."

Well, perhaps it had addled my brain! I waited in a kind of numbness for Winchester to come.

Presently he strode in, his feet silent on the thick rugs.

"Sorry," he began, abruptly. "I wanted to look the children over. Not a scratch on them. You're all right, of course?"

"Oh, yes. But Thalia—"

"She won't even have a doctor. I put her straight to bed—she's so damned nervous, you know. Hot-water bottles . . . she was cold. I think she's asleep now. Said she'd see you in the morning. You'll stay here, of course." He swallowed in a gulp the whisky he had poured. "Have some, Mary? Or would you like something hot?"

"No, thanks. If you're sure she's all right I'll go to bed."

"Sure?" His laugh was defiant. "Did that damn fool on the bridge throw a scare into you? He gave me a bad minute, I'll say. If that car hadn't cut in on me—I told Walter last week the brakes needed looking at. They shouldn't grab like that. Might have been serious."

"Since it wasn't—" I rose, wearily, watching him pour amber liquid slowly into his glass—"if you'll have someone show me my room—"

"After Chinese bandits, a little skid ought not to matter to you." His prominent eyes gleamed hostilely at me; he wanted some assurance offered that the skidding wasn't his fault, that only his skill had saved all our lives.

"I can't see Thalia?" I said.

"She's asleep. Nobody can see her." His eyes moved coldly from my face, down to my muddy shoes. "Better give your clothes to the maid for a pressing. You're smeared quite a bit."

I woke early, with clear September sun at the windows of the room, with blue sky behind the sharp city contours beyond the windows. There was none too much time to make the morning train for Albany, where I had an engagement that day, an interview for an article. The maid who answered my ring insisted on serving breakfast to me in borrowed elegance of satin negligee. Mrs. Corson was resting, and would see me before I left. Something—the formality and luxury, the complicated household so unlike the old days at the Cape—accented the queer dread which had filtered all night through my dreams.

I saw Thalia for only a moment. The heavy silk curtains were drawn against the light and in the dimness her face seemed to gather shadows.

"Are you quite all right, Thalia?" I hesitated beside her bed, as if my voice might tear apart the veils of drowsiness in which she rested.

"Why, yes—" as if she wondered. Then she added, so low that I wasn't sure what I heard, "It is hard to get back in."

"What, Thalia?" I bent toward her.

"I'll be myself once I've slept enough." Her voice was clearer. "Come back soon, won't you, Mary?" Then her eyelids closed and her face merged into the shadows of the room. I tiptoed away, thinking she slept.

It was late November before I returned to New York. Freelancing has a way of drawing herrings across your trail and, when I might have drifted back in early November, a younger sister wanted me to come home to Arlington for her marriage. I had written to Thalia, first a note of courtesy for my week with her, and then a letter begging for news. Like many people of charm, she wrote indifferent letters, stiff and childlike, lacking in her personal quality. Her brief reply was more unsatisfactory than usual. The children were away in school, lots of cold rainy weather, everything was going well. At the end, in writing unlike hers, as if she scribbled the line in haste, "I am lonely. When are you coming?" I answered that I'd show up as soon as the wedding was over.

The night I reached Arlington was rainy, too, and I insisted upon a taxi equipped with chains. My brother thought that amusing, and at dinner gave the family an exaggerated account of my caution. I tried to offer him some futile sisterly advice and, to point up my remarks, told about that drive in from Long Island with the Corsons. I had never spoken of it before; I found that an inexplicable inhibition kept me from making much of a story.

"Well, nothing happened, did it?" Richard was triumphant.

"A great deal might have," I insisted. "Thalia was stunned, and I was disagreeably startled."

"Thalia was stunned, was she?" An elderly cousin of ours from New Jersey picked out that item. I saw her fitting it into some pigeonhole, but she said nothing until late that evening when she stopped at the door of my room.

"Have you seen Thalia Corson lately?" she asked.

"I haven't been in New York since September."

She closed the door and lowered her voice, a kind of avid curiosity riding astride the decorous pity she expressed.

"I called there, one day last week. I didn't know what was the matter with her. I hadn't heard of that accident."

I waited, an old antagonism for my proper cousin blurring the fear that shot up through my thoughts.

"Thalia was always *individual,* of course." She used the word like a reproach. "But she had *savoir faire.* But now she's—well—*queer.* Do you suppose her head was affected?"

"How is she queer?"

"She looks miserable, too. Thin and white."

"But how—"

"I am telling you, Mary. She was quite rude. First she didn't come down for ever so long, although I sent up word that I'd come up to her room if she was resting. Then her whole manner—well, I was really offended. She scarcely heard a word I said to her, just sat with her back to a window so I couldn't get a good look at her. When I said, 'You don't look like yourself,' she actually sneered. 'Myself?' she said. 'How do you know?' Imagine! I tried to chatter along as if I noticed nothing. I flatter myself I can manage awkward moments rather well. But Thalia sat there and I am sure she muttered under her breath. Finally I rose to go and I said, meaning well, 'You'd better take a good rest. You look half dead.' Mary, I wish you'd seen the look she gave me! Really I was frightened. Just then their dog came in, you know, Dorothy's little terrier. Thalia used to be silly about him. Well, she actually tried to hide in the folds of the curtain, and I don't wonder! The dog was terrified at her. He crawled on his belly out of the room. Now she must have been cruel to him if he acts like that. I think Winchester should have a specialist. I didn't know how to account for any of it; but of course a blow on the head can affect a person."

Fortunately my mother interrupted us just then, and I didn't, by my probable rudeness, give my cousin reason to suppose that the accident had affected me, too. I sifted through her remarks and decided they might mean only that Thalia found her more of a bore than usual. As for Nug, perhaps he retreated from the cousin! During the next few days the house had so much wedding turmoil that she found a chance only for a few more dribbles: one that Thalia had given up all her clubs—she had belonged to several—the other that she had sent the children to boarding schools instead of keeping them at home. "Just when her husband is doing so well, too!"

I was glad when the wedding party had departed, and I could plan to go back to New York. Personally I think a low-caste Chinese wedding is saner and more interesting than a modern American affair. My cousin "should think I could stay home with the family," and "couldn't we go to New York together, if I insisted upon gadding off?" We couldn't. I saw to that. She hoped that I'd look up Thalia. Maybe I could advise Winchester about a specialist.

I did telephone as soon as I got in. That sentence, "I am lonely," in her brief note kept recurring. Her voice sounded thin and remote, a poor connection, I thought. She was sorry. She was giving a dinner for Winchester that evening. The next day?

I had piles of proof to wade through that next day, and it was late afternoon when I finally went to the Corson house. The butler looked doubtful but I insisted, and he left me in the hall while he went off with my card. He returned, a little smug in his message: Mrs. Corson was resting and had left word she must not be disturbed. Well, you can't protest to a perfect butler, and I started down the steps, indignant, when a car stopped in front of the house, a liveried chauffeur opened the door, and Winchester emerged. He glanced at me in the twilight and extended an abrupt hand.

"Would Thalia see you?" he asked.

"No." For a moment I hoped he might convoy me past the butler. "Isn't she well? She asked me to come to-day."

"I hoped she'd see you." Winchester's hand smoothed at his little mustache. "She's just tired from her dinner last night. She overexerted herself, was quite the old Thalia." He looked at me slowly in the dusk, and I had a brief feeling that he was really looking at me, no, *for* me, for the first time in all our meetings, as if he considered me without relation to himself for once. "Come in again, will you?" He thrust away whatever else he thought of saying. "Thalia really would like to see you. Can I give you a lift?"

"No, thanks, I need a walk." As I started off I knew the moment had just missed some real significance. If I had ventured a question . . . but, after all, what could I ask him? He had said that Thalia was "just tired." That night I sent a note to her, saying I had called and asking when I might see her.

She telephoned me the next day. Would I come in for Thanksgiving? The children would be home, and she wanted an old-fashioned day, everything but the sleigh ride New York couldn't furnish. Dinner would be at six, for the children; perhaps I could come in early. I felt a small grievance at being put off for almost a week, but I promised to come.

That was the week I heard gossip about Winchester, in the curious devious way of gossip. Atlantic City, and a gaudy lady. Someone having an inconspicuous fortnight of convalescence there had seen them. I wasn't surprised, except perhaps that Winchester chose Atlantic City. Thalia was too fine; he couldn't grow up to her. I wondered how much she knew. She must, years ago, with her sensitiveness, have discovered that Winchester was stationary so far as love went and, being stationary himself, was inclined to move the object toward which he directed his passion.

On Thursday, as I walked across Central Park, gaunt and deserted in the chilly afternoon light, I decided that Thalia probably knew more about Winchester's affairs than gossip had given me. Perhaps that was why she had sent the children away. He had always been conventionally discreet, but discretion would be a tawdry coin among Thalia's shining values.

I was shown up to the nursery, with a message from Thalia that she would join me there soon. Fletcher seemed glad to see me, in a shy, excited way, and stood close to my chair while Dorothy wound up her phonograph for a dance record and pirouetted about us with her doll.

"Mother keeps her door tight locked all the time," whispered Fletcher doubtfully. "We can't go in. This morning I knocked and knocked but no one answered."

"Do you like your school?" I asked cheerfully.

"I like my home better." His eyes, so like Thalia's with their long, arched lids, had young bewilderment under their lashes.

"See me!" called Dorothy. "Watch me do this!"

While she twirled I felt Fletcher's thin body stiffen against my arm, as if a kind of panic froze him. Thalia stood in the doorway. Was the boy afraid of her? Dorothy wasn't. She cried, "See me, Mother! Look at me!" and in her lusty confusion, I had a moment to look at Thalia before she greeted me. She was thin, but she had always been that. She did not heed Dorothy's shrieks, but watched Fletcher, a kind of slanting dread on her white, proud face. I had thought, that week on Long Island, that she shut herself away from me, refusing to restore the intimacy of ten years earlier. But now a stiff loneliness hedged her as if she were rimmed in ice and snow. She smiled. "Dear Mary," she said. At the sound of her voice I lost my slightly cherished injury that she had refused to see me. "Let's go down to the library," she went on. "It's almost time for the turkey." I felt Fletcher break his intent watchfulness with a long sigh, and as the children went ahead of us, I caught at Thalia's arm. "Thalia—" She drew away, and her arm, under the soft flowing sleeve of dull blue stuff, was so slight it seemed brittle. I thought suddenly that she must have chosen that gown because it concealed so much beneath its lovely embroidered folds. "You aren't well, Thalia. What *is* it?"

"Well enough! Don't fuss about me." And even as I stared reproachfully she seemed to gather vitality, so that the dry pallor of her face became smooth ivory and her eyes were no longer hollow and distressed. "Come."

The dinner was amazingly like one of our old holidays. Winchester wore his best mood, the children were delighted and happy. Thalia, under the gold flames of the tall black candles, was a gracious and lovely hostess. I almost forgot my troublesome anxiety, wondering whether my imagination hadn't been playing me tricks.

We had coffee by the library fire and some of Winchester's old Chartreuse. Then he insisted upon exhibiting his new radio. Thalia demurred, but the children begged for a concert. "This is their party, Tally!" Winchester opened the doors of the old teakwood cabinet which housed the apparatus. Thalia sank back into the shadows of a wing chair, and I watched her over my cigarette. Off guard, she had relaxed into strange apathy. Was it the firelight or my unaccustomed Chartreuse? Her features seemed blurred as if a clumsy hand trying to trace a drawing made uncertain outlines. Strange groans and whirs from the radio.

"Win, I can't stand it!" Her voice dragged from some great distance. "Not to-night." She swayed to her feet, her hands restless under the loose sleeves.

"Static," growled Winchester. "Wait a minute."

"No!" Again it was as if vitality flowed into her. "Come, children. You have had your party. Time to go upstairs. I'll go with you."

They were well trained, I thought. Kisses for their father, a curtsy from Dorothy for me, and a grave little hand extended by Fletcher. Then Winchester came toward the fire as the three of them disappeared.

"You're good for Thalia," he said, in an undertone. "She's—well, what do you make of her?"

"Why?" I fenced, unwilling to indulge him in my vague anxieties.

"You saw how she acted about the radio. She has whims like that. Funny, she was herself at dinner. Last week she gave a dinner for me, important affair, pulled it off brilliantly. Then she shut herself up and won't open her door for days. I can't make it out. She's thin—"

"Have you had a doctor?" I asked, banally.

"That's another thing. She absolutely refuses. Made a fool of me when I brought one here. Wouldn't unlock her door. Says she just wants to rest. But"—he glanced toward the door—"do you know that fool on the bridge . . . that little runt? The other night, I swear I saw him rushing down the steps as I came home. Thalia just laughed when I asked about it."

Something clicked in my thoughts, a quick suspicion, drawing a parallel between her conduct and that of people I had seen in the East. Was it some drug? That lethargy, and the quick spring into vitality? Days behind a closed door—

"I wish you'd persuade her to go off for a few weeks. I'm frightfully pressed just now, in an important business matter, but if she'd go off—maybe you'd go with her?"

"Where, Winchester?" We both started, with the guilt of conspirators. Thalia came slowly into the room. "Where shall I go? Would you suggest—Atlantic City?"

"Perhaps. Although some place further south this time of year—" Winchester's imperturbability seemed to me far worse than some slight sign of embarrassment; it marked him as so rooted in successful deceit whether Thalia's inquiry were innocent or not. "If Mary would go with you. I can't get away just now."

"I shall not go anywhere until your deal goes through. Then—" Thalia seated herself again in the wing chair. The hand she lifted to her cheek, fingers just touching her temple beneath the soft drift of hair, seemed transparent against the firelight. "Have you told Mary about your deal? Winchester plans to be the most important man on Automobile Row." Was there mockery in her tone? "I can't tell you the details, but he's buying out all the rest."

"Don't be absurd. Not all of them. It's a big merging of companies, that's all."

"We entertain the lords at dinner, and in some mysterious way that smooths the merging. It makes a wife almost necessary."

"Invite Mary to the next shebang, and let her see how well you do it." Winchester was irritated. "For all your scoffing, there's as much politics to being president of such a concern as of the United States."

"Yes, I'll invite Mary. Then she'll see that you don't really want to dispense with me—yet."

"Good God, I meant for a week or two."

As Winchester, lighting a cigarette, snapped the head from several matches in succession, I moved my chair a little backward, distressed. There was a thin wire of significance drawn so taut between the two that I felt at any moment it might splinter in my face.

"It's so lucky"—malice flickered on her thin face—"that you weren't hurt in that skid on the bridge, Mary. Winchester would just have tossed you in the river to conceal your body."

"If you're going over that again!" Winchester strode out of the room. As Thalia turned her head slightly to watch him, her face and throat had the taut rigidity of pain so great that it congeals the nerves.

I was silent. With Thalia I had never dared intrude except when she admitted me. In another moment she too had risen. "You'd better go home, Mary," she said slowly. "I might tell you things you wouldn't care to live with."

I tried to touch her hand, but she retreated. If I had been wiser or more courageous, I might have helped her. I shall always have that regret, and that can't be much better to live with than whatever she might have told me. All I could say was stupidly, "Thalia, if there's anything I can do! You know I love you."

"Love? That's a strange word," she said, and her laugh in the quiet room was like the shrilling of a grasshopper on a hot afternoon. "One thing I will tell you." (She stood now on the stairway above me.) "Love has no power. It never shouts out across great space. Only fear and self-desire are strong."

Then she had gone, and the butler appeared silently, to lead me to the little dressing room.

"The car is waiting for you, madam," he assured me, opening the door. I didn't want it, but Winchester was waiting, too, hunched angrily in a corner.

"That's the way she acts," he began. "Now you've seen her I'll talk about it. Thalia never bore grudges, you know that."

"It seems deeper than a grudge," I said cautiously.

"That reference to the . . . the accident. That's a careless remark I made. I don't even remember just what I said. Something entirely inconsequential. Just that it was damned lucky no one was hurt when I was putting this merger across. You know if it'd got in the papers it would have queered me. Wrecking my own car . . . there's always a suspicion you've been drinking. She picked it up and won't drop it. It's like a fixed idea. If you can suggest something. I want her to see a nerve specialist. What does she do behind that locked door?"

"What about Atlantic City?" I asked, abruptly. I saw his dark eyes bulge, trying to ferret out my meaning, there in the dusky interior of the car.

"A week there with you might do her good." That was all he would say, and I hadn't courage enough to accuse him, even in Thalia's name.

"At least you'll try to see her again," he said, as the car stopped in front of my apartment house.

I couldn't sleep that night. I felt that just over the edge of my squirming thoughts there lay clear and whole the meaning of it all, but I couldn't reach past thought. And then, stupidly enough, I couldn't get up the next day. Just a feverish cold, but the doctor insisted on a week in bed and subdued me with warnings about influenza.

I had begun to feel steady enough on my feet to consider venturing outside my apartment when the invitation came, for a formal dinner at the Corsons'. Scrawled under the engraving was a line, "Please come. T." I sent a note, explaining that I had been ill, and that I should come—the dinner was a fortnight away—unless I stayed too wobbly.

I meant that night to arrive properly with the other guests, but my watch, which had never before done anything except lose a few minutes a day, had gained an unsuspected hour. Perhaps the hands stuck—perhaps—Well, I was told I was early, Thalia was dressing, and only the children, home for the Christmas holidays, were available. So I went again to the nursery. Dorothy was as plump and unconcerned as ever, but Fletcher had a strained, listening effect and he looked too thin and white for a little boy. They were having their supper on a small table, and Fletcher kept going to the door, looking out into the hall. "Mother promised to come up," he said.

The maid cleared away their dishes, and Dorothy, who was in a beguiling mood, chose to sit on my lap and entertain me with stories. One was about Nug the terrier; he had been sent out to the country because Mother didn't like him any more.

"I think," interrupted Fletcher, "she likes him, but he has a queer notion about her."

"She doesn't like him," repeated Dorothy. Then she dismissed that subject, and Fletcher too, for curiosity about the old silver chain I wore. I didn't notice that the boy had slipped away, but he must have gone down stairs; for presently his fingers closed over my wrist, like a frightened bird's claw, and I turned to see him, trembling, his eyes dark with terror. He couldn't speak but he clawed at me, and I shook Dorothy from my knees and let him pull me out to the hall.

"What is it, Fletcher?" He only pointed down the stairway, toward his mother's door, and I fled down those stairs. *What* had the child seen?

"The door wasn't locked—" he gasped behind me—"I opened it very still and went in—"

I pushed it ajar. Thalia sat before her dressing table, with the three-fold mirrors reiterating like a macabre symphony her rigid, contorted face. Her gown, burnished blue and green like peacock's feathers, sheathed her gaudily, and silver, blue and green chiffon clouded her shoulders. Her hands clutched at the edge of the dressing table. For an instant I could not move, thrust through with a terror like the boy's.

Then I stumbled across the room. Before I reached her, the mirrors echoed her long shudder, her eyelids dragged open, and I saw her stare at my reflection wavering toward her. Then her hands relaxed, moved quickly toward the crystal jars along the heavy glass of the table and, without a word, she leaned softly forward, to draw a scarlet line along her white lips.

"How cold it is in here," I said, stupidly, glancing toward the windows, where the heavy silk damasks, drawn across, lay in motionless folds. "Fletcher said—" I was awkward, an intruder.

"He startled me." Her voice came huskily. She rouged her hollow cheeks. It was as if she drew another face for herself. "I didn't have time to lock the door." Then turning, she sought him out, huddled at the doorway, like a moth on a pin of fear: "It wasn't nice of you, Son. It's all right now. You see?" She rose, drawing her lovely scarf over her shoulders. "You should never open closed doors." She blew him a kiss from her finger tips. "Now run along and forget you were so careless."

The icy stir of air against my skin had ceased. I stared at her, my mind racing back over what I knew of various drugs and the stigmata of their victims. But her eyes were clear and undilated, a little piteous. "This," she said, "is the last time. I can't endure it." And then, with that amazing flood of vitality, as if a sudden connection had been made and current flowed again, "Come, Mary. It is time we were down stairs."

I thought Fletcher peered over the railing as we went down. But a swift upward glance failed to detect him.

The dinner itself I don't remember definitely except that it glittered and sparkled, moving with slightly alcoholic wit through elaborate courses, while I sat like an abashed poor relation at a feast, unable to stop watching Thalia, wondering whether my week of fever had given me a tendency to hallucinations. At the end a toast was proposed, to Winchester Corson and his extraordinary success. "It's done then?" Thalia's gayety had sudden malice—as she looked across at Winchester, seating himself after a slightly pompous speech. "Sealed and cemented forever?"

"Thanks to his charming wife, too," cried a plump, bald man, waving his glass. " A toast to Mrs. Corson!"

Thalia rose, her rouge like flecked scarlet on white paper. One hand drew her floating scarf about her throat, and her painted lips moved without a sound. There was an instant of agitated discomfort, as the guests felt their mood broken so abruptly, into which her voice pierced, thin, high. "I . . . deserve . . . such a toast—"

I pushed back my chair and reached her side.

"I'll take her—" I saw Winchester's face, wine-flushed, angry rather than concerned. "Come, Thalia."

"Don't bother. I'll be all right—now." But she moved ahead of me so swiftly that I couldn't touch her. I thought she tried to close her door against me, but I was too quick for that. The silver candelabra still burned above the mirrors. "Mary!" Her voice was low again as she spoke a telephone number. "Tell him *at once.*" She stood away from me, her face a white mask with spots of scarlet, her peacock dress ashimmer. I did as I was bid and when I had said, "Mrs. Corson wishes you at once," there was an emptiness where a man's voice had come which suggested a sudden leap out of a room somewhere.

"I can never get in again!" Her fingers curled under the chiffon scarf. "Never! The black agony of fighting back— If he—" She bent her head, listening. "Go down to the door and let him in," she said.

I crept down the stairs. Voices from the drawing-room. Winchester was seeing the party through. Almost as I reached the door and opened it I found him there: the little doctor with the pointed beard. He brushed past me up the stairs. He knew the way then! I was scarcely surprised to find Thalia's door fast shut when I reached it. Behind it came not a sound. Fletcher, like an unhappy sleepwalker, his eyes heavy, slipped down beside me, clinging to my hand. I heard farewells, churring of taxis and cars. Then Winchester came up the stairs.

"She's shut you out?" He raised his fist and pounded on the door. "I'm going to stop this nonsense!"

"I sent for a doctor," I said. "He's in there."

"Is it"—his face was puffy and gray—"that same fool?"

Then the door opened, and the man confronted us.

"It is over," he said.

"What have you done to her?" Winchester lunged toward the door, but the little man's lifted hand had dignity enough somehow to stop him.

"She won't come back again." He spoke slowly "You may look if you care to."

"She's dead?"

"She died—months ago. There on the bridge. But you called to her, and she thought you wanted—*her.*"

Winchester thrust him aside and strode into the room. I dared one glance and saw only pale hair shining on the pillow. Then Fletcher flung himself against me, sobbing, and I knelt to hold him close against the fear we both felt.

What Winchester saw I never knew. He hurled himself past us, down the stairs. And Thalia was buried with the coffin lid fast closed under the flowers.

228/Helen R. Hull

Since I Died

Elizabeth Stuart Phelps

Elizabeth Stuart Phelps (1844–1911) took her mother's name out of empathy for the once-popular author of children's stories, magazine articles, and religious books about the frustrations of domesticity. Bibliographers should not be confused by the two authors with the same name, as the younger Phelps was motherless by the age of eight and there was an interval between the end of one's career and the beginning of the other's.

Her first novel, The Gates Ajar *(1868), was a fantasy of afterlife inspired by her Calvinist upbringing and the Civil War. She wrote it at the age of 20 in the barn and attic, wrapped in her mother's coat. Phelps's once considerable reputation has been done a disservice in that only* The Gates Ajar, *wildly successful despite its immaturity, has been kept perpetually in print. Her better work has only recently begun to regain critical and popular attention, with the reissues of* The Silent Partner *(1871) in 1983 and* Doctor Zay *(1882) in 1987, among others. Her stories are filled with exceptional and independent women, some sophisticated, some rustic, many eccentric and alone as in the best work of Mary E. Wilkins Freeman.*

Phelps was an influential supporter of women's rights and in her early career was encouraged by many of her contemporaries, including Harriet Beecher Stowe of Uncle Tom's Cabin *fame and the latter-day Romanticist Harriet Prescott Spofford. Throughout Phelps's long and successful career as a storyteller, essayist and poet, her Calvinist and feminist ideologies battled one another and were never fully reconciled. This places a fascinating tension in much of her work.*

In the early days of her popularity, she was frequently seen in the company of Andover physician Dr. Mary Briggs Harris. Many of her tales from this period are light-hearted and amusing, as evidenced by her first collection, Men, Women and Ghosts *(1869). Later works were increasingly brooding, revealing an unhappier side to the author, who eventually married, but unsuccessfully.*

"Since I Died" first appeared in the February 1873 Scribner's Monthly, *from which it is reprinted here, and was reprinted in Phelps's volume* Sealed Orders *(1879). It has a measured cadence and a decadence that shows some influence by the writings of Parisians Theophile Gautier and Charles Baudelaire, who impressed many New England writers at the time. "Since I Died" explores the theme of lovers separated by death, a theme Phelps repeated near the end of her life in "The Presence" (1910). In the later tale, a woman's husband appears to her as a specter and she struggles toward a difficult reunion. "Since I Died" differs mainly in that its parted lovers are women, clearly partners in a successful "Boston Marriage." Although there is mention of a mother (peripheral and barely seen) who may have been included to imply that these women are merely exceedingly close sisters, erotic undertones are clear, and the resemblance to the later heterosexual version undeniable. It may surprise modern readers that a positive treatment of lesbianism was not uncommon in nineteenth-century periodical fiction, though the subject tended to be approached circumspectly. In the present anthology, Trevanion's "A Ghost Story" and Brown's "There and Here" may be considered supporting examples, but "Since I Died" is by far the most overt.*

⁂

How very still you sit!

If the shadow of an eyelash stirred upon your cheek; if that gray line about your mouth should snap its tension at this quivering end; if the pallor of your profile warmed a little; if that tiny muscle on your forehead, just at the left eyebrow's curve, should start and twitch; if you would but grow a trifle restless, sitting there beneath my steady gaze; if you moved a finger of your folded hands; if you should turn and look behind your chair, or lift your face, half lingering and half longing, half loving and half loth, to ponder on the annoyed and thwarted cry which the wind is making, where I stand between it and yourself, against the half-closed window.—Ah, there! You sigh and stir, I think. You lift your head. The little muscle is a captive still; the line about your mouth is tense and hard; the deepening hollow in your cheek has no warmer tint, I see, than the great Doric column which the moonlight builds against the wall. I lean against it; I hold out my arms.

You lift your head and look me in the eye.

If a shudder crept across your figure; if your arms, laid out upon the table, leaped but once above your head; if you named my name; if you held your breath with terror, or sobbed aloud for love, or sprang, or cried—.

But you only lift your head and look me in the eye.

If I dared step near, or nearer; if it were permitted that I should cross the current of your living breath; if it were willed that I should feel the leap of human blood within your veins; if I should touch your hands, your cheeks, your lips; if I dropped an arm as lightly as a snowflake round your shoulder—

The fear which no heart has fathomed, the fate which no fancy has faced, the riddle which no soul has read, steps between your substance and my soul.

I drop my arms. I sink into the heart of the pillared light upon the wall. I will not wonder what would happen if my outlines defined upon it to your view. I will not think of that which could be, would be, if I struck across your still-set vision, face to face.

Ah me, how still she sits! With what a fixed, incurious stare she looks me in the eye!

The wind, now that I stand no longer between it and yourself, comes enviously in. It lifts the curtain, and whirls about the room. It bruises the surface of the great pearled pillar where I lean. I am caught within it. Speech and language struggle over me. Mute articulations fill the air. Tears and laughter, and the sounding of soft lips, and the falling of low cries, possess me. Will she listen? Will she bend her head? Will her lips part in recognition? Is there an alphabet between us? Or have the winds of night a vocabulary to lift before her holden eyes?

We sat many times together, and talked of this. Do you remember, dear? You held my hand. Tears that I could not see fell on it; we sat by the great hall-window upstairs, where the maple shadow goes to sleep, face down, across the floor upon a lighted night; the old green curtain waved its hands upon us like a mesmerist, I thought; like a priest, you said.

"When we are parted, you shall go," you said; and when I shook my head you smiled—you always smiled when you said that, but you said it always quite the same.

I think I hardly understood you then. Now that I hold your eyes in mine, and you see me not; now when I stretch my hand and you touch me not; now that I cry your name, and you hear it not,—I comprehend you, tender one! A wisdom not of earth was in your words. "To live, is dying; I will die. To die is life, and you shall live."

Now when the fever turned, I thought of this.

That must have been—ah! how long ago? I miss the conception of that for which *how long* stands index.

Yet I perfectly remember that I perfectly understood it to be at three o'clock on a rainy Sunday morning that I died. Your little watch stood in its case of olive-wood upon the table, and drops were on the window. I noticed both, though you did not know it. I see the watch now, in your pocket; I cannot tell if the hands move, or only pulsate like a heart-throb, to and fro; they stand and point, mute golden fingers, paralyzed and pleading, forever at the hour of three. At this I wonder.

When first you said I "was sinking fast," the words sounded as old and familiar as a nursery tale. I heard you in the hall. The doctor had just left, and you went to mother and took her face in your two arms, and laid your hand across her mouth, as if it were she who had spoken. She cried out and threw up her thin old hands; but you stood as still as Eternity. Then I thought again: "It is she who dies; I shall live."

So often and so anxiously we have talked of this thing called death, that now that it is all over between us, I cannot understand why we found in it such a source of distress. It bewilders me. I am often bewildered here. Things and the fancies of things possess a relation which as yet is new and strange to me. Here is a mystery.

Now, in truth, it seems a simple matter for me to tell you how it has been with me since your lips last touched me, and your arms held me to the vanishing air.

Oh, drawn, pale lips! Nerveless, dropping arms! I told you I would come. Did ever promise fail I spoke to you? "Come and show me Death," you said. I have come to show you Death. I could show you the fairest sight and sweetest that ever blessed your eyes. Why, look! Is it not fair? Am I terrible? Do you shrink or shiver? Would you turn from me, or hide your strained, expectant face?

Would she? Does she? Will she? . . .

Ah, how the room widened! I could tell you that. It grew great and luminous day by day. At night the walls throbbed; lights of rose ran round them, and blue fire, and a tracery as of the shadows of little leaves. As the walls expanded, the air fled. But I tried to tell you how little pain I knew or feared. Your haggard face bent over me. I could not speak; when I would I struggled, and you said "She suffers!" Dear, it was so very little!

Listen, till I tell you how that night came on. The sun fell and the dew slid down. It seemed to me that it slid into my heart, but still I felt no pain. Where the walls pulsed and receded, the hills came in. Where the old bureau stood, above the glass, I saw a single mountain with a face of fire, and purple hair. I tried to tell you this, but you said: "She wanders." I laughed in my heart at that, for it was such a blessed wandering! As the night locked the sun below the mountain's solemn watching face, the Gates of Space were lifted up before me; the everlasting doors of Matter swung for me upon their rusty hinges, and the

King of Glories entered in and out. All the kingdoms of the earth, and the power of them, beckoned to me, across the mist my failing senses made,—ruins and roses, and the brows of Jura and the singing of the Rhine; a shaft of red light on the Sphinx's smile, and caravans in sand-storms, and an icy wind at sea, and gold adream in mines that no man knew, and mothers sitting at their doors in valleys singing babes to sleep, and women in dank cellars selling souls for bread, and the whir of wheels in giant factories, and a single prayer somewhere in a den of death,—I could not find it, though I searched,—and the smoke of battle, and broken music, and a sense of lilies alone beside a stream at the rising of the sun—and, at last, your face, dear, all alone.

I discovered then, that the walls and roof of the room had van-ished quite. The night-wind blew in. The maple in the yard almost brushed my cheek. Stars were about me, and I thought the rain had stopped, yet seemed to hear it, up on the seeming of a window which I could not find.

One thing only hung between me and immensity. It was your single, awful, haggard face. I looked my last into your eyes. Stronger than death, they held and claimed my soul. I feebly raised my hand to find your own. More cruel than the grave, your wild grasp chained me. Then I struggled, and you cried out, and your face slipped, and I stood free.

I stood upon the floor, beside the bed. That which had been I lay there at rest, but terrible, before me. You hid your face, and I saw you slide upon your knees. I laid my hand upon your head; you did not stir; I spoke to you: "Dear, look around a minute!" but you knelt quite still. I walked to and fro about the room, and meeting my mother, touched her on the elbow; she only said, "She's gone!" and sobbed aloud. "I have not *gone!*" I cried; but she sat sobbing on.

The walls of the room had settled now, and the ceiling stood in its solid place. The window was shut, but the door stood open. Suddenly I was restless, and I ran.

I brushed you in hurrying by, and hit the little light-stand where the tumblers stood; I looked to see if it would fall, but it only shivered as if a breath of wind had struck it once.

But I was restless, and I ran. In the hall I met the Doctor. This amused me, and I stopped to think it over. "Ah, Doctor," said I, "you need not trouble yourself to go up. I'm quite well to-night, you see." But he made me no answer; he gave me no glance; he hung up his hat, and laid his hand upon the banister against which I leaned, and went pon-derously up.

It was not until he had nearly reached the landing that it occurred to me, still leaning on the banisters, that his heavy arm must have swept against and *through* me, where I stood against the oaken mouldings which he grasped.

I saw his feet fall on the stairs above me; but they made no sound which reached my ear. "You'll not disturb me *now* with your big boots, sir," said I, nodding; "never fear!"

But he disappeared from sight above me, and still I heard no sound. Now the Doctor had left the front door unlatched.

As I touched it, it blew open wide, and solemnly. I passed out and down the steps. I could see that it was chilly, yet I felt no chill. Frost was on the grass, and in the east a pallid streak, like the cheek of one who had watched all night. The flowers in the little square plots hung their heads and drew their shoulders up; there was a lonely, late lily which I broke and gathered to my heart, where I breathed upon it, and it warmed and looked me kindly in the eye. This, I remember, gave me pleasure. I wandered in and out about the garden in the scattering rain; my feet left no trace upon the dripping grass, and I saw with interest that the garment which I wore gathered no moisture and no cold. I sat musing for a while upon the piazza, in the garden-chair, not caring to go in. It was so many months since I had felt able to sit upon the piazza in the open air. "By and by," I thought, I would go in and upstairs to see you once again. The curtains were drawn from the parlor windows and I passed and repassed, looking in.

All this while, the cheek of the east was waning, and the air gathering faint heats and lights about me. I remembered, presently, the old arbor at the garden-foot, where before I was sick, we sat so much together; and thinking, "She will be surprised to know that I have been down alone," I was restless, and I ran again.

I meant to come back and see you, dear, once more. I saw the lights in the room where I had lain sick, overhead; and your shadow on the curtain; and I blessed it, with all the love of life and death, as I bounded by.

The air was thick with sweetness from the dying flowers. The birds woke, and the zenith lighted, and the leap of health was in my limbs. The old arbor held out its soft arms to me—but I was restless, and I ran.

The field opened before me, and meadows with broad bosoms, and a river flashed before me like a scimiter, and woods interlocked their hands to stay me—but being restless, on I ran.

The house dwindled behind me; and the light in my sick-room, and your shadow on the curtain. But yet I was restless, and I ran.

In the twinkling of an eye I fell into a solitary place. Sand and rocks were in it, and a falling wind. I paused, and knelt upon the sand, and mused a little in this place. I mused of you, and life and death, and love and agony;—but these had departed from me, as dim and distant as the fainting wind. A sense of solemn expectation filled the air. A tremor and a trouble wrapped my soul.

"I must be dead!" I said aloud. I had no sooner spoken than I learned that I was not alone.

The sun had risen, and on a ledge of ancient rock, weather-stained and red, there had fallen over against me the outline of a Presence lifted up against the sky, and turning suddenly, I saw......

Lawful to utter, but utterance has fled! Lawful to utter, but a greater than Law restrains me! Am I blotted from your desolate fixed eyes? Lips that my mortal lips have pressed, can you not quiver when I cry? Soul that my eternal soul has loved, can you stand enveloped in my presence, and not spring like a fountain to me? Would you not know how it has been with me since your perishable eyes beheld my perished face? What my eyes have seen or my ears have heard, or my heart conceived without you? If I have missed or mourned for you? If I have watched or longed for you? Marked your solitary days and sleepless nights, and tearless eyes, and monotonous slow echo of my unanswered name? Would you not know?

Alas! would she? Would she not? My soul misgives me with a matchless, solitary fear. I am called, and I slip from her. I am beckoned, and I lose her.

Her face dims, and her folded, lonely hands fade from my sight.

Time to tell her a guarded thing! Time to whisper a treasured word! A moment to tell her that *Death is dumb, for Life is deaf!* A moment to tell her.—

The Little Dirty Girl

ılıı

Joanna Russ

Born in New York city in 1937, a graduate of Cornell and Yale Universities, Joanna Russ is presently a professor at the University of Washington in Seattle, where she teaches creative writing. Her award-winning story "When it Changed" (1972) shook science fiction right off its conservative foundation. Her book The Lesson For Today Is, How To Suppress Women's Writing *(1983) should be consulted for an idea of how it came to be that so few people know that feminist supernatural stories have a long tradition. Her other books include:* Picnic on Paradise *(1968), about a woman trying to lead a group of spoiled tourists out of a deadly, alien landscape;* The Female Man *(1975), a recognized classic of science fiction; a lesbian children's story,* Kittatiny: A Tale of Magic *(1978); a selection of her best short stories,* The Zanzibar Cat *(1983); a selection of novelettes,* Extra (Ordinary) People *(1984), which includes the award-winning "Souls"; and the collection* The Hidden Side of the Moon *(1987).*

"The Little Dirty Girl," from the second volume of Terri Windling and Mark Arnold's Elsewhere *(1983), is a very personal tale, apparently deeply felt by the author. Its portrayal of a single, middle-aged, professional woman's search for her own identity and feelings, and of the barriers that can exist between mothers and daughters, explores two of the feminist concerns of this story. It is also tremendously original. This cannot be said of many ghost stories, which use conventional themes and plot devices, with only subtle variations, more often than wholly unique approaches. Though Russ is widely known as a science fiction writer,*

"The Little Dirty Girl" suggests that she should be known as a writer of the supernatural as well.

⫶

Dear——— ,

Do you like cats? I never asked you. There are all sorts of cats: elegant, sinuous cats, clunky, heavy-breathing cats, skinny, desperate cats, meatloaf-shaped cats, waddling, dumb cats, big slobs of cats who step heavily and groan whenever they try to fit themselves (and they never do fit) under something or in between something or past something.

I'm allergic to all of them. You'd think they'd know it. But as I take my therapeutic walks around the neighborhood (still aching and effortful after ten months, though when questioned, my doctor replies, with the blank, baffled innocence of those Martian children so abstractedly brilliant they've never learned to communicate about merely human matters with anyone, *that my back will get better*) cats venture from alleyways, slip out from under parked cars, bound up cellar steps, prick up their ears and flash out of gardens, all lifting up their little faces, wreathing themselves around my feet, crying *Dependency! Dependency!* and showing their elegantly needly little teeth, which they never use save in yearning appeal to my goodness. They have perfect confidence in me. If I try to startle them by hissing, making loud noises, or clapping my hands sharply, they merely stare in interested fashion and scratch themselves with their hind legs: how nice. I've perfected a method of lifting kitties on the toe of my shoe and giving them a short ride through the air (this is supposed to be alarming); they merely come running back for more.

And the children! I don't dislike children. Yes I do. No I don't, but I feel horribly awkward with them. So of course I keep meeting them on my walks this summer: alabaster little boys with angelic fair hair and sky-colored eyes (this section of Seattle is Scandinavian and the Northwest gets very little sun) come up to me and volunteer such compelling information as:

"*I'm* going to my friend's house."

"I'm going to the store."

"My name is Markie."

"I wasn't really scared of that big dog; I was just *startled.*"

"People leave a lot of broken glass around here."

The littler ones confide; the bigger ones warn of the world's dangers: dogs, cuts, blackberry bushes that might've been sprayed. One came up to me once—what do they see in a tall, shuffling, professional, intellectual woman of forty?—and said, after a moment's thought:

"Do you like frogs?"

The Little Dirty Girl/237

What could I do? I said yes, so a shirt-pocket that jumped and said *rivit* was opened to disclose Mervyn, an exquisite little being the color of wet, mottled sea-sand, all webbed feet and amber eyes, who was then transferred to my palm where he sat and blinked. Mervyn was a toad, actually; he's barely an inch long and can be found all over Seattle, usually upside down under a rock. I'm sure he (or she) is the Beloved Toad and Todkins and Todlekrancz Virginia Woolf used in her letters to Emma Vaughan.

And the girls? O they don't approach tall, middle-aged women. Little girls are told not to talk to strangers. And the little girls of Seattle (at least in my neighborhood) are as obedient and feminine as any in the world; to the jeans and tee-shirts of Liberation they (or more likely their parents) add hair-ribbons, baby-sized pocketbooks, fancy pins, pink shoes, even toe polish.

The liveliest of them I ever saw was a little person of five, coasting downhill in a red wagon, her cheeks pink with excitement, one pony-tail of yellow hair undone, her white tee-shirt askew, who gave a decorous little squeak of joy at the sheer speed of it. I saw and smiled; pink-cheeks saw and shrieked again, more loudly and confidently this time, then looked away, embarrassed, jumped quickly out of her wagon, and hauled it energetically up the hill.

Except for the very littlest, how neat, how clean, how carefully dressed they are! with long, straight hair that the older ones (I know this) still iron under waxed paper.

The little, dirty girl was different.

She came up to me in the supermarket. I've hired someone to do most of my shopping, as I can't carry much, but I'd gone in for some little thing, as I often do. It's a relief to get off the hard bed and away from the standing desk or the abbreviated kitchen stools I've scattered around the house (one foot up and one foot down); in fact it's simply such a relief—

Well, the little, dirty girl *was* dirty; she was the dirtiest eight-year-old I've ever seen. Her black hair was a long tangle. Her shoes were down-at-heel, the laces broken, her white (or rather grey) socks belling limply out over her ankles. Her nose was running. Her pink dress, so ancient that it showed her knees, was limp and wrinkled and the knees themselves had been recently skinned. She looked as if she had slid halfway down Volunteer Park's steepest, dirtiest hill on her panties and then rolled end-over-end the rest of the way. Besides all this, there were snot-and-tear-marks on her face (which was reddened and sallow and looked as if she'd been crying) and she looked—well, what can I say? *Neglected.* Not poor, though someone had dressed her rather eccentrically, not physically unhealthy or underfed, but messy, left alone, ignored, kicked out, bedraggled, like a cat caught in a thunderstorm.

She looked (as I said) tear-stained, and yet came up to my shopping cart with perfect composure and kept me calm company for a minute or so. Then she pointed to a box of Milky Way candy bars on a shelf above my head, saying "I like those," in a deep, gravelly voice that suggested a bad cold.

I ignored the hint. No, that's wrong; it wasn't a hint; it was merely a social, adult remark, self-contained and perfectly emotionless, as if she had long ago given up expecting that telling anyone she wanted something would result in getting it. Since my illness I have developed a fascination with the sheer, elastic wealth of children's bodies, the exhaustless, energetic health they don't know they have and which I so acutely and utterly miss, but I wasn't for an instant tempted to feel this way about the Little Dirty Girl. She had been through too much. She had Resources. If she showed no fear of me, it wasn't because she trusted me but because she trusted nothing. She had no expectations and no hopes. Nonetheless she attached herself to me and my shopping cart and accompanied me down two more aisles, and there seemed to be hope in that. So I made the opening, social, adult remark:

"What's your name?"

"A. R." Those are the initials on my handbag. I looked at her sharply but she stared levelly back, unembarrassed, self-contained, unexpressive.

"I don't believe that," I said finally.

"I could tell you lots of things you wouldn't believe," said the Little Dirty Girl.

She followed me up to the cashier and as I was putting out my small packages one by one by one, I saw her lay out on the counter a Milky Way bar and a nickel, the latter fetched from somewhere in that short-skirted, cap-sleeved dress. The cashier, a middle-aged woman, looked at me and I back at her; I laid out two dimes next to the nickel. She really did want it! As I was going into the logistics of How Many Short Trips From The Cart To The Car And How Many Long Ones From The Car To The Kitchen, the Little Dirty Girl spoke: "I can carry that." (Gravelly and solemn.)

She added hoarsely, "I bet I live near you."

"Well, *I* bet you don't," I said.

She didn't answer, but followed me to the parking lot, one proprietary hand on the cart, and when I unlocked my car door, she darted past me and started carrying packages from the cart to the front seat. I can't move fast enough to escape these children. She sat there calmly as I got in. Then she said, wiping her nose on the back of her hand:

The Little Dirty Girl/239

"I'll help you take your stuff out when you get home."

Now I know that sort of needy offer and I don't like it. Here was the Little Dirty Girl offering to help me, and smelling in close quarters as if she hadn't changed her underwear for days: demandingness, neediness, more annoyance. Then she said in her flat, crow's voice: "I'll do it and go away. I won't bother you."

Well, what can you do? My heart misgave me. I started the car and we drove the five minutes to my house in silence, whereupon she grabbed all the packages at once (to be useful) and some slipped back on the car seat; I think this embarrassed her. But she got my things up the stairs to the porch in only two trips and put them on the unpainted porch rocker, from where I could pick them up one by one, and there we stood.

Why speechless? Was it honesty? I wanted to thank her, to act decent, to make that sallow face smile. I wanted to tell her to go away, that I wouldn't let her in, that I'd lock the door. But all I could think of to say was, "What's your name, really?" and the wild thing said stubbornly, "A. R." and when I said, "No, really," she cried *"A. R. !"* and facing me with her eyes screwed up, shouted something unintelligible, passionate and resentful, and was off up the street. I saw her small figure turning down one of the cross-streets that meets mine at the top of the hill. Seattle is grey and against the massed storm clouds to the north her pink dress stood out vividly. She was going to get rained on. Of course.

I turned to unlock my front door and a chunky, slow, old cat, a black-and-white Tom called Williamson who lives two houses down, came stiffly out from behind an azalea bush, looked slit-eyed (bored) about him, noticed me (his pupils dilated with instant interest) and bounded across the parking strip to my feet. Williamson is a banker-cat, not really portly or dignified but simply too lazy and unwieldy to bother about anything much. Either something scares him and he huffs under the nearest car or he scrounges. Like all kitties he bumbled around my ankles, making steam-engine noises. I never feed him. I don't pet him or talk to him. I even try not to look at him. I shoved him aside with one foot and opened the front door; Williamson backed off, raised his fat, jowled face and began the old cry: *Mrawr! Mrawr!* I booted him ungently off the porch before he could trot into my house with me, and as he slowly prepared to attack the steps (he never quite makes it) locked myself in. And the Little Dirty Girl's last words came suddenly clear:
I'll be back.

Another cat. There are too many in this story but I can't help it. The Little Dirty Girl was trying to coax the neighbor's superbly elegant half-Siamese out from under my car a few days later, an animal tiger-marked on paws and tail and as haughty-and-mysterious-looking as all cats are supposed to be, though it's really only the long Siamese body and small head. Ma'amselle (her name) still occasionally leaps onto my dining room windowsill and stares in (the people who lived here before me used to feed her). I was coming back from a walk, the Little Dirty Girl was on her knees, and Ma'amselle was under the car; when the Little Dirty Girl saw me she stood up, and Ma'amselle flashed Egyptianly through the laurel hedge and was gone. Someone had washed the Little Dirty Girl's pink dress (though a few days back, I'm afraid) and made a half-hearted attempt to braid her hair: there were barrettes and elastic somewhere in the tangle. Her cold seemed better. When it rains in August our summer can change very suddenly to early fall, and this was a chilly day; the Little Dirty Girl had nothing but her mud-puddle-marked dress between her thin skin and the Seattle air. Her cold seemed better, though, and her cheeks were pink with stooping. She said, in the voice of a little girl this time and not a raven, "She had *blue* eyes."

"She's Siamese," I said. "What's your name?"

"A. R."

"Now look, I don't—"

"*It's A.R. !*" She was getting loud and stolid again. She stood there with her skinny, scabbed knees showing from under her dress and shivered in the unconscious way kids do who are used to it; I've seen children do it on the Lower East Side in New York because they had no winter coat (in January). I said, "You come in." She followed me up the steps—warily, I think—but when we got inside her expression changed, it changed utterly; she clasped her hands and said with radiant joy, "Oh, they're *beautiful!*"

These were my astronomical photographs. I gave her my book of microphotographs (cells, crystals, hailstones) and went into the kitchen to put up water for tea; when I got back she'd dropped the book on my old brown-leather couch and was walking about with her hands clasped in front of her and that same look of radiant joy on her face. I live in an ordinary, shabby frame house that has four rooms and a finished attic; the only unusual thing about it is the number of books and pictures crammed in every which way among the (mostly second-hand) furniture. There are Woolworth frames for the pictures and cement-block bookcases for the books; nonetheless the Little Dirty Girl was as awed as if she'd found Aladdin's Cave.

She said, "It's so . . . sophisticated!"

Well, there's no withstanding that. Even if you think: what do kids know? She followed me into the kitchen where I gave her a glass of milk and a peach (she sipped and nibbled). She thought the few straggling rose bushes she could see in the back garden were wonderful. She loved my old brown refrigerator; she said, "It's so big! And such a color!" Then she said anxiously, "Can I see the upstairs?" and got excited over the attic eaves which were also "so big" (wallboard and dirty pink paint) to the point that she had to run and stand under one side and then run across the attic and stand under the other. She liked the "view" from the bedroom (the neighbor's laurel hedge and a glimpse of someone else's roof) but my study (books, a desk, a glimpse of the water) moved her so deeply and painfully that she only stood still in the center of the room, struggling with emotion, her hands again clasped in front of her. Finally she burst out, "It's so . . . *swanky!*" Here my kettle screamed and when I got back she had gotten bold enough to touch the electric typewriter (she jumped when it turned itself on) and then walked about slowly, touching the books with the tips of her fingers. She was brave and pushed the tabs on the desk lamp (though not hard enough to turn it on) and boldly picked up my little mailing scale. As she did so, I saw that there were buttons missing from the back of her dress; I said, "A. R., come here."

She dropped the scale with a crash. "I didn't mean it!" Sulky again.

"It's not that, it's your buttons," I said, and hauled her to the study closet where I keep a Band-Aid box full of extras; two were a reasonable match: little, flat-topped, pearlized, pink things you can hardly find anymore. I sewed them onto her, not that it helped much, and the tangles of her hair kept falling back and catching. What a forest of lost barrettes and snarls of old rubber bands! I lifted it all a little grimly, remembering the pain of combing out. She sat flatly, all adoration gone:

"You can't comb my hair against my will; you're too weak."

"I wasn't going to," I said.

"That's what *you* say," the L.D.G. pointed out.

"If I try, you can stop me," I said. After a moment she turned around, flopped down on my typing chair, and bent her head. So I fetched my old hairbrush (which I haven't used for years) and did what I could with the upper layers, managing even to smooth out some of the lower ones, though there were places near her neck nearly as matted and tangled as felt; I finally had to cut some pieces out with my nail scissors.

L.D.G. didn't shriek (as I used to, insisting my cries were far more artistic than those of the opera singers on the radio on Sundays) but finally asked for the comb herself and winced silently until she was decently braided, with rubber bands on the ends. We put the rescued barrettes in her shirt pocket. Without that cloud of hair her sallow face and pitch-ball eyes looked bigger, and oddly enough, younger; she was no more a wandering Fury with the voice of a Northwest-coast raven but a reasonably human (though draggly) little girl.

I said, "You look nice."

She got up, went into the bathroom, and looked at herself in the mirror. Then she said calmly, "No, I don't. I look conventional."

"Conventional?" said I. She came out of the bathroom, flipping back her new braids.

"Yes, I must go."

And as I was wondering at her tact (for anything after this would have been an anti-climax):

"But I shall return."

"That's fine," I said, "but I want to have grown-up manners with you, A. R. Don't ever come before ten in the morning or if my car isn't here or if you can hear my typewriter going. In fact, I think you had better call me on the telephone first, the way other people do."

She shook her head sweetly. She was at the front door before I could follow her, peering out. It was raining again. I saw that she was about to step out into it and cried "Wait, A. R.!" hurrying as fast as I could down the cellar steps to the garage, from where I could get easily to my car. I got from the back seat the green plastic poncho I always keep there and she didn't protest when I dumped it over her and put the hood over her head, though the poncho was much too big and even dragged on the ground in the front and back. She said only, "Oh, it's swanky. Is it from the Army?" So I had the satisfaction of seeing her move up the hill as a small, green tent instead of a wet, pink draggle. Though with her tea-party manners she hadn't really eaten anything; the milk and peach were untouched. Was it wariness? Or did she just not like milk and peaches? Remembering our first encounter, I wrote on the pad by the telephone, which is my shopping list:

Milky Way Bars

And then:

1 doz.

She came back. She never did telephone in advance. It was all right, though; she had the happy faculty of somehow turning up when I wasn't working and wasn't busy and was thinking of her. But how often is an invalid busy or working? We went on walks or stayed home and on these occasions the business about the Milky Ways turned out to be a brilliant guess, for never have I met a child with such a passion for junk food. A. R.'s formal, disciplined politeness in front of milk or fruit was like a cat's in front of the mass-produced stuff; faced with jam, honey, or marmalade, the very ends of her braids crisped and she attacked like a cat flinging itself on a fish; I finally had to hide my own

The Little Dirty Girl/243

supplies in self-defense. Then on relatively good days it was ice cream or Sara Lee cake, and on bad ones Twinkies or Mallo-bars, Hostess cupcakes, Three Musketeers bars, marshmallow cream, maraschino chocolates, Turkish taffy, saltwater taffy, or—somewhat less horribly— Doritos, reconstituted potato chips, corn chips, pretzels (fat or thin), barbecued corn chips, or onion-flavored corn chips, anything like that. She refused nuts and hated peanut butter. She also talked continuously while eating, largely in polysyllables, which made me nervous as I perpetually expected her to choke, but she never did. She got no fatter. To get her out of the house and so away from food, I took her to an old-fashioned five-and-ten nearby and bought her shoelaces. Then I took her down to watch the local ship-canal bridge open up (to let a sailboat through) and we cheered. I took her to a department store (just to look; "I know consumerism is against your principles," she said with priggish and mystifying accuracy) and bought her a pin shaped like a ladybug. She refused to go to the zoo ("An animal jail!") but allowed as the rose gardens ("A plant *hotel,")* were both pleasant and educational. A ride on the zoo merry-go-round excited her to the point of screaming and running around dizzily in circles of half an hour afterwards, which embarrassed me—but then no one paid the slightest attention; I suppose shrieky little girls had happened there before, though the feminine youth of Seattle, in its Mary Jane shoes and pink pocketbooks, rather pointedly ignored her. The waterfall in the downtown park, on the contrary, sobered her up; this is a park built right on top of a crossing over one of the city's highways and is usually full of office-workers; a walkway leads not only up to but actually behind the waterfall. A. R. wandered among the beds of bright flowers and passed, stopping, behind the water, trying to stick her hand in the falls; she came out saying:

"It looks like an old man's beard," (pointing to one of the ragged Skid Row men who was sleeping on the grass in the rare, Northern sunlight). Then she said, "No, it looks like a lady's dress without any seams."

Once, feeling we had become friends enough for it, I ran her a bath and put her clothes through the basement washer-dryer; her splashings and yellings in the bathroom were terrific and afterwards she flashed nude about the house, hanging out of windows, embellishing her strange, raucous shouts with violent jerkings and boundings-about that I think were meant for dancing. She even ran out the back door naked and had circled the house before I—voiceless with calling, *"A. R., come back here!"*—had presence of mind enough to lock both the front and back doors after she had dashed in and before she could get out again to make the entire *tour de Seattle* in her jaybird suit. Then I had to get her back into that tired pink dress, which (when I ironed it) had *finally* given up completely, despite the dryer, and sagged into two sizes too big for her.

Unless A. R. was youthifying.

I got her into her too-large pink dress, her baggy underwear, her too-large shoes, her new pink socks (which I had bought for her) and said:

"A.R., where do you live?"

Crisp and shining, the Little Clean Girl replied, "My dear, you always ask me that."

"And you never answer," said I.

"O yes I do," said the Little Clean Girl. "I live up the hill and under the hill and over the hill and behind the hill."

"That's no answer," said I.

"Wupf merble," said she (through a Mars Bar) and then, more intelligibly, "If you knew, you wouldn't want me."

"I would so!" I said.

L.D.G.—now L.C.G.—regarded me thoughtfully. She scratched her ear, getting, I noticed, chocolate in her hair. (She was a fast worker.) She said, "You want to know. You think you ought to know. You think you have a right. When I leave you'll wait until I'm out of sight and then you'll follow me in the car. You'll sneak by the curb way behind me so I won't notice you. You'll wait until I climb the steps of a house—like that big yellow house with the fuchsias in the yard where you think I live and you'll watch me go in. And then you'll ring the bell and when the lady comes to the door you'll say, 'Your little daughter and I have become friends,' but the lady will say, 'I haven't got any little daughter,' and then you'll know I fooled you. And you'll get scared. So don't try."

Well, she had me dead to rights. Something very like that had been in my head. Her face was preternaturally grave. She said, "You think I'm too small. I'm not.

"You think I'll get sick if I keep on eating like this. I won't.

"You think if you bought a whole department store for me, it would be enough. It wouldn't."

"I won't—well, I can't get a whole department store for you," I said. She said, "I know." Then she got up and tucked the box of Mars Bars under one arm, throwing over the other my green plastic poncho, which she always carried about with her now.

"I'll get you anything you want," I said; "No, not what you want, A. R., but anything you really, truly need."

"You can't," said the Little Dirty Girl.

"I'll try."

She crossed the living room to the front door, dragging the poncho across the rug, not paying the slightest attention to the astronomical photographs that had so enchanted her before. Too young now, I suppose. I said, "A. R., I'll try. Truly I will." She seemed to consider it a moment, her small head to one side. Then she said briskly, "I'll be back," and was out the front door.

And I did not—would not—could not—did not dare to follow her.

Was this the moment I decided I was dealing with a ghost? No, long before. Little by little, I suppose. Her clothes were a dead giveaway, for one thing: always the same and the kind no child had worn since the end of the Second World War. Then there was the book I had given her on her first visit, which had somehow closed and straightened itself on the coffee table, another I had lent her later (the poems of Edna Millay) which had mysteriously been there a day afterwards, the eerie invisibility of a naked little girl hanging out of my windows and yelling; the inconspicuousness of a little twirling girl nobody noticed spinning round and shrieking outside the merry-go-round, a dozen half-conscious glimpses I'd had, every time I'd got in or out of my car, of the poncho lying on the back seat where I always keep it, folded as always, the very dust on it undisturbed. And her unchildlike cleverness in never revealing either her name or where she lived. And as surely as A.R. had been a biggish eight when we had met, weeks ago, just as surely she was now a smallish, very unmistakable, unnaturally knowledgeable five.

But she was such a *nice* little ghost. And so solid! Ghosts don't run up your grocery bills, do they? Or trample Cheez Doodles into your carpet or leave gum under your kitchen chair, large smears of chocolate on the surface of the table (A. R. had) and an exceptionally dirty ring around the inside of the bathtub? Along with three (count 'em, three) large, dirty, sopping-wet bath towels on the bathroom floor? If A. R.'s social and intellectual life had a tendency to become intangible when looked at carefully, everything connected with her digestive system and her bodily dirt stuck around amazingly; there was the state of the bathroom, the dishes in the sink (many more than mine), and the ironing board still up in the study for the ironing of A.R.'s dress (with the spray starch container still set up on one end and the scorch mark where she'd decided to play with the iron). If she was a ghost, she was a good one and I liked her and wanted her back. Whatever help she needed from me in resolving her ancient Seattle tragedy (ancient ever since nineteen-forty-two) she could have. I wondered for a moment if she were connected with the house, but the people before me—the original owners—hadn't had children. And the house itself hadn't even been built until the mid-fifties; nothing in the neighborhood had. Unless both they and I were being haunted by the children we hadn't had; could I write them a psychotherapeutic letter about it? ("Dear Mrs. X, How is your inner space?") I went into the bathroom and discovered that A. R. had relieved herself interestingly in the toilet and had then not flushed it, hardly what I would call poetical behavior on the part of somebody's unconscious. So *I* flushed it. I picked up the towels one by one and dragged them to the laundry basket in the bedroom. If the Little Dirty Girl was a ghost, she was obviously a bodily-dirt-and-needs ghost traumatized in life by never having been given a proper bath or allowed to eat marshmallows until she got sick. Maybe this was it and now she could rest (scrubbed and full of Mars Bars) in peace. But I hoped not. I was nervous; I had made a promise ("I'll give you what you need") that few of us can make to anyone, a frightening promise to make to anyone. Still, I hoped. And she was a businesslike little ghost. She would come back.

For she, too, had promised.

Autumn came. I didn't see the Little Dirty Girl. School started and I spent days trying to teach freshmen and freshwomen not to write like Rod McKuen (neither of us really knowing why they shouldn't, actually) while advanced students pursued me down the halls with thousand-page trilogies, demands for independent study, and other unspeakables. As a friend of ours said once, everyone will continue to pile responsibility on a woman and everything and everyone must be served except oneself; I've been a flogged horse professionally long enough to know that and meanwhile the dishes stay in the sink and the kindly wife-elves do *not* come out of the woodwork at night and do them. I was exercising two hours a day and sleeping ten; the Little Dirty Girl seemed to have vanished with the summer.

Then one day there was a freak spell of summer weather and that evening a thunderstorm. This is a very rare thing in Seattle. The storm didn't last, of course, but it seemed to bring right after it the first of the winter rains: cold, drenching, ominous. I was grading papers that evening when someone knocked at my door; I thought I'd left the garage light on and my neighbor'd come out to tell me, so I yelled "Just a minute, please!", dropped my pen, wondered whether I should pick it up, decided the hell with it, and went (exasperated) to the door.

It was the Little Dirty Girl. She was as wet as I've ever seen a human being be and had a bad cough (my poncho must've gone heaven knows where) and water squelching in her shoes. She was shivering violently and her fingers were blue—it could not have been more than fifty degrees out—and her long, baggy dress clung to her with water running off it; there was a puddle already forming around her feet on the rug.

Her teeth were chattering. She stood there shivering and glowering miserably at me, from time to time emitting that deep, painful chest cough you sometimes hear in adults who smoke too much. I thought of hot baths, towels, electric blankets, aspirin—can ghosts get pneumonia? "For God's sake, get your clothes off!" I said, but A. R. stepped back against the door, shivering, and wrapped her starved arms in her long, wet skirt.

"No!" she said, in a deep voice more like a crow's than ever. "Like this!"

"Like what?" said I helplessly, thinking of my back and how incapable I was of dragging a resistant five-year-old anywhere.

"You hate me!" croaked A. R. venomously; "You starve me! You do! You won't let me eat anything!"

Then she edged past me, still coughing, her dark eyes ringed with blue, her skin mottled with bruises, and her whole body shaking with cold and anger, like a little mask of Medusa. She screamed:

"You want to clean me up because you don't like me!

"You like me clean because you don't like me dirty!

"You hate me so you won't give me what I need!

"You won't give me what I need and I'm dying!

"I'm dying! I'm dying!

"I'M DYING!"

She was interrupted by coughing. I said, "A. R.—" and she screamed again, her whole body bending convulsively, the cords in her neck standing out. Her scream was choked by phlegm and she beat herself with her fists, then wrapping her arms in her wet skirt through another bout of coughing, she said in gasps:

"I couldn't get into your house to use the bathroom, so I had to shit in my pants.

"I had to stay out in the rain; I got cold.

"All I can get is from you and you won't give it."

"Then tell me what you need!" I said, and A. R. raised her horrid little face to mine, a picture of venomous, uncontrolled misery, of sheer, demanding starvation.

"You," she whispered.

So that was it. I thought of the pleading cats, whose open mouths *(Dependency! Dependency!)* reveal needle teeth which can rip off your thumb; I imagined the Little Dirty Girl sinking her teeth into my chest if I so much as touched her. Not touched for bathing or combing or putting on shoelaces, you understand, but for touching only. I saw— I don't know what; her skin ash-grey, the bones of her little skull coming through her skin worse and worse every moment—and I knew she would kill me if she didn't get what she wanted, though she was suffering far worse than I was and was more innocent—a demon child is still a child, with a child's needs, after all. I got down on one knee, so as to be nearer her size, and saying only, "My back—be careful of my back," held out my arms so that the terror of the ages could walk into them. She was truly grey now, her bones very prominent. She was starving to death. She was dying. She gave the cough of a cadaver breathing its last, a phlegmy wheeze with a dreadful rattle in it, and then the Little Dirty Girl walked right into my arms.

And began to cry. I felt her crying right up from her belly. She was cold and stinky and extremely dirty and afflicted with the most surprising hiccough. I rocked her back and forth and mumbled I don't know what, but what I meant was that I thought she was fine, that all of her was fine: her shit, her piss, her sweat, her tears, her scabby knees, the snot on her face, her cough, her dirty panties, her bruises, her desperation, her anger, her whims—all of her was wonderful, I loved all of her, and I would do my best to take good care of her, all of her, forever and forever and then a day.

She bawled. She howled. She pinched me hard. She yelled, "Why did it take you so long!" She fussed violently over her panties and said she had been humiliated, though it turned out, when I got her to the bathroom, that she was making an awfully big fuss over a very little brown stain. I put the panties to soak in the kitchen sink and the Little Dirty Girl likewise in a hot tub with vast mounds of rose-scented bubble bath which turned up from somewhere, though I knew perfectly well I hadn't bought any in years. We had a shrieky, tickly, soapy, toe-grabby sort of bath, a *very* wet one during which I got soaked. (I told her about my back and she was careful.) We sang to the loofah. We threw water at the bathroom tiles. We lost the soap. We came out warm in a huge towel (I'd swear mine aren't that big) and screamed gaily again, to exercise our lungs, from which the last bit of cough had disappeared. We said, "Oh, floof! there goes the soap." We speculated loudly (and at length) on the possible subjective emotional life of the porcelain sink, American variety, and (rather to my surprise) sang snatches of *The Messiah* as follows:

Every malted
Shall be exalted!

and:

Behold and see
Behold and see

If there were e'er pajama
Like to this pajama!

and so on.

My last memory of the evening is of tucking the Little Dirty Girl into one side of my bed (in my pajamas, which had to be rolled up and pinned even to stay on her) and then climbing into the other side myself. The bed was wider than usual, I suppose. She said sleepily, "Can I stay?" and I (also sleepily) "Forever."

But in the morning she was gone.

Her clothes lasted a little longer, which worried me, as I had visions of A. R. committing flashery around and about the neighborhood, but in a few days they too had faded into mist or the elemental particles of time or whatever ghosts and ghost-clothes are made of. The last thing I saw of hers was a shoe with a new heel (oh yes, I had gotten them fixed) which rolled out from under the couch and lasted a whole day before it became—I forget what, the shadow of one of the ornamental tea-cups on the mantel, I think.

And so there was no more five-year-old A. R. beating on the door and demanding to be let in on rainy nights. But that's not the end of the story.

As you know, I've never gotten along with my mother. I've always supposed that neither of us knew why. In my childhood she had vague, long-drawn-out symptoms which I associated with early menopause (I was a late baby); then she put me through school, which was a strain on her librarian's budget and a strain on my sense of independence and my sense of guilt, and always there was her timidity, her fears of everything under the sun, her terrified, preoccupied air of always being somewhere else, and what I can only call her furtiveness, the feeling I've always had of some secret life going on in which I could never ask about or share. Add to this my father's death somewhere in pre-history (I was two) and then that ghastly behavior psychologists call The Game of Happy Families—I mean the perpetual, absolute insistence on How Happy We All Were that even aunts, uncles, and cousins rushed to heap on my already bitter and most unhappy shoulders, and you'll have some idea of what's been going on for the last I-don't-know-how-many years.

Well, this is the woman who came to visit a few weeks later. I wanted to dodge her. I had been dodging academic committees and students and proper bedtimes; why couldn't I dodge my mother? So I decided that *this time I would be openly angry* (I'd been doing that in school, too).

Only there was nothing to be angry about, this time.

Maybe it was the weather. It was one of those clear, still times we sometimes have in October: warm, the leaves not down yet, that in-

and-out sunshine coming through the clouds, and the northern sun so low that the masses of orange pyracantha berries on people's brick walls and the walls themselves, or anything that color, flame indescribably. My mother got in from the airport in a taxi (I still can't drive far) and we walked about a bit, and then I took her to Kent and Hallby's downtown, that expensive, old-fashioned place that's all mirrors and sawdust floors and old-fashioned white tablecloths and waiters (also waitresses now) with floor-length aprons. It was very self-indulgent of me. But she had been so much better—or I had been—it doesn't matter. She was seventy and if she wanted to be fussy and furtive and act like a thin, old guinea-hen with secret despatches from the C.I.A. (I've called her worse things) I felt she had the right. Besides, that was no worse than my flogging myself through five women's work and endless depressions, beating the old plough horse day after day for weeks and months and years—no, for decades—until her back broke and she foundered and went down and all I could do was curse at her helplessly and beat her the more.

All this came to me in Kent and Hallby's. Luckily my mother squeaked as we sat down. There's a reason; if you sit at a corner table in Kent and Hallby's and see your face where the mirrored walls come together—well, it's complicated, but briefly, you can see yourself (for the only time in your life) as you look to other people. An ordinary mirror reverses the right and left sides of your face but this odd arrangement re-reflects them so they're back in place. People are shocked when they see themselves; I had planned to warn her.

She said, bewildered, "What's that?" But rather intrigued too, I think. Picture a small, thin, white-haired, extremely prim ex-librarian, worn to her fine bones but still ready to take alarm and run away at a moment's notice; that's my mother. I explained about the mirrors and then I said:

"People don't really know what they look like. It's only an idea people have that you'd recognize yourself if you saw yourself across the room. Any more than we can hear our own voices; you know, it's because longer frequencies travel so much better through the bones of your head than they can through the air; that's why a tape recording of your voice sounds higher than—"

I stopped. Something was going to happen. A hurricane was going to smash Kent and Hallby's flat. I had spent almost a whole day with my mother, walking around my neighborhood, showing her the University, showing her my house, and nothing in particular had happened; why should anything happen now?

She said, looking me straight in the eye, "You've changed."

I waited.

She said, "I'm afraid that we—like you and I were not—are not—a happy family."

I said nothing. I would have, a year ago. It occurred to me that I might, for years, have confused my mother's primness with my mother's self-control. She went on. She said:

"When you were five, I had cancer."

I said, *"What? You had what?"*

"Cancer," said my mother calmly, in a voice still as low and decorous as if she had been discussing her new beige handbag or Kent and Hallby's long, fancy menu (which lay open on the table between us). "I kept it from you. I didn't want to burden you."

Burden.

"I've often wondered—" she went on, a little flustered; "they say now—but of course no one thought that way then." She went on, more formally, "It takes years to know if it has spread or will come back, even now, and the doctors knew very little then. I was all right eventually, of course, but by that time you were almost grown up and had become a very capable and self-sufficient little girl. And then later on you were so successful."

She added, "You didn't seem to want me."

Want her! Of course not. What would you feel about a mother who disappeared like that? Would you trust her? Would you accept anything from her? All those years of terror and secrecy; maybe she'd thought she was being punished by having cancer. Maybe she'd thought she was going to die. Too scared to give anything and everyone being loudly secretive and then being faced with a daughter who wouldn't be questioned, wouldn't be kissed, wouldn't be touched, who kept her room immaculate, who didn't want her mother and made no bones about it, and who kept her fury and betrayal and her misery to herself, and her schoolwork excellent. I could say only the silliest thing, right out of the movies:

"Why are you telling me all this?"

She said simply, "Why not?"

I wish I could go on to describe a scene of intense and affectionate reconciliation between my mother and myself, but that did not happen—quite. She put her hand on the table and I took it, feeling I don't know what; for a moment she squeezed my hand and smiled. I got up then and she stood too, and we embraced, not at all as I had embraced the Little Dirty Girl, though with the same pain at heart, but awkwardly and only for a moment, as such things really happen. I said to myself: *Not yet. Not so fast. Not right now,* wondering if we looked—in Kent and Hallby's mirrors—the way we really were. We were both embarrassed, I think, but that too was all right. We sat down: *Soon. Sometime. Not quite yet.*

The dinner was nice. The next day I took her for breakfast to the restaurant that goes around and gives you a view of the whole city and then to the public market and then on a ferry. We had a pleasant, affectionate quiet two days and then she went back East.

We've been writing each other lately—for the first time in years more than the obligatory birthday and holiday cards and a few remarks about the weather—and she sent me old family photographs, talked about being a widow, and being misdiagnosed for years (that's what it seems now) and about all sorts of old things: my father, my being in the school play in second grade, going to summer camp, getting moths to sit on her finger, all sorts of things.

And the Little Dirty Girl? Enclosed is her photograph. We were passing a photographer's studio near the University the other day and she was seized with a passionate fancy to have her picture taken (I suspect the Tarot cards and the live owl in the window had something to do with it), so in we went. She clamors for a lot lately and I try to provide it: flattens her nose against a bakery window and we argue about whether she'll settle for a currant bun instead of a do-nut, wants to stay up late and read and sing to herself so we do, screams for parties so we find them, and *at* parties impels me towards people I would probably not have noticed or (if I had) liked a year ago. She's a surprisingly generous and good little soul and I'd be lost without her, so it's turned out all right in the end. Besides, one ignored her at one's peril. I try not to.

Mind you, she has taken some odd, good things out of my life. Little boys seldom walk with me now. And I've perfected—though regretfully—a more emphatic method of kitty-booting which they seem to understand; at least one of them turned to me yesterday with a look of disgust that said clearer than words: "Good Heavens, how you've degenerated! Don't you know there's nothing in life more important than taking care of Me?"

About the picture: you may think it odd. You may even think it's not her. (You're wrong.) The pitch-ball eyes and thin face are there, all right, but what about the bags under her eyes, the deep, downward lines about her mouth, the strange color of her short-cut hair (it's grey)? What about her astonishing air of being so much older, so much more intellectual, so much more professional, so much more—well, competent—than any Little Dirty Girl could possibly be?

Well, faces change when forty-odd years fall into the developing fluid.

The Little Dirty Girl/253

And you have always said that you wanted, that you must have, that you commanded, that you begged, and so on and so on in your interminable, circumlocutory style, that the one thing you desired most in the world was a photograph, a photograph, your kingdom for a photograph—of me.

Envoi

For Emily D.

The only ghost I ever saw
   was white and palely shining
She stood beside my writing desk
   apparently reciting
Lines of verse I could not hear
   although she begged attention
Expressing with dramatic pose
   her soundless recitation
I clapped my hands and yelled "Bravo!"
   (how bright her face was beaming)
She blew a kiss and curtsied low
   then vanished from the evening.

Recommended Reading

I hope that this recommended reading list, together with titles mentioned in the headnotes, will form a want-list for the establishment of the reader's own core library, or for library and interlibrary requests. Because multi-author anthologies, especially in the United States, tend to feature only one or two women per volume (if that!), I find it counterproductive to send feminist readers to horror anthologies other than those exceptions mentioned in the Preface and headnotes (they are not repeated here). However, in the few cases in which an author does not have her own collection, stories are cited from anthology appearances. Individual stories of particular merit, within each author's collection, have been indicated. In some cases this will be the volume's only supernatural piece, in the context of a broader range of that author's short works. In other cases, the indicated story is the most representative of several that are apropos. In all cases, the individually cited stories have strong feminist value in addition to their macabre content. Some of these books, especially the older ones, are rare, while others are easily obtained. Rarities are included not to frustrate the eager reader, but so that these books will not have to remain not only rare but virtually unknown as significant feminist works.

Asterisked titles are currently in print or have been in print very recently.

Adisa, Opal Palmer. "Duppy Get Her," in *Bake-Face and Other Guava Stories*★ (Berkeley, Calif.: Kelsey Street, 1986).

Aichinger, Ilse. "Story in a Mirror," "Moon Story," and others, in *The Bound Man* (New York: Farrar Straus Giroux, 1955).

Aiken, Joan. "The Green Flash," in *The Green Flash* (New York: Holt Rinehart Winston, 1971); "A Taxi to Solitude," in *The Far Forests* (New York: Viking, 1977); "Lodgers," in *A Touch of Strange*★ (New York: Delacorte, 1980); many others.

Allen, Mary Ann. "The Gravedigger and Death," "Joan," and others, in *The Angry Dead* (Liverpool: Dark Dreams, 1987).

Asquith, Cynthia. "God Grante that She Lye Still," in *The Mortal Coil* (Sauk City, Wis.: Arkham House, 1947).

Atherton, Gertrude. "Natalie Ivanhoff," in *Splendid Idle Forties*★ (New York: Fredrick Stokes, 1902; Boston: Gregg Press, 1968); "The Dead and the Countess" and "Death and the Woman," in *The Bell in the Fog*★ (New York: Harper and Brothers, 1905; New York: Irvington, 1968); "The Foghorn," in *The Foghorn*★ (New York: Houghton Mifflin, 1934; Salem, N. H.: Ayers, 1970).

Bacon, Josephine Dodge Daskam. "The Children," in *The Strange Cases of Dr. Stanchon* (Toronto: McLeod & Allen, 1913).

Beck, L. Adams. "Juana," in *The Ninth Vibration* (New York: Dodd Mead, 1923); others.

Bowen, Elizabeth. "The Evil Men Do," "The Cat Jumps," "The Apple Tree," and "The Demon Lover," in *Collected Stories* (New York: Knopf, 1981).

Bowen, Marjorie. "Dark Ann," in *Dark Ann* (London: Bodley Head, 1928); "The Last Bouquet," in *The Last Bouquet* (London: Bodley Head, 1933); "The Crown Derby Plate" and others, in *Kecksies*★ (Sauk City, Wis.: Arkham House, 1976).

Broster, D. K. "Clairvoyance," in *A Fire in Driftwood* (London: Heineman, 1932); "From the Abyss," in *The Couching by the Door* (London: Heineman, 1942).

Buxton, Meg. "The Flora Stone," in *One Footprint in the Sand*★ (London: William Kimber, 1979).

Carter, Angela. "The Loves of Lady Purple" and others, in *Fireworks*★ (New York: Harper and Row, 1974; rev. ed. London: Chatto and Windus, 1987); others.

Cholmondeley, Mary. "Votes for Men," in *The Romance of His Life* (New York: Dodd Mead, 1921); others.

Christie, Agatha. "The Last Seance" and "The Hound of Death," in *The Hound of Death* (London: Odhams, 1933); others.

Clingerman, Mildred. "First Lesson," "The Day of the Green Velvet," and others, in *A Cupful of Space* (New York: Ballantine, 1961).

Corelli, Marie. "The Lady with Carnations," in *Cameos*★ (London: Hutchinson, 1986; Salem, N. H.: Ayer, 1970); "A Sculptor's Angel," in *The Love of Long Ago* (New York: Doubleday Page, 1921).

Crabtree, Lou V. "Prices' Bewitched Cow," in *Sweet Hollow*★ (Baton Rouge: Louisiana State University Press, 1984).

Dilke, Emilia Frances. "The Secret" and "The Shrine of Death," in *The Shrine of Death* (London: Routledge, 1886).

Dinesen, Isak. "The Monkey," in *Seven Gothic Tales*★ (New York: Smith & Haas, 1934; New York: Random House, n.d.); "The Sailor-boy's Tale," in *Winter's Tales*★ (New York: Random House, 1942, 1961); "The Cloak," in *Last Tales*★ (New York: Random House, 1955, 1975); "Carnival," in *Carnival*★ (Chicago: University of Chicago Press, 1977).

du Maurier, Daphne. "The Chamois," in *Echoes from the Macabre*★ (New York: Doubleday, 1976; New York: Pocket Books, 1978).

Duras, Marguerite. *The Malady of Death*★ (New York: Grove, 1986).

Erskine, Ella. "The Waxen Image," in *Shadow-Shapes* (London: Elkin Mathews, 1909).

Farjeon, Eleanor. "Faithful Jenny Dove," in *Faithful Jenny Dove* (New York: Collins, 1925; Salem, N. H.: Ayer, 1970).

Fisher, M. F. K. "The Lost, Strayed, Stolen" and others, in *Sister Age*★ (New York: Knopf, 1983).

Fitzgerald, M. J. "Creases" and others, in *Rope-Dancer*★ (New York: Random House, 1985).

Fox, Janet. "Witches," in *Tales by Moonlight*★ (Chicago: Garcia Press, 1983; New York: Tor, 1985); "Screaming to Get Out," in *Year's Best Horror Stories Series VII*★ (New York: DAW, 1978); others, all uncollected.

Gibbons, Stella. "The Butterfly Net," in *Roaring Tower* (London: Longmans, 1937).

Gilchrist, Ellen. "The Young Man," in *Drunk with Love*★ (Boston: Little Brown, 1986).

Glasgow, Ellen. "The Shadowy Third" and "Dare's Gift," in *The Collected Stories of Ellen Glasgow* (Baton Rouge: Louisiana State University Press, 1963).

Greenberg, Joanne. "Certain Distant Suns," in *High Crimes and Misdemeanors*★ (New York: Holt Rinehart Winston, 1980); others.

Hawthorne, Hildegard. "Legend of Sonora" and others, in *Faded Gar-*

den: *Collected Ghost Stories of Hildegard Hawthorne*★ (Madison, Wis.: Dream House, 1985).

Haynes, Dorothy K. "Thou Shalt Not Suffer a Witch," in *Thou Shalt Not Suffer a Witch* (London: Methuen, 1949).

Henderson, Zenna. "Walking Aunt Daid," in *The Anything Box*★ (New York: Doubleday, 1969; New York: Avon, 1986).

Highsmith, Patricia. "The Empty Birdhouse," in *Eleven*★ (London: Heineman, 1970).

Hunt, Violet. "The Corsican Sisters," in *More Tales of the Uneasy* (London: Heineman, 1928).

Ingalls, Rachel. "Blessed Art Thou," in *I See a Long Journey*★ (New York: Simon & Schuster, 1985); others.

Irwin, Margaret. "Monsieur Seeks a Wife," in *Bloodstock*★ (London: Chatto & Windus, 1953; Hornchurch, Essex: Ian Henry Publications, 1978).

Jackson, Shirley. "The Summer People," in *Come Along with Me*★ (New York: Viking, 1968); "The Daemon Lover," in *The Lottery*★ (New York: Farrar Straus Giroux, 1972).

Jesse, F. Tennyson. "A Shepherdess of Fauns" and others, in *Beggars on Horseback* (New York: Doran, 1915); "The Canary," in *Solange Stories* (London: Heineman, 1931).

Jewett, Sarah Orne. "Lady Ferry," in *Funeral Seasons: Complete Uncanny Stories of Sarah Orne Jewett*★ (Los Angeles: Scream/Press Grim Maids, in press).

Kallas, Aino. "The Legend of Young Odele and the Leper," in *The White Ship* (New York: Knopf, 1924).

Kavan, Anna. "Fog," "Obsessional," and "Clarita," in *Julia and the Bazooka*★ (New York: Knopf, 1975).

Kerruish, Jessie Douglas. "She Who Was Late for Her Funeral," in *Babylonian Nights' Entertainment* (London: Denis Archer, 1934).

Kincaid, Jamaica. "In the Night," "At the Bottom of the River," and others, in *At the Bottom of the River*★ (New York: Farrar Straus Giroux, 1983).

Lagerlöf, Selma. "The King's Grave," in *Invisible Links* (Boston: Little Brown, 1899); "Old Agnete" in *From a Swedish Homestead*★ (New York: McClure, Philips, 1901; Salem, N. H.: Ayer, 1970).

Lee, Tanith. "Chund Veda" and others, in *Tamastra or the Indian Nights*★ (New York: DAW, 1983); "The Gorgon" and others, in *The Gorgon*★ (New York: DAW, 1983); many others.

Lofts, Nora. "A Visit to Claudia" and others, in *Hauntings: Is There Anybody There?* (New York: Doubleday, 1975).

Lowndes, Marie Bellock. "The Woman from Purgatory," in *Studies in Love and Terror* (London: Methuen, 1913); "The Duenna," in *The*

Ghost Book (London: Hutchinson, 1926); "An Unrecorded Instance," in *The Black Cap*★ (London: Hutchinson, 1927; Darby, Pa.: Darby Books, 1981).

Marryat, Florence. "The Ghost of Charlotte Gray," in *The Ghost of Charlotte Gray* (Leipzig, Germany: Tauchnitz, 1883).

Mayor, F. M. "Tales of Widow Weeks" and "The Spectre de la Rose," in *The Room Opposite* (London: Longman's, 1935).

Mew, Charlotte. "The Smile," in *Collected Poems and Prose*★ (London: Virago Press, 1982).

Myers, Jane Pentzer. "The Corn Fairy," in *Stories of Enchantment or The Ghost Flower* (Chicago: McLurg, 1901).

Nicholas, Anna. "Out of the Past," in *The Making of Thomas Barton* (New York: Bobbs-Merrill, 1913).

Oates, Joyce Carol. "Nightside," in *Nightside*★ (New York: Vanguard, 1977; New York: Fawcett, 1980).

Oliphant, Margaret. "Lady Mary," in *Tales of the Seen and Unseen* (Boston: Roberts, 1889; Salem, N. H.: Ayer, 1970).

Ozick, Cynthia. "Levitation," in *Levitation*★ (New York: Knopf, 1982; New York: Dutton, 1983); others.

Peattie, Elia Wilkinson. "On the Northern Ice," in *Shape of Fear*★ (Philadelphia: Lippincott, 1898; Salem, N. H.: Ayer, 1969).

Plath, Sylvia. "All the Dead Dears," in *Johnny Panic and the Bible of Dreams*★ (New York: Harper and Row, 1979).

Rhys, Jean. "I Used to Live Here Once," "A Spiritualist," "Pioneers, Oh, Pioneers," and others, in *The Collected Short Stories of Jean Rhys*★ (New York: Norton, 1979).

Salmonson, Jessica Amanda. "Nights in the City" and others, in *A Silver Thread of Madness*★ (New York: Ace, 1989); "Angela's Love," in *John Collier and Fredric Brown Went Quarrelling Through My Head*★ (Buffalo: W. Paul Ganley, 1989).

Schwartz, Lynn Sharon. "Sound is Second Sight," in *Acquainted with the Night*★ (New York: Harper and Row, 1984).

Slosson, Annie Trumbull. "Dumb Foxglove," in *Dumb Foxglove*★ (New York: Harpers, 1898; Salem, N. H.: Ayer, 1970); "A Dissatisfied Soul," in *A Local Colorist*★ (New York: Scribner, 1912; Salem, N. H.: Ayer, 1971).

Spoffard, Harriet Prescott. "The Godmothers," "The Moonstone Mass," and others, in *"The Amber Gods" and Other Stories*★ (New Brunswick, N. J.: Rutgers University Press, 1989).

Squier, Emma-Lindsay. "The Leopard Queen Smiles" and "Rose Amarila," in *The Bride of the Sacred Well* (New York: Cosmopolitan, 1928).

Stead, Christina. "The Rightangle Creek," in *The Puzzleheaded Girl* (New York: Holt Rinehart Winston, 1967).

Stuart, Ruth McEnery. "The Haunted Photograph," in *The Haunted Photograph*★ (New York: Century, 1911; Salem, N. H.: Ayer, n.d.).

Taylor, Constance G. "Prisoner in Venice," in *Four Stories*★ (New York: Vantage, 1984).

Vivien, Renee. "Crocodile Lady," in *The Woman of the Wolf*★ (New York: The Gay Press, 1983).

Vorse, Mary Heaton. "The Halfway House" and others, in *Sinister Romance: Collected Ghost Stories of Mary Heaton Vorse*★ (Los Angeles: Scream/Press Grim Maids, in press).

Water, Elizabeth. "Dead Woman," in *Dead Woman* (New York: St. Martin's, 1975); many others.

Wells, Jess. "Succubus," in *Dress and the Sharda Stories*★ (San Francisco: Library B. Productions, 1984).

Wharton, Edith. "The Lady's Maid Bell," "Bewitched," and "Afterward" in *Ghost Stories*★ (London: Constable & Co., 1975).

White, Antonia. "The Saint," in *Strangers*★ (London: Harvill, 1954; New York: Dial, 1981).

Williams, Mary. "Ghostly Carnival," in *Ghostly Carnival*★ (London: William Kimber, 1980); many others.

Woolf, Virginia. "The Mysterious Case of Miss V" and "Lapin and Lapinova," in *The Complete Shorter Fiction of Virginia Woolf*★ (New York: Harcourt Brace Jovanovich, 1985).

Wormser, G. Ranger. "Mutter Schwegel," in *The Scarecrow* (New York: Dutton, 1918).

Yarbro, Chelsea Quinn. "Disturb Not My Slumbering Fair" in *Cautionary Tales* (New York: Doubleday, 1978).

Yourcenar, Marguerite. "Kali Beheaded," in *Oriental Tales*★ (New York: Farrar Straus Giroux, 1985).

Acknowledgments

᚛

I gratefully acknowledge permission to print the following material:

Barbara Burford, "Dreaming the Sky Down," from her collection *The Threshing Floor* (Ithaca, N. Y.: Firebrand Press, 1988). ©1987 by Barbara Burford. Reprinted by permission of the author.

Leonora Carrington, "The Debutante," from her collection *The Oval Lady* (Santa Barbara, Calif.: Capra Press, 1975). ©1975 by Capra Press. Reprinted by permission of Capra Press.

Phyllis Eisenstein, "Attachment." ©1974 by Phyllis Eisenstein. Reprinted by permission of the author.

Jules Faye, "Pandora Pandaemonia." ©1989 by Jules Faye. By permission of the author.

Joanna Russ, "The Little Dirty Girl," from *Elsewhere*, Terri Windling and Mark Alan Arnold, editors (New York: Ace Books, 1981). ©1981 by Joanna Russ. Reprinted by permission of the author.

Vita Sackville-West, "An Unborn Visitant," from her collection *Thirty Clocks Strike the Hour* (New York: Doubleday, 1932). © 1932 by Vita Sackville-West. Reprinted by permission of Curtis Brown London on behalf of the Estate of Vita Sackville-West.

Anne Sexton, "The Ghost," from *Anne Sexton's Words for Dr. Y: Uncollected Poems*, Linda Gray Sexton, editor. ©1978 by Linda Gray Sexton and Loring Conant. Reprinted by permission of Sterling Lord Literistic, Inc.

Lady Eleanor Smith, "Tamar," from her collection *Satan's Circus* (London: Golancz, 1932). © 1932 by Eleanor Smith. Reprinted by permission of Aitken and Stone London on behalf of the Estate of Eleanor Smith.

Armonía Somers, "The Fall," from *Other Fires: Short Fiction by Latin American Women*, Alberto Manguel, editor (New York: Clarkson N. Potter, 1986). ©1967 by Armonía Somers. Translation ©1985, 1986 by Alberto Manguel. Reprinted by permission of Alberto Manguel.

Lisa Tuttle, "A Friend in Need," from *The Year's Best Fantasy Stories: 8* (New York: DAW, 1982). ©1981 by TZ Publications. Reprinted by permission of the author.

Luisa Valenzuela, "The Teacher," from her collection *Clara: Thirteen Short Stories and a Novel* (New York: Harcourt, Brace, Jovanovich, 1976). ©1976 by Harcourt, Brace, Jovanovich, Inc. Reprinted by permission of the author.

The Feminist Press at The City University of New York offers alternatives in education and in literature. Founded in 1970, this nonprofit, tax-exempt educational and publishing organization works to eliminate sexual stereotypes in books and schools and to provide literature with a broad vision of human potential. The publishing program includes reprints of important works by women, feminist biographies of women, and nonsexist children's books. Curricular materials, bibliographies, directories, and a quarterly journal provide information and support for students and teachers of women's studies. Through publications and projects, The Feminist Press contributes to the rediscovery of the history of women and the emergence of a more humane society.

New and Forthcoming Books

Always a Sister: The Feminism of Lillian D. Wald, a biography by Doris Groshen Daniels. $24.95 cloth.

Bamboo Shoots after the Rain: Contemporary Stories by Women Writers of Taiwan, edited by Anne C. Carver and Sung-sheng Yvonne Chang. $29.95 cloth, $12.95 paper.

A Brighter Coming Day: A Frances Ellen Watkins Harper Reader, edited by Frances Smith Foster. $29.95 cloth, $13.95 paper.

The Daughters of Danaus, a novel by Mona Caird. Afterword by Margaret Morganroth Gullette. $29.95 cloth, $11.95 paper.

The End of This Day's Business, a novel by Katharine Burdekin. Afterword by Daphne Patai. $24.95 cloth, $8.95 paper.

Families in Flux (formerly *Household and Kin*), by Amy Swerdlow, Renate Bridenthal, Joan Kelly, and Phyllis Vine. $9.95 paper.

How I Wrote Jubilee *and Other Essays on Life and Literature*, by Margaret Walker. Edited by Maryemma Graham. $29.95 cloth, $9.95 paper.

Lillian D. Wald: Progressive Activist, a sourcebook edited by Clare Coss. $7.95 paper.

Lone Voyagers: Academic Women in Coeducational Institutions, 1870–1937, edited by Geraldine J. Clifford. $29.95 cloth, $12.95 paper.

Not So Quiet: Stepdaughters of War, a novel by Helen Zenna Smith. Afterword by Jane Marcus. $26.95 cloth, $9.95 paper.

Seeds: Supporting Women's Work in the Third World, edited by Ann Leonard. Introduction by Adrienne Germain. Afterwords by Marguerite Berger, Vina Mazumdar, Kathleen Staudt, and Aminita Traore. $29.95 cloth, $12,95 paper.

Sister Gin, a novel by June Arnold. Afterword by Jane Marcus. $8.95 paper.

These Modern Women: Autobiographical Essays from the Twenties, edited, and with a revised introduction by Elaine Showalter. $8.95 paper.

Truth Tales: Contemporary Stories by Women Writers of India, selected by Kali for Women. Introduction by Meena Alexander. $22.95 cloth, $8.95 paper.

We That Were Young, a novel by Irene Rathbone. Introduction by Lynn Knight. Afterword by Jane Marcus. $29.95 cloth, $10.95 paper.

Women Composers: The Lost Tradition Found, by Diane Peacock Jezic. $29.95 cloth, $12.95 paper.

For a free, complete backlist catalog, write to The Feminist Press at The City University of New York, 311 East 94 Street, New York, NY 10128. Send book orders to The Talman Company, Inc., 150 Fifth Avenue, New York, NY 10011. Please include $1.75 postage and handling for one book, $.75 for each additional.